Cyber Trail

R J Jeffery

Bloomington, IN　　Milton Keynes, UK
authorHOUSE

AuthorHouse™
1663 Liberty Drive, Suite 200
Bloomington, IN 47403
www.authorhouse.com
Phone: 1-800-839-8640

AuthorHouse™ UK Ltd.
500 Avebury Boulevard
Central Milton Keynes, MK9 2BE
www.authorhouse.co.uk
Phone: 08001974150

© 2006 R J Jeffery. All rights reserved.

No part of this book may be reproduced, stored in a retrieval system, or transmitted by any means without the written permission of the author.

First published by AuthorHouse 8/7/2006

ISBN: 1-4259-1402-0 (sc)

Printed in the United States of America
Bloomington, Indiana

This book is printed on acid-free paper.

ACKNOWLEDGEMENTS

I wish to thank my daughter, Marie Hutchinson, for her interest in the book, and her ideas to improve the storyline as she edited the manuscripts for me. My son in law, Paul Hutchinson, provided me with important information on the workings of computers.

Coralee Walker proved helpful in correcting the grammar and punctuation.

My wife Doreen's aid in finding the information I required to register the book, and sending the manuscript to the publishing house. and supporting me throught the various stages of the book from start to finish.

I must not forget Vid Beldavs of Author House. His expertise proved to be invaluable in enabling me to publish the story in a timely manner.

Table of Contents

Discovery 1

Surveillance 7

Garage Sale 17

Something Missing 25

Home Invasion 29

The Investigation 37

Controlling the Investigation 56

The Surveillance Continues 60

The Plan 69

Disguise 87

Problems 90

Contact 95

Security 100

On The Job 102

Spies and Counterspies 104

New Job 113

The Proof 115

The Unwitting Assistant 117

The Mistress 125

The Recruit 128

Two Ladies – One Divorce 134

The Trojan Horse Program 140

Discovering the Camera 143

Putting the Horse to Work 155

Another Ally	158
Enlisting Powerful Allies	171
Hamed Ahmidam	177
Ambush	179
More C.S.I.S.	189
The Argument	193
"Why Joe Ferguson?"	196
Disguises	205
Posting Bail	211
The House of Parliament	218
Money, Money Everywhere	226
A New Client	227
Wheels Within Wheels	233
Take Care	235
The Arrest	242
Belle River	252
Strangers in the Night	258
Sowing Dissention	267
Civil Rights	271
Dissention	274
The Beginning of the Plan	278
Pilfering	284
Terrorist Attack	292
Night Shift	295
The Search	302

Channel Islands	*305*
The Airplane	*310*
Time to Relax	*315*
Cayman Islands	*317*
No Time for Complacency	*324*
The Evidence Search Continues	*326*
Learning the Truth	*330*
Election Call	*335*
Time to Leave	*343*
Cecil	*346*
Scandal	*350*
Terrorist Strike	*354*
Epilogue	*360*
Six Months Later	*367*

Forward

The story you are about to read is a work of fiction; it is not a fairy tale. Political corruption is a reality of life and no country is exempt from the degradation of corrupt elected officials and civil servants.

United States President Richard Nixon was forced to resign and the Republican Party lost the ensuing election because of Watergate.

The integrity of the citizens of America demanded a higher standard from their elected officials.

The Liberal Party of Canada is embroiled in Adscam – a far more scandalous affair – stealing money from the citizens of Canada.

After the Auditor General Report, the Prime Minister of Canada was forced by the ensuing scandal to appoint a Royal Commission, under the auspices of Judge Gomery, to look into government 'mishandling' of funds in contracts granted to Quebec companies. Judge Gomery overstepped his mandate when he allowed testimony showing the Liberal party overpaid the contracts in return for clandestine cash kickbacks from the companies. The final destination of the cash, delivered in envelopes, is unknown at this time. Judge Gomery's mandate did not allow the Gomery Commission to pursue the kickbacks within the government.

Gomery's mandate did not allow testimony on a similar scheme with other Canadian advertisers, kickbacks in the gun registry, or money paid to Crown Corporations.

From 1992 until Hong Kong reverted to China in 1997, the Canadian Government granted 'Landed Immigrant' status to known criminals from that British Protectorate. The criminals paid on average, $500,000 to the Department of Foreign Affairs for their Canadian citizenship. This practice began under the 'Progressive Conservative' banner when Brian Mulrooney was the Prime Minister and Joe Clark the Minister of Foreign Affairs and continued under the Jean Chretien 'Liberal' regime (1993). One of the criminals was the 'Ice Lady', the largest underground manufacturer of 'Crystal Meth' in Hong Kong. Today the police in Canada are battling major 'Methamphetamine' and 'Asian Gang' problems.

Canadian Press Edmonton Sun-2004

Ahmed Ressam, terrorist, arrested in the US in December 1999. He was part of a larger group of Montreal-based terrorists, aimed at striking at U.S. targets during millennium celebrations. Ahmed Ressam and others obtained fraudulent Canadian passports at will. The inability of Canadian authorities to detect him for almost two years sparked the U.S. Congress to call for tighter restrictions along the Canada-U.S. border.

Canadian Press Robert Russo - Readers Digest-2002

Prime Minister Jean Chretien personally went to Pakistan to obtain the release of Ahmed Said Khadr from prison. Chretien spoke to President Bhutto in Pakistan. When released Khadr immediately returned to Afghanistan to fight with al-Qaeda forces against the UN coalition forces.

Red Deer Conservative Constituency Office

Prime Minister Jean Chretien denied there are any terrorists in Canada and claimed the documents the U.S. government have are American lies to discredit the Canadian government.

Canadian Press 2004

The database with names of suspected terrorists linked to the United States crashed for 17 months during the 28-month period monitored by the Auditor General leaving **14,500** names off the list.

How many terrorist names remained on the list?

Canadian Press Calgary Sun-2004

The names of all the characters in this book are fictitious except for a few acknowledged terrorists. One of the most prominent names is **Ayman al-Zawahri** whose alias' have included the names Mahmoud el-Hafnawi, Amin Othman, and Adbed Moez. This confederate of Osama bin-Ladin is second in command of the al Qaeda terrorist organization and bears the dubious distinction of having planned the attacks on the World Trade Center and the U.S. White House. A second terrorist is Abu Zubaydah, a known al-Qaeda recruiter believed killed in Afghanistan battling coalition forces.

Canadian Press, 2004

I have used the Liberal Party and the Alliance Party because the Liberal Party was in power and the Alliance Party was in opposition in 2001, the time the story began.

Some statements used by politicians in the story came directly from statements made by politicians and quoted in the Canadian Press.

Now we have a story.

Discovery

On May 3, 2001, Joe Ferguson flips on his computer to begin working. Suddenly appearing in immigration documents on his monitor is a face he recognizes, Ayman al-Zawahri, second in command of the terrorist organization al Qaeda. The document reveals Ayman al-Zawahri is now living in West Van, an upscale community of Vancouver. The signature, Joseph P. Ferguson, is on the document – but that is impossible. Joe's work in the department involves researching the requirements needed to fill positions where there is a shortage of qualified Canadians. The Immigration Department uses this information to locate properly qualified immigrants to fill these positions. Joe has never seen this file before and could never have signed any papers regarding this, or any other individual's immigration to Canada. He copies the documents onto a computer disk intending to discuss this error with his superiors. As he watches, the screen begins to change. The photograph remains the same but the name of the terrorist changes to Mahmoud el-Hafnawi and the address changes to a location in Montreal, Quebec. Joe adds this information to the disk. The documentation disappears from his monitor as quickly as it appeared. Joe removes the disk from the computer and slips it into his pants pocket.

This information really concerns Joe. 'Who aided that terrorist to get into Canada?' There are only fifteen people able to access his file name and these were illegal documents bearing his signature.

"Good morning Fergie."

Joe freezes – then recognizing the voice, smiles and swivels around slowly in his chair.

"Good morning Betty. Is there any news on the new grandchild yet?"

"Yes. It's a baby girl. They named her Elizabeth-Anne after both grandparents." Betty places her hands on her hips and flicks her head flouncing her hair. "My name's first."

Joe laughs at the antics of his friend.

"It's hard to believe you're a grandmother – you're so young and beautiful and vivacious."

"Now you know that's not true Fergie… but keep on talking…. I just had to tell you about our new granddaughter before I started work." Betty glances at her watch. "Woops, I'm late. I'll join you for coffee."

Betty waves and bounces out the door.

Joe is glad for the break Betty has afforded him. Her flamboyant attitude has helped dispel the shock and then the anger he'd experienced finding the terrorist file in his documents.

Joe prints off the information he will require today and gathers some papers he no longer requires. At the office printer, he collects the new material, then to the paper shredder to dispose of his scrap. Later that morning, a superior summons Joe to his office to further explain some information he has documented. Returning to his office he is offended to discover a man rifling through his paperwork.

"What do you think your doing?"

The man whirls around startled and Joe recognizes the Senior Official in the Immigration Department, Pierre Montague.

"Who do you think you are, speaking to me in that tone of voice!" The Senior Immigration Official barks back at Joe. Pierre Montague, an imposing figure, angrily glares down at Joe from his height of well over six feet.

Joe is contrite. "I'm sorry. I didn't recognize you from the back. I thought it was someone else rifling through my paperwork."

Montague's face is hard – hard as granite. "Have you seen anything unusual on your computer this morning?"

"No. Should I have?" Joe replies innocently, not willing to reveal anything.

Angrily Pierre turns back to the computer and pages through Joe's files. Finding nothing, he stalks from the office.

Joe realizes that his superior, Pierre Montague, is involved in the criminal activities he has just uncovered in the Immigration Department. Murray Jones, the individual who summoned him to the fifth floor under the pretense of requiring more information on a file must also be involved. Members of the Department of Foreign Affairs must also be in on the scheme. After all, they begin the immigration process. Joe realizes he needs the information on the disk to expose the individuals bringing this and probably other terrorists into Canada; however, this same information could jeopardize his career in the Immigration Department.

At four o'clock, Eileen Ferguson enters Joe's office.

Placing her handbag on the desk, Eileen turns to the family photograph hanging on the wall. She doesn't notice Joe covertly removing the floppy disk from his pants pocket and slipping it into a side pocket of her handbag. After looking at the picture for a few more moments, Eileen turns "We need to get a new family photo. Our boys have sure grown since that picture was taken."

"Yes, Keith was just telling me he's five foot seven. I think he wants to be taller than me."

"I think he'll make it. Jerry definitely will." Eileen replies, her pride evident for Joe to see.

"Are we a little too proud of our sons?" Joe chides his wife.

"Definitely not," Eileen merrily replies. "We could never be too proud of those two boys. I'm in parking lot G at stall #39. I'll wait for you there."

"I'll be about 20 minutes before I'm finished here."

"That's fine. I have a pocketbook I'll read 'til you get there."

Eileen retrieves her handbag and blows her husband a kiss as she leaves.

Joe prepares to depart for the evening. He files the papers he is currently documenting and exits his office. Before he can close the door, Pierre Montague and a stranger accost him.

"Step back into your office Ferguson," orders Montague. "We need to talk."

Montague and the stranger crowd Joe closely, forcing him back into the office. They close the door.

"Give me your jacket," growls Montague.

Joe, puzzled, takes off the coat and hands it to the Senior Official in the Immigration Department.

After emptying the pockets onto the desk, Montague throws the jacket onto the chair in disgust.

"Now give me your pants and shirt."

"You must be kidding!"

The stranger produces a badge and bellows. **"I'm from C.S.I.S. Now do as your told. Take off your damn pants and shirt."**

Joe steps to the desk, and picks up the phone.

The stranger, stepping forward and hovering over Joe like a demon from the depths of Hell, bellows, **"Put down that damn phone and strip right now."**

4

Joe looks up at the C.S.I.S. agent knowing this man is big trouble. He carefully puts back the phone handset. Hastily removing his shirt and pants, Joe places them on the chair.

The stranger quickly examines the clothes and then angrily fires them back on the chair. He and Montague leave the room.

Joe quickly dresses, then starts to leave. The stranger from C.S.I.S. dominates the doorway, glowering down on Joe.

"Don't you ever tell anybody about this! Have you got that straight?"

Joe recoils from the belligerent tone of the C.S.I.S. agent's voice then storms angrily past the man, dismayed over the events of the last few minutes.

The C.S.I.S. agent enters Joe's office to conduct a thorough search of the premises.

Joe stalks into the lunchroom to retrieve his lunchbox and head home. Unlocking his personal locker he discovers it has been ransacked and the person made no attempt to hide his efforts. Even his lunch box is turned upside down.

Arriving home, Joe changes while Eileen is preparing supper. He retrieves the computer disk with the incriminating evidence, slipping it into an envelope and sealing the flap. Looking around the garage for a place to hide the disk he spots the attic hatch. Using the stepladder, Joe raises the attic hatch and places the envelope under the insulation…. nobody will want to look for it there.

Returning the ladder to the corner of the garage, he glances up at the sealed attic hatch – satisfied with his choice. The disk with the information about the al Qaeda terrorist, Ayman al-Zawahri, is safely hidden where it won't accidentally be discovered.

Joe, after cleaning up, speaks to his wife.

"I'm feeling better now."

"I noticed you were upset when you got in the car," Eileen responds quietly. "I didn't say anything because I assumed it was government business."

"No, somebody broke into my locker and left it a mess."

Keith and Jerry Ferguson bound in from baseball practice. Jerry asks, "Dad, will you and mom be coming to our game on Saturday?"

"I'm counting on seeing you and Keith playing, and I will definitely be there."

"How about you mom? Will you be coming?" Keith quietly inquires.

" I've already cancelled my hairdresser appointment to be there."

Jerry, never missing a chance to tease, jokes to his mother. "We must be pretty important for you to cancel that appointment for us."

"Don't get feeling too important, I'm only going so I can laugh at all your mistakes," Eileen teases back. "Now the two of you get cleaned up because dinner's ready."

Surveillance

The following morning Pierre Montague calls Marie Fontaine, the member of the secretarial staff seated closest to the communal office equipment, into his private office.

Montague pushes aside the papers he is presently working on and rises smiling as Marie enters the room.

"Please come in and sit down Mrs. Fontaine. May I call you Marie?"

"Why certainly, Mr. Montague."

"We're supposed to have nice weather this weekend. Will you be out taking advantage of it?"

"It was my daughter's birthday yesterday. We have a party planned for tomorrow."

"She must be excited. How old is she?"

"She turned four. Annie keeps asking when Saturday will be here."

"Marie, it's come to my attention that you will soon be receiving a well-deserved raise in wages. Your work ethic and the quality of your work are well known throughout the department and I might add the envy of some of your colleagues. I wanted to tell you personally because you have done such a wonderful job, and I know you will continue to perform at your same level of excellence."

"Thank you Mr. Montague."

"It's me that must thank you Marie. You're so conscientious in your duties and attitude you make my job much easier."

"I'm always pleased when I'm able to compliment staff for their accomplishments. I've really enjoyed conversing with you Marie, but (Montague begins moving some papers back in front of himself) I'm afraid I must return to my work."

While Marie rises to leave Pierre's office, he solicits the information she was summoned to the office to provide.

"Oh, before you run Marie, could you tell me if Joe Ferguson was at the office printer early yesterday morning?"

"Yes," she nods. "I saw him pick up some papers and glance at them, then he disposed of the papers at the shredder."

"Are you certain of that?"

"Yes, I particularly noticed because he went directly from the printer to the shredder, and I heard it running for a few pages."

"Thank you Marie, I compliment you on your memory, but please don't mention our conversation to anyone – it's confidential."

"Is Joe in trouble?"

"Definitely not," Pierre smiles, "I just required confirmation on the status of some highly classified documents he's been working on. Joe is a very sensitive about his work; I thought you might be able to confirm the information he passed on to me, which you have. Again, please don't mention our conversation. I wouldn't want Joe to be needlessly upset."

"I wouldn't want that either, Mr. Montague. Joe's a very nice man."

"And thank you again Marie for the terrific work you are doing in your department. We really need more people of your calibre."

Marie leaves, completely enamoured by the praise and attention from her superior.

Pierre phones Jean Perrault, the stranger from C.S.I.S.

"It looks like Ferguson copied some documents yesterday, but he must have changed his mind because he shredded them immediately."

"How positive are you?"

"One of the staff seated next to the printer saw him, and that bitch doesn't miss a thing."

"Is there any way we can examine the papers Pierre?"

"No, it's incinerated by the cleaning staff when they come in each evening. I should have thought of that yesterday morning."

"Is there any opportunity to bring Ferguson into the organization?" Perrault asks. "That would certainly clear up the problem for us."

"No. He works in the wrong department to help us. Anyway, that bastard has too much integrity."

"We'll keep Ferguson under surveillance for a while and see what happens. If he starts acting furtive, we'll have to dispose of him. If nothing suspicious happens you'd be smart to fire him in a year or so – not too soon – it would look suspicious. Besides, it's much easier to watch him from inside the department."

"The firing is a good idea. I'd already planned to keep an eye on him from this end.

"I've arranged with my technician for a surveillance camera and a bug to be installed in Ferguson's office over the weekend. That will give the technician ample opportunity to do a neat job without being observed. The recording unit will be installed in your office. Also, two of our agents will be monitoring the Ferguson residence to install bugs while the family's out."

On Friday evening, Joe and Eileen Ferguson plan to meet with friends, John and Marjorie Thatcher, for supper and the theatre. Joe and Eileen arrive first. A vase of flowers is placed on their table.

"What lovely flowers," smiles Marjorie as she and her husband sit down. "I wonder what the occasion is?"

Joe glances around and notices theirs is the only table containing the centerpiece but gives it no more thought as he becomes engrossed in the dinner conversation.

When the Fergusons and the Thatchers enter the theatre the surveillance team tailing the Fergusons waits patiently in their vehicle. The two C.S.I.S. agents conducting the surveillance of Joe and Eileen follow them back to their home after leaving the theatre. Again, Joe is oblivious of the vehicle following them.

Saturday afternoon, while cheering on their sons at the baseball game, a C.S.I.S. agent enters the Ferguson home and installs the audio surveillance equipment.

On Monday morning, Marc Leblanc, the departmental head of C.S.I.S. in Ottawa, has three reports on his desk. The first confirms Joe Ferguson's office phone has a tap on it and a video camera has been installed in his office. The second deals with a tap on the home phone and the additional five pieces of audio surveillance equipment installed in the Ferguson residence and garage complete with tapes of all conversations on the phones and in the residence. There is also confirmation of a satellite tracer placed on Joe Ferguson's car making it easier to follow. The third is a complete dossier on Joe's activities for the past week including the meeting with the Thatchers and the tape of the conversations between the Thatcher and the Ferguson families during their dinner engagement. Leblanc will pass this information on to Jean Perrault, the Senior Official of the Canadian Security and Intelligence Service, later today.

By Wednesday, Joe is becoming curious about the van parked in front of his neighbour's residence since Saturday afternoon. Spotting the neighbour, Tom Jackson, taking his dog for a walk, Joe strolls out to the sidewalk to greet him.

"Hi Tom, I See Ralph is giving you your daily exercise."

"Yeah, Ralph takes me walking three or four times a day. If I didn't have him, I wouldn't be enjoying nearly enough exercise. I'll be getting more exercise shortly though. Harold is coming over on Saturday to work my garden, then I'll plant some veggies."

"I see you bought a van. Are you planning to use it on a holiday?"

"That's not my van Fergie, I don't know whose it is. Last Saturday afternoon I saw it stop in front of my house. A man came from behind your house and climbed in the back of it. A few minutes later both men left the van, got in a car parked on the street in front of your house, and drove away. I'm wondering what's going on because the man who drove the van comes back every morning, carries a briefcase into the rear of the vehicle for ten to fifteen minutes and then leaves."

Joe ponders to himself why anybody would do that. "That's bizarre, does he do anything else or just go to the van?"

"So far that's all he's done. He's got me so curious I've taken pictures of him and his car. I plan to watch him really close until I figure out just what on earth he's doing. If I find something out I'll let you know."

Thanks Tom. I appreciate that. I'm curious as to the reason why a stranger would park his van so close to our homes and visit it every day." Joe glances at his watch then changes the subject. "Ralph seems anxious to be on his way and I have to run to an Elks meeting tonight. I'll talk to you later Tom."

Joe is mystified about the information Tom had just given him, then realizes it must be tied to the computer disk in the garage attic. This was becoming dangerous. Montague's actions indicate the documents have to be the tip of a very large criminal activity in his department and Joe is already set up to be a scapegoat if it is ever uncovered.

Joe proceeds down to the basement of his home and turns on the stereo in the family room. Searching diligently, he discovers an electronic device under the coffee table. His suspicions are confirmed. How many more of these devices are in their home? A search of the office and spare bedroom fails to turn up the phone tap. Joe's feelings are changing from nervous to angry. Slowly he calms himself down. Shutting off the stereo, Joe goes up to the living room to continue his search. He discovers an identical device under the coffee table in the living room. He's now found two. Joe sits down, his mind in a turmoil as he processes the implications of his discovery. He deduces they are most likely some type of listening device. Joe heads upstairs to the bathroom. He requires the opportunity to regain his composure before sitting down with his family for dinner. Joe realizes he cannot tell his wife and sons about the problem that has invaded their lives. A slip of the tongue will place their lives in jeopardy – a danger he dares not impose on them.

At six thirty Joe leaves early for his monthly meeting of the Elks Lodge. He is still anguishing over the latest development when he spots his friend Maurice Solinger, proprietor of Confidential Investigations.

"Hello Maurice. Could we talk in private for a few minutes? I was going to phone but realized it could be dangerous from home."

"Sure. Let's go out to my car."

"This information is highly confidential. I've got a problem that started at the Immigration Department. I was working on the computer and some landed immigration papers appeared showing Aymon al-Zawahri, an al Qaeda terrorist, has been granted Canadian Landed Immigrant status and is living in Vancouver."

"Ayman al-Zawahri. I've heard of him. That guy is pure poison. Isn't the U.S. Government looking for him? Well, it certainly can't get any worse than that."

"The documents bore my signature."

"It just got worse. Do you have any more information Fergie?"

"Yes. Somebody changed the terrorist's name to Mahmoud el-Hafnawi, and his address to Montreal, Quebec. My signature remained on the papers. Later I was called...." Joe freezes.... His eyes register movement behind the car. Three men walk past, headed for the lodge. Both men relax and grin nervously. "Later I was called to the office of a superior to clarify a problem. When I returned to my desk, I surprised the head of the Immigration Department pawing through the papers on my desk. When I confronted Montague, he became very angry. I wasn't supposed to catch him there. He searched through my computer files before leaving."

"Why would he go through your files?"

"To find out if I'd recorded the information."

"Did you?"

"As I was leaving for the evening, Montague and a stranger forced me back into my office. They demanded my jacket and emptied the pockets onto my desk. When I challenged their order to strip off my pants and shirt an argument ensued."

"I'll just bet it did. Keep talking."

"The stranger produced a badge showing that he was with C.S.I.S. and demanded that I do as I'm told. They went through the rest of my clothes and left. After dressing, I left the office, only to be confronted by the man from C.S.I.S. again. He told me to forget what had happened. He's a scary character – well over six feet tall and must weigh 300 pounds. His looks as mean as a pro wrestler posturing for the camera. As I left, the C.S.I.S. agent entered my office."

"You've just described the Senior Official of C.S.I.S. I've heard he's as mean as he looks. The agents working in Ottawa have a very low opinion of him – in fact, they hate his guts. I hear he's very cozy with the Prime Minister…. That's how he got the job – it certainly wasn't by his ability…. Go on."

"Saturday afternoon I noticed a strange van parked on the street in front of my neighbor's house. I questioned him about it tonight, and he told me a stranger parked it there. My neighbor told me the man comes back every morning and goes into the vehicle. That got me thinking. I started checking in my house and I found a strange electronic device under the coffee table in the family room."

"Probably a bug. Did you check in your phones?"

"No I didn't. I was afraid the noise would alert the people that installed the devices. That could pose a greater danger."

"You're right. I never thought of that."

"Searching further, I discovered another identical device under a coffee table in the living room. There are probably more of those things scattered throughout the house. I have no idea what they are or how they operate but I believe they must be some type of listening device – as you called them – a bug. My biggest concern is to protect my family and then I need to clear myself."

"Go back into the meeting Joe. I'll contact a friend and we'll discuss your options once he arrives."

Later that evening Maurice Solinger signals Joe, and the two men leave the meeting. Neither one speaks as they wend their way towards Maurice's vehicle. Once inside, a stranger in the back seat speaks.

"We can talk without fear of being overheard. There's no surveillance equipment on us right now, but I'll keep monitoring."

"Joe Ferguson, meet Alex Johansen. Alex has been in the audio and video surveillance business for the last twenty years and has operated his own business for fourteen of those years. I've used him for years – his work is excellent. He'll check your car and house to find out if the devices you discovered in your home are some type of surveillance monitor."

"Would you write down your address for us and then wait here for ten minutes?" Alex asks Joe. "We'll meet you at your residence, but I need to arrive first. Maurice will watch to see if anybody is tailing you. I'll check your car right now, before we leave."

Alex finds the tracer on Joe's vehicle.

"That tracer allows them to follow you at a distance," Alex informs Joe, "and also tells them via satellite everywhere the car has been."

Alex arrives at the Ferguson house first. He uses his equipment to examine the van and finds an audio surveillance recording system installed inside it.

Joe arrives home, drives into the garage, and closes the overhead door. He opens the garage entrance door and turns on the light. Alex enters and quickly finds a listening device located under a small kitchen table stored in the garage. He finds a second device under the dining room table, and a third unit attached to the bottom of the coffee table in the living room. In the basement, Alex discovers a fourth device in the telephone in the office, and another in the family room under the coffee table. Joe Ferguson, using the monitor, enters the master bedroom where his wife is sleeping and discovers the last unit in the hollow base of a lamp. The boy's rooms are clean. The two men leave the Ferguson residence to discuss with Maurice the problems Joe faces with the surveillance equipment in the house.

"Those audio surveillance bugs are used almost exclusively by the R.C.M.P. and C.S.I.S.," Alex informs the two men. "You're a top priority with those guys Joe. You must have stumbled onto something very incriminating for them to take this much interest in you. I can try to check at your office, but you need to assume that your phone is bugged, and they might even have installed video surveillance equipment to monitor everything you do in your office. I'm going to do some research on how to counteract these devices. I need your home phone number and your office phone number including your extension. My secretary will phone you just before lunch with a wrong number. I'll see if my equipment can pick up any bugs but that type can be almost impossible to detect through a telephone exchange."

"Go for a walk each day and I'll meet you at the service station on Carling Avenue at seven p.m.," Maurice advises Joe. "We'll be able to pass any information we acquire on to you at that time."

Monday evening Maurice meets with Joe at the appointed rendezvous. As they cross the street on the walk signal Maurice slips a piece of paper into Joe's hand saying, "read this when you're alone and then destroy it." Both men walk their respective ways. At home, Joe goes into the bathroom to read the note.

Strong possibility your office phone is bugged. If they use a surveillance camera, it will be located in a light fixture above your head. Take a short walk each Monday and Thursday evening and we will meet you as required. To contact us with any pertinent information, phone Maurice's cell from a pay phone and leave the message "Joe here." We'll meet you in the Deli section of the Carlingwood Plaza Loblaw store at seven p.m. the following evening.

Garage Sale

Saturday, while Joe is mowing the lawn, a neighbor, Jerry Adams stops to speak.

"We're holding a garage sale next weekend Fergie. Are you interested in buying or selling anything?"

"I just might be. I have some household items cluttering up the garage. I need the space more than the furniture. Are you running an ad in the newspaper?"

"We sure are. The ad will bring more people than just using signs."

"If you add a twin bed with a dresser and a small kitchen table with three chairs to the list, I'll split the cost of the ad with you."

"Thanks Fergie. That's fair enough."

That evening, Joe leaves the house for a walk. Stopping at a pay phone, he places the call to Maurice.

"Confidential Investigations, Maurice speaking."

"Joe here."

Both parties hang up.

Sunday evening Joe arrives at the Loblaw store at the predetermined time to rendezvous with Maurice and Alex in the deli section of the store. Alex is seated, eating a salad. Maurice joins Alex, then Joe strolls over.

Joe sits down and "The Three Mumbles" huddle close together to hear his scheme. Joe glances furtively around, making sure no one can overhear their conversation then speaks quietly to his fellow conspirators.

"My neighbor is holding a garage sale this coming weekend. I was wondering what would happen if I sold a couple of items?"

"Someone might have a heart attack," says Alex, with a conniving grin.

"I take it you like the idea as much as I do."

"I love the idea. They never dreamed of this eventuality. I can just see their faces when they discover their precious equipment gone. Lets plan this out right now Joe. What day would you be selling the articles?"

"Saturday. The mystery man usually arrives at the van between eight and nine and stays for fifteen minutes. I'll take the items to the Adams sale after he leaves. They're not likely to notice the disappearance of their equipment until Monday morning and even if they do find out Sunday it's too late."

Alex thinks for a moment, visualizing the placement of the surveillance devices in his mind. Leaning closer, he mumbles.

"Sell the table and chairs from the garage, the coffee and end table from the basement, and the telephone from your office. Then move the coffee and end table from the living room downstairs. Gloria and Shannon will be at the sale to buy those items."

"Are you planning to sell the dresser and twin bed you have stored in the garage?" Maurice softly inquires. "I could use those items myself."

"Yes. In fact I've included the bed and dresser and the table and chairs in my neighbor's advertisement."

"This is better still," Alex gloats. "We'll pick up those goodies as well and Gloria and Shannon can talk about Shannon being transferred to Toronto and renting a bachelor suite. That will throw them completely off the track. When you go for your walk on Thursday, meet me here. I'll show you a picture of Gloria, Shannon and the pick-up truck so you'll recognize them. My wife will dicker with you on the prices to make it more authentic. Everything said during the transactions and loading will be recorded on the tapes in the van so Gloria and Shannon will have to use aliases. If it's C.S.I.S. or the R.C.M.P. involved, those agents will be absolutely beside themselves with rage. They both believe their taps are so damned important this will screw up their whole day. We can assume the bugs are illegal. Anything we do will make them nervous, maybe even enough to remove the rest of the audio surveillance equipment from your home."

Joe glances at his watch. "I'd better get my shopping done. I'll come past on my way to the till. If you think of anything else let me know."

"I'm sure were finished here." Alex continues speaking. "When you leave I'll take a picture of you to show Gloria and Shannon. They should arrive at the sale shortly after nine o'clock."

Maurice and Alex are still laughing over this turn of events as Joe wheels his shopping cart away to pick up the rest of his groceries.

As Joe leaves the Loblaw grocery, he observes Alex standing between two cars directly in front of him. Joe walks nonchalantly toward the camera and after the first picture is taken turns towards his car. Alex snaps another photo.

Arriving home, Joe carries the groceries into the house. "Is there anything else you need Eileen?"

"I'm sorry, I forgot to mention the milk."

"I picked up milk. With those two calves around the house we're always short."

A voice is heard, bellowing from the living room.

"Fresh milk."

Keith comes streaming towards the fridge. Joe grabs him.

"Quick Eileen, padlock the fridge."

The laughter and the banter continues as the family walks out the back door to relax and enjoy the cool Ottawa evening. The boys are carrying their baseball gloves, so Joe grabs a spare glove to join them in a game of catch, while Eileen dives back into her book. Joe, relaxed and is enjoying himself, suddenly realizes the heavy load he has been carrying is much lighter in his mind.

During the ensuing week, Joe gathers children's books, tapes, and old records and stores them in boxes in the garage. Thursday afternoon Joe carries them to the neighbor, Jerry Adams, for the garage sale.

"Could you sell these items in your sale? Just put whatever price you think they're worth on them and sell them for whatever you can get. There are some children's books and videos in those boxes. If you have any use for them just take them. Your kids should enjoy them."

"Thanks Fergie. Have you changed your mind on the furniture?"

"No, I'm bringing them over Saturday morning. I won't be too early. We'll be late getting home Friday evening, but I'll definitely bring them over."

"Would you mind helping me bring the chesterfield up from the basement to the garage for the sale? I don't have two big men to help me like somebody I know."

"You were outside for a few minutes. Were you talking to a neighbor?" Eileen asks her husband.

"I was talking to Jerry. I helped him carry an old chesterfield from his basement to the garage."

Saturday morning Joe sees the man entering the van. The operative leaves quickly because people are arriving for the sale and he doesn't want any scrutiny of himself or the vehicle. From the living room, Joe watches him leave.

"Eileen, Jerry and Connie Adams are holding a garage sale. Why don't we get rid of the old coffee and end tables from the family room? They've become a real eyesore. I've seen you checking out that new set from Sears and I think they'd look great in the living room."

Eileen eyes him speculatively. "So, what do you want?"

Well… I've been thinking… I'd like a cordless phone in the dining room. We could move that phone to the office. Selling the table and chairs and the bed and dresser from the garage would give us more room for the cars. Do you boys want to sell anything?"

"We need the coffee table," interjects Jerry.

"We could take the coffee and end table from the living room downstairs," suggests Joe. "Would that work for you?"

"No probleemo – they hold food just as well!"

Keith and Jerry head for the stairs to the basement.

"Hey you two. Why don't you carry the coffee and end table downstairs with you?"

While Joe is conferring with his sons Eileen disappears up the stairs. Joe is extricating the table and chairs for the sale when Eileen gaily dances into the garage holding the lamp like her dance partner and singing, "The lamp is gone, the lamp is gone."

Joe is laughing at his wife's antics when the boys charge past them making the first delivery to the Adams' garage sale.

Joe and his sons are setting up the sale items when a mother and her daughter begin examining the furniture.

The mother turns to her daughter "We could be in luck. Take a look at this bed and dresser and the dinette and see what you think."

"I'd rather have new stuff."

"Whatever you can afford darling."

"Well I tried," Shauna admits. "The bed and dresser look very good and they're small enough to fit in the bachelor suite. The table and chairs are fine. How much are you asking for the phone?"

"$5.00 for the phone, $50.00 for the dresser and bed and $25.00 for the table and chairs."

"That lamp is cute," Shauna says to her mother.

"It's ugly."

"Alright," Shauna admits. "It's so ugly that it's cute. How much is it?"

"$5.00 but you can't return it," quips Joe.

"I don't want to return it. How much for these two items?"

"$5.00 for the coffee table and $10.00 for the end table."

"How much does that come to?" Shauna asks.

"$100.00."

Shauna's mother bargains, "Would you take $75.00 for all the items we just discussed?"

"I'll take $80.00."

"Pay the man Shauna, That's a very good deal."

"Mom, would we have time to take these things to Toronto today?

"That's an excellent idea. It will save us hauling everything up and down three flights of stairs. We could visit with my sister tonight and come home tomorrow. We'll need to load a few items from the apartment first, and I'll phone Ellen from home. Try to get me a parking spot to load the pick-up and I'll bring it closer."

Joe and his sons carry the sold items to the curb where two people are preparing to leave.

"Would you mind waiting for a minute?" Joe asks the driver of the car. "The lady who bought this stuff is bringing her vehicle and it's hard to hold a parking stall."

"No problem. Just let me know when to pull out."

With the truck loaded Joe, Keith and Jerry help the Adams family sell the rest of the goods at the garage sale.

Gloria Johansen drives into the Carlingwood Plaza parking lot, and then continues to the far side of the lot. The two ladies alite from the truck.

"I have the list of groceries I need." Shannon informs her mother.

As the ladies walk toward the grocery store, Alex intersects their paths, handing Gloria a set of keys.

"Maurice just phoned and gave me the all clear. It's safe for me to remove the bugs but wait here until I'm finished."

Alex shuts down the audio surveillance units as he removes them from the lamp and phone, and repeats the process on the coffee table and kitchen table in the back of the truck. The job finished, he climbs into the truck, and drives away followed by Gloria and Shannon in the Solinger car. Alex stops the pick-up before entering Saville Row and Maurice jumps into the passenger seat. Arriving at the Solinger residence, the Johansens and Maurice Solinger unload the furniture, carrying the items into the basement of the house. Maurice picks up the lamp.

"Don't even think of touching that lamp," Shannon states emphatically, "it's mine."

"I'll rassle you for it," Maurice jokes, hugging it in his arms.

"If you don't put that lamp back I'll tear off your arm and beat you sillier than you already are," Shannon fires back at him.

The four proceed laughing into the house where Kathleen Solinger has prepared lunch.

"How's the sale going Joe?" Eileen Ferguson asks her husband, having just arrived at the scene.

"We sold all the larger items," Joe responds. "A lady and her daughter bought all of them."

"Did you know the buyers?"

"No. I've never seen them before in my life. I gathered from their conversation the daughter is moving to Toronto."

"Would you be able come with me and we could look at some end tables?"

"Sure. We've sold almost everything we brought." Joe turns to his sons, "could you boys help Jerry and Connie while we go shopping?

"We have a ball practice at four-thirty. Can you be back before then?" Jerry asks his father.

"If they're not back we'll look after the sale," Connie interjects. "We plan to close down at five o'clock."

Something Missing

Sunday the stranger again visits the van and again leaves quickly.

Monday he picks up the tapes and drives to the office. Playing the Saturday tape, he can't believe what he's hearing. After listening to the truck pull away, he plays the tape again, then makes a phone call.

"Jean Perrault here."

"It's John Winston. You'd better come down and listen to the Ferguson recordings for Saturday."

"I'll be there at three o'clock. I'm too busy to come right now."

"They sold some furniture and there's four surveillance bugs missing."

"**WHAT!**"

John removes the phone from his ear to lessen the reverberations of Perrault's angry outburst.

"They sold some…

"**I damn well heard you. I'm coming right down.**"

When John Winston hangs up he is smiling. He doesn't like Perrault and enjoys his discomfort. Perrault has made it a point to belittle John because he is only a technician with C.S.I.S. John takes satisfaction in the knowledge that the service he provides, the agents with their university degrees in law and criminology are incapable of handling."

Perrault storms through the doorway bellowing, **"Let's hear the tape!"**

John starts the recording.

"Play it again."

After listening to the recording a second time Perrault asks, "Are you positive it was a garage sale?"

"There were signs up and people hauling stuff away four doors down from the marks home."

"Why didn't you listen to this on Sunday?"

"My brother and his family were visiting us over the weekend. I had a hard time getting away to even pick up the recordings. Anyways from all the previous recordings, there was no way I could foresee this problem. Regardless, there is nothing I could have done to stop him from selling his own possessions without being obvious."

From his office, Perrault places a call to one of the secretaries.

"Hello, Erin Henley here."

"Erin, I need you to pick up your daughter and clarify a problem for me. Come up to my office and I'll give you the information and the address you'll require to do some clandestine research."

Jean knows that Erin is trustworthy and will be discreet. They have been lovers for three years and the baby girl is his.

Erin Henley parks the car two blocks from the Ferguson residence and fastens her daughter in the baby stroller. Meandering down the street, they wander up to the Adams residence at 21 Rowanwood Avenue. Erin rings the doorbell and a young lady answers the door. Huddled behind her are two very inquisitive children staring at the strange lady with the baby.

"Hello, my name is Erin. We just moved in three blocks away and I heard you were having a garage sale."

"No. We had the sale last weekend," Connie informs Erin.

"Oh. I'm sorry for bothering you. I was hoping to buy a table and chairs but I guess I'm out of luck."

"One of our neighbors did sell a kitchenette."

"Do you know who bought them? Maybe I could talk them into selling them to me. If not they might sell me their old set."

"I'd never seen them before." Connie continues speaking, "and I heard our neighbor tell his wife they were strangers to him. I know the young lady also bought a dresser and bed and a coffee table from Joe. She bought an electric frying pan from me as well, and a toaster and electric kettle from another neighbor."

"I'm sorry I bothered you. Thank you for your time. This looks like a beautiful neighbourhood. I sure hope to see you again."

Erin wanders slowly back to her car with her baby tucked safely in the stroller.

She returns her daughter to the daycare, drives back to the headquarters of the Canadian Security and Intelligence Service, and heads directly to Perrault's office.

"Were you able to learn anything about the surveillance equipment that disappeared during the garage sale?"

"Yes. The lady bought a bed and dresser from Joseph Ferguson as well as the dinette. She also purchased various household items from other neighbours. From the items she purchased I believe she was moving from her parent's home to her own place. The neighbour had never seen the people before and she overheard Ferguson telling his wife they were strangers to him."

"Thank you dear, I knew I could count on you." Jean envelops Erin in an enthusiastic embrace to which she responds passionately. Erin has thoroughly enjoyed the role she played while helping her lover procure the information he required.

As Erin is leaving, Perrault picks up the phone to contact John Winston.

"Install listening devices in the living room and in the office phone. We don't need to worry about putting bugs in the garage and bedroom."

"I'm not going into the Ferguson house. Get one of your field agents to do it."

"I'm not pulling an agent off another project just to install two bugs in a house, so you're stuck with the job."

"It's not part of my job description."

"It is now so do as I damn well tell you! One more bitch out of you and you'll find yourself working out of our Winnipeg office and freezing you're nuts off. Have I made myself clear?"

"Yeah," John grumbles. "We'll need another court order to re-enter the Ferguson premises."

"Don't you worry your pretty little head about that." The Senior Official continues sarcastically. "It's not part of your job description. I'll have the office staff pick up the court order. When can you install the bugs?"

"Hopefully next Sunday while they're in church."

Sunday morning, the C.S.I.S. technician again enters the van. While furtively waiting, he observes Joe, Eileen and Jerry leaving their home to attend worship. Keith isn't with them. John Winston cannot take a chance on entering the residence while it could be occupied. With a sense of relief, he leaves the site, planning to enter the residence later.

Tom observes the agent entering the van and then leaving an hour later. He records the information as he has been doing ever since talking to Joe a few weeks ago. He had previously recorded the license plate number on the car, and using a telephoto lens, has taken a picture of the operative.

Home Invasion

Thursday morning Tom Jackson observes Joe backing his wife's car out of the garage. When the C.S.I.S. technician arrives, he enters the van but doesn't leave. Ralph, wanting to go for a walk, starts to fuss. Tom releases his golden retriever into the back yard, then continues his stealthy observation of the man waiting covertly in the van.

At eleven, o'clock Eileen leaves the house. The technician slips from the van and quickly moves into the back yard of the residence. Ralph, his head held high and his ears alertly perked, trots over to the fence. The dog lowers his ears, drops his head and begins sniffing along the fence as he moves away. Tom, seeing the change in Ralph's demeanor, realizes the man must have entered the house. Stepping out his back door confirms his suspicions – the stranger is nowhere to be seen. Moving back into his own home, Tom quickly dials 911.

"My name is Tom Jackson. A stranger broke into my neighbor's home. The address is 29 Rowanwood Avenue." Hanging up the phone he spots Keith and Jerry Ferguson and three of their friends running across the lawn to the front door of their home. Tom rushes downstairs. Opening the gun case, he removes the shotgun, loads it, and then heads up the stairs and out the front door.

John Winston watches Eileen Ferguson departing from her home. This is the dreaded opportunity he has spent the morning nervously anticipating.

Leaving the van, John walks apprehensively to the back door of the residence. This is field agent work and he won't be bullied into doing it again. John easily gains entry with the key provided by C.S.I.S. In the living room, he installs a listening device under one of the new end tables. He runs down the stairs, anxious to be finished. Dismantling the phone in the office, he is all thumbs. A screw falls. 'Where? There…. Footsteps! Voices! Hide…. Nothing! Trapped!' Setting the phone down, John creeps to the door and silently closes it. Searching… searching…. 'Window… too small… too small…. Searching… searching…. Windows… remove windows – escape….'

John almost stumbles moving a chair under the window. He steps up on it, and begins removing the sliding glass panels…. 'Careful…. Careful….' Muscles tense with the nervous strain, he sweats profusely. His hands want to slip…. 'Careful…. Careful….'

'Footsteps… someone coming… hide…. Trapped….' John steps off the chair and pulls out his weapon. Like a cornered animal, he crouches – waiting for the door to open… crouching… waiting…. Muscles tighten to the breaking point. The room, like a giant constrictor crushing in on him, holds John in its deadly grasp. The footsteps quietly glide past the doorway – their ghostly passage bringing an icy sweat to the brow of the man hiding in his lair.

The boys race into the house and Keith runs up the stairs to the washroom.

Art Condor speaks to Jerry inquiring, "Can I use the bathroom?"

"Sure Art, use the one in the basement. You know where it is."

Art heads downstairs. As he enters the washroom Jerry sneaks down the stairs to the landing, hiding there to scare his friend as he returns.

John nervously replaces the gun in the holster. He steps quickly back on the chair to remove the rest of the window panels. Every little scrape exaggerates his anxiety. He is panicking in his fight to quickly and silently remove the last panel when he hears the toilet flush. Ghostly footsteps once more kcs – kcs – kcs – kcs – inexorably towards him. With each step, icy tendrils probe *deeper... d e e p e r... d e e p e r...* into his soul. Tension freezes his muscles – constricting his movements. Nervously, John steps down from the chair. The chair scrapes.... Icy sweat covers his shivering body.... He can barely move.... He can't breathe.... His wildly pounding heart thunders in his ears.... John awkwardly pulls out his firearm – fumbling and almost dropping it.

Art, walking towards the stairs, hears the scrape of chair and assumes his friends are in the office. Smiling, he reaches for the doorknob....

Slowly it turns.... Slowly it turns....

A wildly gyrating demon flies screaming into John's presence, threatening to devour the life inside him. Its menacing descent clawing into his soul. The crack of the weapon in his hand sends its deadly projectile, slamming this spirit of evil, lifeless, into the floor.

Jerry, hearing the shout and the shot, steps out onto the landing. His eyes searching... searching... searching....

The technician, like a trapped animal seeing an escape route opening up before him, leaps wildly over the crumpled body – out through doorway – the harbinger of death poised in his hand.

"What are you doing here?"

The stranger in a wild panic swings around, raising his weapon, his path to freedom blocked once more. Jerry, like a cat, leaps to the side. The weapon crackles again sending its deadly messenger of death in search of another victim – to no avail. The missile, buzzing harmlessly through now empty space, slams into the wall.

'RUN!'

Their silent scream dominates the boys very being.... Their legs pump in slow motion, weighted down by leaden feet.... Their bodies being clutched at – clutched at – clutched at.... Holding them back from their flight to freedom.

'RUN!'

The silent scream continues. Slowly the leg rises, drags ahead, and plunges deep into the ground as the other leg begins its slow forward motion. Their chests shrink until they cannot breathe. The pounding hearts try to explode. They force themselves through the dense air clutching them.... Holding them back.... Holding them back....

HWAK!

Another fiery messenger of death whistles after the fleeing boys. Search and destroy.... Search and destroy....

'RUN!'

The scream rings in their panic stricken minds as they   s—l—o—w—l—y,   s—l—o—w—l—y,   s—l—o—w—l—y,   f—l—e—e   i—n   t—e—r—r—o—r. Their feet continue their leaden motions forward. Drag the foot from the clutches of the ground. Push the heavy, heavy foot forward. Drive the foot into the clutches of the ground. Drag the other foot slowly, slowly forward….

BO-O-O-OM.

'RUN, RUN, RUN!'

The silent screams continue…. Their legs continue their slow, inexorable drive for life….

'R-U-U-U-N!'

Silence!!!!!

Slowly, ever so slowly, the different sound of the last shot sinks into the terrified minds of the fleeing boys. Glancing back, they slowly realize that Tom Jackson is the lone figure standing in the Ferguson yard.

The three boys streak out the front door of the house. They fly across the lawn, and down the sidewalk, away from Tom Jackson rushing towards the lilac bushes dividing the two properties.

Twack! The terrified man exits the house firing at the boys. He leaps wildly from the step into the yard, stumbles, stops, and again raises his deadly weapon.

Tom, seeing the man firing the third shot, raises his shotgun. As the man stops to fire again, Tom pulls both triggers. **BOOM! Twack!** The man falls forward pulling the trigger of his weapon as he falls.

Silence descends eerily onto the scene. The birds have fled. A cat crouches – ready to flee for its life…. Nothing moves…. Nothing makes a sound….

Tom reloads and then rushes up to the man lying on the lawn.

Keith peeks out the door… then explodes from the house racing towards Tom.

"Keith – In the kitchen – Grab my camera."

Keith hesitates, then races into Tom's home.

Tom removes the live shells from his gun, placing them in his pocket. Keith returns and hands Tom the camera as Tom hands Keith the empty shotgun.

"Put the gun in the closet by the front door and phone your dad. Don't say a word about what happened but tell him to come home immediately."

Keith charges back into the Jackson residence to contact his father. His trembling hands dial the number.

"Joe Ferguson here."

"Could you come home right now? We need you and mom isn't home."

Hearing the panic in Keith's voice but also realizing that his office phone is likely bugged, Joe doesn't question Keith any further.

"Yes! I'm leaving now!"

Tom takes a picture of the dead man, and then rolling him over, takes another photo. The intruder's jacket is open and Tom, seeing the man's wallet, removes it and examines the contents. He is stunned to discover a C.S.I.S. badge pinned to the inside of the pocketbook. Placing the opened wallet on the corpse, Tom takes pictures of the dead technician's badge, his C.S.I.S. identification and his driver licence, before cautiously replacing the articles and placing the wallet back inside the jacket pocket. Tom then carefully rolls the man back to his original position.

The three boys, fleeing in panic from the gunman, hear the louder boom of the shotgun. Slowly the different sound registers in their minds. Jerry, now in the lead, glances back towards the house. No longer able to see the man with the gun menacing them, he slows down and then stops running. The other boys, seeing Jerry slowing down, follow suit. They turn around and recognize Tom Jackson standing over something lying on the ground. The three boys wait, then cautiously retrace their steps back to Tom. He herds them into his own residence, and dials his lawyer.

"Jones, Smythe and Watson Law Offices."

"I have to speak to Bob Watson right now."

"That's not possible," the receptionist, explains, "Mr. Watson is busy with a client at the present time."

Tom is thoroughly agitated and his voice begins to rise. "I just killed a man, get him for me immediately."

A moment later, a male voice is on the line. "Bob Watson."

"Tom Jackson here. I just killed a man." His voice continues to rise as his speech accelerates. "He broke into my neighbor's home. The neighbor's sons surprised him. He was shooting at the boys when I shot him. I discovered he works for C.S.I.S. You'll have to come over right now."

" Slow down and give me your address."

"27 Rowanwood Avenue."

Bob speaks slowly in a soothing voice.

"Take a deep breath and relax."

"Now give me that address again."

"27 Rowanwood Avenue."

"I'll be right there."

Keith, looking around, suddenly realizes one of his friends is missing. "Where's Art?"

"He was ddddown the bbbbasement wwhere the shshshooting started," Jerry stammers, seized by the realization of the tragedy that has befallen his friend.

"You wait here." Tom again takes charge of the situation, his voice back to normal. "I'll check on him right now."

Picking up his camera, Tom hurries over to the Ferguson house, then down into the basement. Art lies crumpled on the office floor. Tom, after ascertaining the boy is dead, takes pictures of him. He also takes pictures of the window, the chair, the partially dismantled phone, a plastic box containing various electronic devices, and the shell casings on the office floor and at the foot of the stairs.

As he leaves the Ferguson residence, Tom finds the four boys huddled outside the front door, anxiously waiting for him. Despair written all over their features.

"Let's go back to my place." Tom's voice is quiet as he feels the excruciating pain expressed on the faces of the boys. "I'm sorry. Your friend is dead."

Back in the Jackson residence, Tom removes the memory disk from the camera, switching it with a new memory disk. The disk containing the photo evidence he hides at the back of the kitchen closet shelf.

Tom quietly takes the boys into his confidence.

"Don't tell anybody about the pictures I took. That man lying on your lawn is a C.S.I.S. agent. If the government tries to cover up what has happened here we'll need the pictures to prove our own innocence. When the police question you, answer only their questions, don't volunteer any information until you have a chance to talk to a lawyer and then let the lawyer do the talking for you. This could get real dicey with a federal agent involved."

The Investigation

The wail of approaching sirens draws Tom and the boys onto the front lawn of the Jackson residence. Some neighbours are on the Ferguson lawn, drawn to the scene by the sounds of the gunshots and their own morbid curiosity.

The Ottawa City Police arrive – two detectives – two uniforms. A detective takes command as they begin securing the area around the dead man and his firearm.

Tom Jackson begins walking over to the detective in charge of the investigation.

Rene Dubois, observing Tom advancing towards him, asks, "Are you the person who dialed in the 911 call?"

"I am."

"Why didn't you say it was a homicide?"

"He wasn't dead at the time."

"Who shot him?"

"I did," is Tom's quiet answer to the police detective. "He was shooting at three boys, one of whom lives in that home."

"Wait here. I'll need to talk to you as soon as I finish securing the crime scene."

"Maybe first, you should check on the dead boy in the basement of the house." Tom informs the detective.

The detectives mouth drops. Swearing, he turns and runs for the house shouting over his shoulder to the other detective.

"Marcel, come with me."

As the Detectives enter the Ferguson residence, Tom Jackson's solicitor, Bob Watson, and a stranger arrive and hurry up to the Jackson residence. Tom and the boys join them as they enter the home.

Bob Watson introduces the stranger. "Tom Jackson, I want you to meet William Smythe. He's a criminal lawyer and handles all our litigation cases. His expertise will prove invaluable for us today."

Tom shakes hands with Bob's partner as they exchange greetings. Introductions are made between the lawyers and the four boys.

"Let's sit at the table in the dining room," William Smythe advises. "First I need to find out very quickly what has happened." He starts a tape recorder saying, "June 7, 2002, 11.47am. We're in the Tom Jackson residence. First give me your names."

"Tom Jackson."

"JJJJerry Ferguson."

"Keith Ferguson."

"Andre Dupree`."

"SSSSandy Hanger."

"My friend AAAArt CCCCCondor is laying ddddead in the basement of our hhhhome." Jerry Ferguson is choking as he talks. "That man llllying on our lawn kkkkkilled him."

William glances around the table at the four remorse stricken boys. Knowing the boys need time to collect themselves, he speaks quietly to Tom Jackson, asking him to give his information first.

Tom begins to relate his story "I watched the man enter the van at eight-thirty this morning."

William questions Tom further to clarify his answer.

"Are you referring to the van parked in front of your house?"

"Yes he's been coming there every morning for close to a month."

William shuts off the tape recorder. "That van has to be a key piece of evidence. We have to find out what's in it. There has to be a reason why that C.S.I.S. agent comes here every day. Tom and Bob come with me. You boys wait here. Get some water or juice to drink and make yourselves a sandwich. That should help you handle the pain and shock you're now experiencing."

Tom grabs two large cans of juice from a cabinet and a can opener from a drawer. After placing four glasses and the two juice containers on the counter, he informs the boys that bread and jam are in the fridge. Picking up his camera, Tom follows the two lawyers into the Ferguson yard where William Smythe is speaking to the police constable guarding the dead C.S.I.S. agent.

"Tom Jackson informs me that dead man was waiting in that van for an hour and a half before entering the house. One of the keys to solving this dilemma will be tied directly to that vehicle."

"I'll tell Rene."

"That will sure help Rene's career," is the response by William. "Why don't you look yourself and further your own career?"

"I said, I'll tell Rene."

"The answer of a typical bureaucrat," is Bob Watson's sarcastic response. "Get a hammer Tom."

Tom heads for the house.

"You can't break into the van."

"Why not?"

"It's part of the crime scene."

"What proof do you have of that?"

"You told me it was."

William Smythe corrects the policeman. "No, I told you the man was in the van. That doesn't make it part of the crime scene. If I'd told you he came by bus would that make the bus part of the crime scene. Here's Tom now."

"I'll open it."

The policeman starts searching for a master key in his personal key ring.

"Why don't you get the keys from the corpse?" William continues speaking. "If one of them unlocks the door it will tie him directly to the vehicle."

The policeman finds two sets of keys in the pockets of the dead technician and unlocks the van with the set containing two keys. Inside they find an array of electronic equipment.

Neighbors peer into the vehicle to satisfy their own curiosity.

Tom photographs the interior of the van with the audio surveillance recording devices. These photos will aid in explaining the natural progression of the crime to its culmination in the death of the C.S.I.S. agent.

While Bob and the policeman are discussing the contents of the van, William is on the phone to his office.

"Offices of Jones, Smythe and Watson."

"Kathy get Rae for me right now."

"Yes sir Mr. Smythe."

"Rae Jones here."

"Check with the Court of the Queens Bench to see if a permit has been issued to place audio surveillance equipment in the Joseph Ferguson residence at 29 Rowanwood Ave. Get the information as quickly as you can and get back to me on my cell phone."

William turns to the police constable. "It will be prudent to lock up the van before the press arrives. You know it's involved so go ahead and secure it. That looks like a house key on the same key ring. The dead C.S.I.S. agent must have used a key to enter the house where the shooting started. It would be sensible to see if that key fits the door to the Ferguson home."

The Police Constable locks and unlocks the door – verifying Williams hunch.

Back in the Jackson residence, William begins his line of questioning again.

"How many shots did the dead agent fire?"

"Three shots." Jerry replies. "Tttwo in the house and one outside."

The other the boys verify Jerry's statement.

"He fired four shots," interjects Tom quietly, still trying to quell the feelings of pain in the boys. "Two inside the house, one as he was coming out of the door, and the last round just as I fired. The boys may not have noticed the last shot because it blended in with my shotgun blast."

"We need to find those two spent cartridge casings. They'll help us affirm the necessity of Tom shooting the man," reasons William. "You boys search beside the front door of the house and we'll search beside the body of the agent. Be very careful where you step and kneel. We can't have you moving or burying the shell casings with your actions. The casing should be to the right of the door as you leave the house but if it struck the door jamb it could be anywhere."

As both parties move to their respective search areas to look for the evidence, Tom takes a picture of the shotgun casings beside the lilac bushes. Keith sees his dad hurrying down the sidewalk towards them. Nudging his brother, they both leave the search to explain to Joe the circumstance surrounding the death of their comrade by the C.S.I.S. technician.

The men begin their search beside the security tape strung around the body.

"I don't want the boys near the body," William advises his fellow searchers. "They've suffered enough trauma for one day."

"There's the shell casing just inside the tape, straight out from the man's waist," Bob informs William.

"Keep your eyes on it. Constable could you come over here for a minute? We've found a spent shell casing."

The policeman pushes a flag into the ground next to the designated shell casing.

Tom takes one photograph showing the proximity of the 45-calibre shell casing to the body and gun, and then leans under the tape to take a close-up shot of it.

Two reporters arrive. They start by taking pictures of the body and asking questions of the policemen. Receiving no answers, they move up to the door of the house where they are barred from entering by security tape.

Andre finds the spent shell casing where it bounced, in a cluster of pansies. The police constable secures the area with a flag and security tape.

Tom takes more photographs of the second spent cartridge.

William notices the reporters trying to corner the two boys, Andre and Sandy, and knows the boys might reveal information that would prove detrimental to their own, or Tom Jackson's best interest.

"Bob, Let's get the boys back in the house before the reporters start pumping them for information. Right now they are extremely vulnerable and don't need hassling from reporters.

Tom hurries over to Joe and his sons.

"Lets get inside my house before those news hounds get here."

As they enter the house, Tom closes the door. Everybody relaxes a little.

"Is there anything else I should know before we get back to recording?" William asks.

"Well maybe," Tom replies. "While I was in Fergie's office I saw his phone partially dismantled and a small plastic box beside it with little electronic components in compartments in the box. Would he have been trying to bug the phone?"

"With C.S.I.S. involved and the audio surveillance equipment in the van there's an excellent possibility of that scenario. We'll need to find out how many bugs are in the house and their location"

After placing a telephone book on the table in front of William, Joe points to Alex Johansen's business ad.

"Excellent idea." William acknowledges. He dials the number on his cell phone.

"Johansen Surveillance Equipment, Alex speaking."

"My name is William Smythe. I'm an attorney. There have been two deaths in a home invasion and I need to protect my client, who is a neighbor. I firmly believe that there is audio surveillance equipment in the neighbour's residence, where a murder was committed, but I require absolute proof. Could you come to 27 Rowanwood Ave. immediately and search the residence? The police are here now, so you would also be aiding their investigation."

"Give me the address again."

"We're at 27 Rowanwood Ave."

"I can be there in about half an hour."

Sirens announce the arrival of the forensic police. Tom leaves the house and walks quickly over to Rene Dubois, the detective in charge of the investigation.

"I have the boys in my house to keep them away from the body. When I first shot the man, I rolled the body over to see if he was still alive, then moved him back into the position he's in now, so the boys wouldn't remember his face and see it in their nightmares."

"I'll pass that information on to forensics," Rene replies "I'll have to get statements from you and the boys later. Until then try to relax and drink lots of water to counteract shock."

"I'll do that. The boys are still showing signs of shock, but they are beginning to feel a little better. The death of their friend hit them very hard. Those five boys did everything together."

"I saw the boy downstairs. Thanks for shooting the bastard."

"He was shooting at the boys. I did what I had to do." Tom continues, "We believe he was installing audio surveillance equipment in the house. We have an expert coming to check the house. Will that pose a problem to your investigation?"

"Not at all. It will actually aid our investigation. We lack the equipment and expertise to conduct that type of search. If you have any problem with the forensic police see me," Rene advises Tom. "I'll get him in."

Rene walks back to the Jackson residence with Tom.

"My name is Detective Rene Dubois, my partner is Detective Marcel St. Croix. I need to know the name and address of the dead boy. The office will have to contact his parents and inform them of the tragedy."

"His name is Art Condor, he lives at…" Keith stops talking, devastated once more by the full realization he will never enjoy the company of his friend again…. Gathering inner strength, he continues speaking to the detective. "He lived at 32 Keenan Ave. His mother, Alice, works at the Carlingwood Plaza Loblaw store and his father, George, is a mechanic at Shultz Motors."

Rene records the information.

"There's mom."

Jerry pushes past the policeman and runs to his mother on the sidewalk. They talk as they slowly move towards Tom's residence.

"I'll have Art's parents contacted," Rene informs the boys. "Phone your parents and let them know you're okay but stay here until I read your statements. Don't mention the death of Art Condor until we contact his parents."

The reporters, spotting Eileen and Jerry moving towards the Jackson residence stream towards their quarry, surrounding and harassing them until it's impossible for them to move.

Rene, leaving the house, sees the reporters impeding the progress of Eileen and Jerry. Pushing through the throng, he spies Jerry attempting to keep the reporters away from his mother, to no avail.

Grabbing Jerry and pushing him forward, Rene hollers to Jerry, "You're the problem! Get in the house!"

Jerry pushes through the impeding throng and races to the house followed by the ravenous reporters. The reporters ring the doorbell and bang on the door. Rene uses the opportunity to escort Eileen across the lawn and through the gate into Tom's back yard. Eileen stands by the gate crying, her anguish over the death Art Condor tearing at her soul.

"Get into the house. The reporters will soon be looking for you. If you continue to dawdle you'll be held here for hours and you'll be able to see your bawling face on the evening news."

Rene leaves and Eileen heads for the back door of the house

William opens the front door. "I have informed everybody in the house that I'm the only person to speak to reporters and I'm not saying anything. You're on private property. Get lost!"

The door closes.

"We keep getting interrupted and it looks like it will continue." William rips some pages from a notebook and spreads them around the table. "I want each of you to write your own account of everything as it transpired. Record it twice – the police will require one copy. Write your name, address, and the date at the top of the page. Write down your memory of what transpired and then sign the paper. Remember, you only heard three shots fired by the dead agent, even though we later proved he fired four shots. Tom will record the fourth shot on his statement. Bob and I will review the information with you when we have time."

The doorbell rings.

"I'm Alex Johansen. Somebody here phoned for me."

"I'm William Smythe, counsel for Tom Jackson, the owner of this home. I phoned for you. Step inside so we can talk without being harassed by that horde of news reporters."

"We found audio surveillance recording equipment in the van outside this residence. Because of the circumstances, it would be very advantageous if we found corresponding audio surveillance transmitters in the Ferguson house where the forensic police are working. Tom Jackson told me there were electronic devices in the office where the C.S.I.S. agent was dismantling a phone. If you will bring your equipment, we'll check the premises."

"I'll get my wand and meet you at the front door."

In the dining room of the Jackson residence, William addresses Joe.

"Would you speak to the forensics specialist so Alex Johansen and I can enter your home and do a search of the premises?"

"Do you want me to go in with you?"

"Do you have a need to go into the house?"

"No. I really liked Art Condor. Being in the same house where he is lying dead would be even more upsetting to me than I'm already feeling. My main concern is to help the boys handle this tragedy."

William accompanies Joe to the crime scene.

"Joe Ferguson this is Alex Johansen. He's going to conduct the search in your residence for audio surveillance equipment."

Joe addresses the forensic investigator inside his house. "Pardon me. I've given Alex Johansen and William Smythe permission to enter my home and search the premises for electronic surveillance equipment. Alex is a…"

"Get lost."

The three men walk toward Rene Dubois, who is talking to the lead forensic specialist, Reuben Stang. Rene, having observed the confrontation by the forensic policeman, is watching them move towards him.

"Well Alex, I guess Johansen Surveillance Equipment needs to do a search of the house."

"It looks that way Rene," is Alex's response to the query. "The other forensic specialist told us to get lost."

Reuben Stang interrupts their conversation. "You can go in. Eventually Steve will learn the value of using other professionals. He's new to the business and on a power trip."

"I'll grab a camera and come with you," interjects Rene.

Joe returns to Tom's house while Rene, William, and Alex enter Joe's residence. In the living room, Alex quickly finds the first receptor and places it on the end table saying, "This receptor has just been installed. The adherent is still tacky."

Rene snaps a picture of it. The trio moves to the dining room and locate another receptor under the kitchen table. There are no receptors in the bedrooms on the second floor of the house. In the basement, Alex begins the search in the family room. The forensic investigator, hearing the men moving about, appears in the office doorway.

"I told you to stay out, now get out, and that means you too Rene."

"Reuben gave permission for us to come in.

"I've got one under the coffee table."

The Investigator moves back into the office. Alex flips over the coffee table to reveal the surveillance device, which Rene photographs. Alex leaves the device for the forensic specialist to remove. Widening his search downstairs, Alex then enters the office, advancing towards the desk waving the wand.

"No active equipment here."

"Where's the plastic box with the electronic parts that was on the desk?" Rene sharply questions the forensic investigator.

"Why? It has nothing to do with the murder investigation."

"Where is it?" demands Rene.

"In the center drawer of the desk."

"Take it out!"

The forensic investigator places the box on the desk. Rene snaps the picture.

"Dust the inside and outside of the box and the contents for prints."

"Why?" asks the investigator, being argumentative.

"Because the C.S.I.S. agent brought it with him." Rene is disgusted with the attitude of the forensic agent. "Are you really as incompetent as you sound?"

Detective Marcel St. Croix has been observing the surveillance equipment in the van, while Alex was finding and removing the bugs in the house. The police now have proof the equipment was monitoring the Ferguson home. Once more outside the residence, Alex speaks to Rene and William.

"It might be a good idea to check Joe's car while I'm here."

"That's a good idea," William acknowledges. "I'll get Joe to identify his vehicle for you."

Alex sweeps Joe's vehicle with his wand. He locates a tracking device under the hood. After Rene Dubois and Tom Jackson take pictures of the electronic gadget, Alex removes the transmitter from the location in which it was hidden. Both men take a second picture of the device.

"This gadget is for tracing the car when they follow it," Alex informs William then asks Joe, "Do you have a second vehicle I should check?"

There is no satellite-tracking device on the second car.

Detective Dubois collects the statements, written by Tom and the four boys and witnessed by Bob Watson, for the police file.

"I also require the shotgun and the spent shell casings. Come in tomorrow morning and make application to get it back Tom. That way you'll get the gun before it disappears in the system."

"The shotgun casings are beside the lilacs where I fired the gun," Tom informs Rene. "The shotgun is in the closet by the front door. I'll get it for you."

"Detective Dubois," Joe Ferguson interjects, "Tom Jackson mentioned that the phone was partially dismantled and there was electronic paraphernalia in a box on the desk."

"That's correct."

"I sold the office phone, along with some other items, at a garage sale the weekend before last and then bought a new phone. It looks like they were trying to replace the receptor that was lost when I sold the phone."

Rene records the information then asks, "Did you happen to sell any living room furniture at the garage sale?"

"No I didn't. Although I did sell the coffee table and end table that were in the family room. Then we moved the coffee table and end table from the living room to the family room."

"As of this afternoon no one has applied for a permit to install audio surveillance equipment in the Ferguson residence," William advises Rene. "You might want to check that out for your own investigation."

"While protecting your clients William, you've certainly made my investigation much simpler. Alex, send your bill in to the Greenbank Road Station. I'll inform them it was me who contacted you. It will look good on my report and if C.S.I.S. pokes their nose in, they won't be trying to question you about it. C.S.I.S. knows better than to push me."

Rene goes back to the investigation. Alex presents William and Bob with business cards before leaving.

*"Joe, you and Eileen might want to make plans for supper and find a friend to spend the night with away from your home." Bob continues speaking. "You won't get much rest in your own home tonight with forensics spending most of the night doing their examination of the of the crime scene. It would be best for the boys to spend the night elsewhere, preferably with their friends. Everybody is going to need somebody to talk to this evening. I'm planning to speak to the Chief of Police about everybody receiving trauma counseling to help them handle this crisis."

"Why don't you and your wife stay here with me Fergie? Tom asks. "I know I definitely need somebody to talk to tonight and you'll need the same."

"I'd like that. How about you Eileen?"

"That's fine with me. Tom, would it be okay if I rested for a little while right now? I'm exhausted and have a headache."

"I'll take you to the spare bedroom and get you an aspirin. Come with me."

The boys finish discussing their plans and leave quietly via the back door, not wishing to alert the reporters. Moving away from the scene of the murder, and the exercise provided by walking, will help to alleviate their feelings of loss.

Joe, realizing he can no longer sit on the information contained on the floppy disk sitting in the attic of his garage, makes the decision to confide in the two lawyers.

"Could I show you some data I have on a computer disk that will explain the home invasion? This has to be completely confidential."

"The best place to meet will be in our office. Could you bring the disk and meet us there in fifteen minutes?"

"I'll come right now." Joe is anxious to speak to others about the terrorist information on the disk. He also requires direction on the course of action required to hinder or suppress the illegal activities inside the Department of Immigration and C.S.I.S.

Tom returns from settling Eileen Ferguson in the spare bedroom.

"We aren't needed here any more, so Bob and I will head back to the office. Keep us posted on any new developments Tom."

"Do you like Chinese food Tom?"

"Very much Fergie, unless I have to cook it myself."

Would you phone the Chinese restaurant in the Carlingwood Plaza and order? Tell them I'll pick it up in one hour. I have two things I've got to do right now but I'll be back shortly."

Joe enters his garage and locks the door. After retrieving the computer disk, he drives to the offices of Jones, Smythe and Watson, where the two lawyers are waiting for him.

"Lets see what you have," William inquires as Joe enters the office.

Joe slides the disk into the computer and Bob accesses the information.

"My God! Is that really who this paper says it is?" Bob is flabbergasted. "Is Ayman al Zawahri really in Vancouver?"

Joe pages down.

Both lawyers are staring in disbelief.

"He's living under a new identity in Montreal." William is worried. "These papers have your signature on them Joe."

"It's my signature but I never signed the papers. Now I'll tell you how I found this information."

Joe relates the whole episode of May 3rd to the lawyers. "Since that day I've seen the picture of the man from C.S.I.S. in the newspaper. His name is Jean Perrault and he's the Senior Official in charge of C.S.I.S. I've done some investigating and discovered he is a close friend of Pierre Montague, the mandarin in charge of the Department of Immigration. Another very close friend of Pierre Montague and Jean Perrault is Guy Trembley, head of the R.C.M.P."

"I believe the information I have is only an indication of a very large operation. There is too much work involved, and too many people involved, to limit the illegal immigrants to just one man. Immigration is involved, and C.S.I.S., by their actions, have proven their culpability. Foreign Affairs has to be involved. They begin the immigration process. The close friendship of Pierre Montague, Jean Perrault and Guy Tremblay implicates the R.C.M.P.

I'll tell you how involved I believe this whole operation is. Beginning June 21st, the top members of government are having a golf tournament at the Eagle Creek Golf Course. One foursome is Pierre Montague, Jean Perrault, the Minister of Immigration, Henri Jolliette, and the Prime Minister, Patrick Champlain."

"That pretty well covers all the bases," muses Bob, "and it wouldn't surprise me to find the Prime Minister involved. All three of those mandarins were hand picked by the Prime Minister, as was the Minister of Immigration. It's no wonder you're under surveillance with this kind of evidence of their criminal activities. They're worried just how much solid proof you have of their culpability."

Bob removes the disk from the computer and hands it back to Joe. Placing a new disk in the computer, he records the material before erasing the information from his computer's hard drive.

"Give us some time to think about this and contact us on Monday," William advises Joe. "I will know better at that time, what precautions we will be able to undertake to protect you from further harassment. Four days should also give me time to formulate a plan to counteract the illegal immigration swindle, in which this government is presently involved."

While Joe is conversing with Bob and William at the law firm, Tom re-enters the Ferguson's residence with camera in hand, slipping in unnoticed by the forensic police. Snapping pictures of the surveillance devices in the dining room and the living room completes his photographic evidence trail. Returning to his residence, Tom removes the memory card from the camera and installs it on the computer to download the pertinent information onto his hard drive. After examining the evidence, he saves the pictures onto a computer disk to present to his lawyers on Friday.

Pierre Montague is enjoying his Thursday afternoon business luncheon with Henri Jolliette, Minister of Immigration, at the Rideau Club, a favorite haunt of Ottawa's elite. Both men enjoy the privileges accorded them by their $500 per year memberships. Of course, these were not the only memberships conferred on these men courtesy of the Canadian taxpayers.

With their luncheon over, Henri Jolliette enters the lounge to visit with some of his contemporaries while Pierre Montague uses this opportunity to visit Caroline Tremblay, the beautiful young lady he keeps hidden from his wife.

Exiting the elevator on the ninth floor, Pierre sees Caroline framed in the doorway of her suite, properly dressed for the occasion in a pale blue, sheer, negligee and matching slippers. 'She is indeed a beauty, a prize worthy of a man of his stature in the governing body of Canada.' Hurrying towards Caroline, she runs to Pierre with outstretched arms and throws herself into his arms, kissing him passionately. Releasing each other, they run, holding hands, into her suite. In the bedroom, they again begin kissing passionately as she removes his clothing.

At five o'clock, Adrian Montague receives a phone call from her husband.

"I'm tied up with Henri and I probably won't be home until seven or later."

"The girls and I will eat," is Adrian's response. "I'll warm up your supper when you arrive."

"Henri has ordered in some lunch. Don't bother with anything for me."

Montague shuts off the cell phone again, not wishing to be disturbed.

Smiling at his beautiful young lover waiting in anticipation for his return to the nest, Montague slips back into the bed. Later Caroline enters the bathroom and begins running the water for a shower. Pierre phones for the delivery of a Chinese dinner. After placing thirty dollars on the table, Pierre joins the jewel of his passions in the shower. They are busy drying each other when the apartment buzzer sounds, announcing the arrival of their meal. Pierre quickly slips into his pants and meets the deliveryman at the door, giving him the money and receiving their meal. Enjoying their Chinese dinner together is the fitting climax for a lovely afternoon of lovemaking. Pierre leaves his mistress for the drive home to his wife and two daughters.

"Jean Perrault has been trying to reach you," Adrian Montague informs her husband as he strides through the front door. "Give him a call."

In the basement of his home, Montague enters his office, locks the door and places the call to his confederate.

"Jean Perrault here."

"It's Pierre "

"Where the hell have you been? Have you heard the news?"

"What news?"

"My technician was killed at Ferguson's house. He killed one boy inside the house and was in the yard firing at three other boys when he was dispatched by a neighbor."

"Oh my God! Is there anything to tie him to our operation?"

"I don't know yet," Perrault responds. "In the morning our office will take over the investigation. I'll talk to you when I have more information."

After putting down the phone, Montague sits brooding in his office chair, worried about the events that have transpired at the Ferguson residence, and fearful of the discovery of his own involvement.

Adrian knows her husband is keeping a mistress and she is planning very carefully to leave her husband, but she will leave under her own terms. She was a chartered accountant before marrying Pierre and has a dossier of all the bank records that are not part of their joint accounts. She has set up the paperwork to divert those funds into her own accounts on very short notice, and to divert all their assets invested in stocks and bonds.

Adrian has hired a private investigator, 'Confidential Investigations', to place her husband under surveillance. Adrian plans to nail her husband for his dalliances. This current mistress is not the first time her husband has strayed, but it will be the last. When she is finished, her husband will be paying alimony and child support to two ex-wives and living in his third home.

Adrian realized the Senior Official of C.S.I.S. has been trying to locate her husband all afternoon and the panic Perrault was feeling registered with her. Rather than pass the information on to Pierre when he phoned, and ruin his tête-à-tête, she waited to tell her husband later in the evening, when it would ruin his sleep.

Controlling the Investigation

On Friday, Joe, feeling remorseful about the death of his sons' companion, telephones home to Eileen. "There is no point in my staying in the office today, I can't concentrate on my work. Maybe we could do something this afternoon that will help me get my mind off Art being killed by that Canadian Security and Intelligence Service agent."

"I'll have lunch ready when you arrive. We could take a walk down to the river. The exercise and the conversation will help to relieve the remorse we are both feeling at this time. Sitting here alone in the house has my mind in a constant whirl."

Early Friday morning, Crown Prosecutor Joshua Campbell makes a special trip to speak to one of the Judges of the Supreme Court of Canada. The Crown Prosecutor has with him all the faxed evidence collected on the murder of Art Condor and the shooting of the C.S.I.S. operative.

Judge Marilyn Kaleen (after reading the evidence) "Would you explain the concerns you have about this case being placed under the jurisdiction of C.S.I.S. instead of being handled by the Ottawa Police force?"

"Yes your Honor. In the last four years there have been twenty-seven cases with C.S.I.S. involvement, turned over to C.S.I.S., that have gone cold, including one where a murder was committed and the killer, a C.S.I.S informant, was apprehended with the weapon at the site. In this case, a sixteen-year old boy was murdered by an on duty C.S.I.S. operative who was illegally re-installing audio surveillance equipment inside a residence. Right now we have no idea why C.S.I.S installed audio surveillance equipment without first obtaining a court order, or why they were re-installing the equipment, again without a court order. If C.S.I.S. obtains the evidence and the jurisdiction over this case, they will be able to cover up their own illegal involvement and this case will then disappear. I don't believe that justice will be served for the dead boy or his family by allowing this travesty of justice to occur. I believe C.S.I.S. will attempt to circumvent any court order we receive. The harder they try the more their guilt will be proven."

"I have found, over the years, that you are an extremely conscientious and honest judge. That is why I have chosen you to hear my case. Once you have made a decision on a case you do not lightly change your rulings. Had I gone to a lower court for the ruling it could have been easily overturned. By coming to you the ruling cannot be overturned without a formal hearing."

Judge Marilyn Kaleen writes out her decision, places her signature and seal on the document and then addresses the Crown Prosecutor.

"I would take it as a personal favour if you would keep me informed on any new developments in this case."

"Thank you for your help," Joshua Campbell responds. "I'll pass that information on to the detectives in charge of the investigation and ask them to forward any new evidence they uncover."

Joshua Campbell proceeds into the reception area of the courthouse and has a clerk fax the document to the Greenbank Road Police Station.

At the Greenbank Station, Chief Henri Montford is engaged in an intense argument with Jean Perrault, Director of C.S.I.S.

"We can't find the evidence," states the Chief of Police, "and without a court order there is no way you're getting the evidence."

"You give me that evidence or I'll see that you receive your walking papers."

Rene Dubois and Marcel St. Croix are observing the argument when the fax from the Crown Prosecutor is received. The secretary photocopies the document and places both copies on Rene's desk.

"You'd better give one copy to Chief Montford. He could use a little sunshine."

Rene peruses the communiqué, then, stepping over to the chief, hands him the document.

"What's this?" asks the exasperated police chief.

Chief Henri Montford reads the paper and smiles. Handing the Court Document to the Senior Official of C.S.I.S. he sarcastically states, "This paper is definitely for you."

Perrault reads the court document. Hate contorts his features with the realization he is thwarted. Ripping the document in half and then crumbling the paper into a ball, he fires it at a wall and storms cursing out of the police station. The two C.S.I.S. officials accompanying Perrault scamper behind him like baby chicks following a mother hen.

Chief Henri Montford carefully picks up the pieces of the document and places them in a file folder. Turning, he hands Rene the folder.

"Put this in the evidence file on the murder at the Ferguson residence. Handle it very carefully. When C.S.I.S. files a motion to change control of the investigation to their jurisdiction, I want the judge to see this document, as it is, torn by 'Mister C.S.I.S. Man.' His contempt for the courts could weigh heavily in our favor."

Rene Dubois takes the file proffered by Chief Montford and carries it into the dead file storage, where he just happens to discover the missing file folder. Rene carries the folder back to the office and locks it in his own filing cabinet.

Early Friday morning, in the private office of William Smythe, Tom Jackson hands William the pictures he took at the crime scene. He places the computer disk containing the same pictures on the desk.

"These pictures will provide evidence crucial to the case," William reiterates. "You also have photographs of the shell casings in the house, the killer's badge, and the audio surveillance equipment in the Ferguson residence."

"I took the picture of the surveillance equipment in the dining room and living room after you and Bob left."

"Excellent. Would you be willing to keep an eye on the Ferguson house while we try to figure out why C.S.I.S. has such an interest in Joe?"

"That's certainly no problem," Tom replies. "Fergie is a great neighbor and is honest to a fault. A bit of surveillance work will give me an excuse for being snoopy."

"With the preponderance of evidence supporting you, I can't see the courts laying any charges against you. They're more likely to give you a letter of commendation. Would you leave this evidence with me until we decide what we require for our records?"

"That's why I brought it in. I have to leave now because I have another engagement."

From the law office of William Smythe, Tom proceeds directly to the Greenbank Road Police Station. The Chief of Police produces the necessary paperwork, previously filed by Detective Dubois, to allow Tom to retrieve his shotgun. After completing the paperwork and Tom signing the document, the police chief informs him that Detective Dubois will return the shotgun within thirty days.

The Surveillance Continues

After lunch, Joe and Eileen take a short walk to the end of the block. Joe spots a C.S.I.S. agent, Jean Goullet, sitting in a car engrossed in a newspaper. Joe and Eileen stop and talk for a few minutes then turn and slowly retrace their steps. They continue walking past their home then come to the other corner of their block on Rowanwood Avenue, where Joe spies the second operative, Cecil Mann. Their all too nonchalant attitude doesn't fool him. Although Joe had never seen these agents before, the only reason they are present, waiting in their vehicles on a Friday afternoon, must be to spy on him. Joe and Eileen continue wandering down the avenue a short distance, then turn and begin walking home. Joe watches the second C.S.I.S. operative turn the corner and hurry down the avenue, preceding him towards his home.

Cecil phones his partner as he walks "The marks have left. Keep a watch for me."

At the Ferguson sidewalk, Cecil Mann glances back before committing himself to move onto the property. He catches sight of Joe and Eileen following behind him, engrossed in their conversation. He continues down Rowanwood Avenue.

John Goullet standing at the corner speaks into his cell phone. "The marks are behind you."

"I saw them."

Cecil continues walking to the end of the block and as he turns the corner towards John Goullet, he glances back. Joe and Eileen are no longer behind him, having returned to their home, where they sit conversing on the front step. The operative sits in the car with his partner, talks to him for a few minutes, then returns to his own vehicle. Eileen, deep in conversation, notices Cecil walking past the front of the house, but gives him little thought. Joe sees him and realizes that C.S.I.S. is attempting to place more surveillance equipment in his home. Tom recognizes him as the man he had previously spotted, turning as if to walk onto the Ferguson sidewalk, and then continue walking down Rowanwood Avenue. Shortly thereafter, Joe and Eileen came into view.

Tom picks up Ralph's leash to take a stroll around the block.

Sunday morning, Joe and Eileen leave for worship. Keith and Jerry remain home to study for final exams. Their friends, Sandy Hanger and Andre Dupree, will be arriving shortly to study with them. Cecil Mann watches Joe and Eileen leave and starts walking down Rowanwood Avenue towards the Ferguson residence. As he approaches the residence, he can hear music coming from the living room. He continues past the house, knowing there is no way he can install the audio surveillance equipment at this time.

Tom Jackson observes the agent walking past the house, and recognizes him from Friday. Gathering up his camera and Ralph's leash, he calls to his golden retriever and heads for the door. Tom and Ralph meander in the opposite direction the agent is walking. The golden retriever stops at a tree. Tom watches the agent turn the corner as Ralph keeps himself busy, sniffing the morning news. Tom takes pictures of the agent's car and then continues walking around the block. As the agent draws close, Ralph examines another bush. Tom faces the agent with his camera dangling from his neck. As the agent enters his focal range Tom speaks to him pleasantly.

"Good morning."

The agent looks over in surprise. With the remote shutter control located in his pocket, Tom snaps the photograph.

"Uh. Good morning." The agent continues walking.

Ralph and Tom continue around the block and return to their home. Tom removes the memory chip from his camera and replaces it with the memory chip he uses to take pictures of birds, then places the camera on the coffee table in the living room.

Early Monday afternoon, Tom Jackson observes the Ferguson family leave to attend the funeral of their friend Art Condor. A car, proceeding slowly down the street, parks in front of the Ferguson residence. The driver is the C.S.I.S. agent, Cecil Mann. Picking up his camera Tom Jackson switches memory disks, slipping the disk he removed from the camera into his pocket. Tom snaps a picture of the agent leaving the car. A bird lands in the lilac bushes between the Jackson and Ferguson residences. Tom exits the house keeping the lilacs between himself and the agent. The agent rings the bell, then produces a key and unlocks the door. Tom, stepping from behind the bush, snaps a picture of the C.S.I.S. agent entering the house. Tom waits, keeping an eye on both the bird and the door of the house.

Marie St. Clair, kneeling in her flowerbed, watches the car stop and a stranger unlock and enter the Ferguson home. She scurries up the steps into her own home to continue her observations from behind the living room curtain.

The agent exits the house and locks the door. As he turns to leave, Tom snaps the picture.

"HEY!"

The bird flees from the bushes, flittering past Tom Jackson to land in a tree further down the avenue.

Tom steps behind the lilacs and switches memory chips all the while watching the flight of the bird. The agent hurries up to Tom.

"I'm sorry I startled the bird."

"You startled more than the bird. You startled me too. I was concentrating on the bird and hadn't seen you."

"Wasn't the bird a Warbling Vireo?"

"No," Tom corrects the C.S.I.S. agent. "It was a Red Eyed Vireo. They look very similar."

"I enjoy a bit of bird watching myself. Could I look at the pictures you have?"

Tom extricates the camera from his neck using the straps, and hands Cecil the camera. Cecil quickly pans through the photographs on the camera memory chip and then hands the camera back to Tom. Again taking the camera by the straps, Tom places it back around his neck.

"Those pictures are terrific. You've taken some beautiful photographs."

"Thank you. The Vireo just flew into that cherry tree down the street. I'm going to attempt to photograph him if I can.

Cecil Mann walks back to his car satisfied the amateur birdwatcher never snapped a picture of him.

Tom, back in his house, removes the memory card from his pocket. Downloading the information onto the computer, he prints off the pictures onto a disk. Tom types out the events of the last few days, printing the information onto the same disk.

Cecil Mann enters the car of his fellow operative, John Goullet, outside the United Church building – the location of the Art Condor funeral service.

"Did you get the equipment installed?"

"It's done."

"They're still in the church conducting the service," notes Goullet.

After the funeral, the Ferguson boys stay in the church hall to visit with their friends. The solace they gather from their group helps them through the agony of this day. They still can't comprehend how the loss of their friend will affect them in the days and years ahead, but for now they will have to take one day at a time.

Joe and Eileen, feeling intensely the loss of their close friend, begin to drive home. Overcome by grief, they fail to notice the C.S.I.S. agents tailing them. The two agents, intent on following their quarry, fail to notice a car pulling away from the curb at the church and begin its clandestine tailing of the C.S.I.S. vehicle. At their home, Eileen picks up her grocery list and walks back to the car. The two agents, in the alley behind the Ferguson home and tuned into the bugs Cecil has just planted, hear the door open and close and Eileen moving about in the house. Again, the door opens and closes and the house is silent. Realizing the Fergusons are leaving again, the agents drive to the end of the alley and fall in behind Joe and Eileen. The vehicle with its clandestine occupants again slips in behind the C.S.I.S. vehicle. The three cars wend their passage through the residential area on their way to Carlingwood Plaza. The Fergusons enter the Loblaw store to begin shopping.

One of the men from the car tailing the C.S.I.S. agents, enters the store and asks, "Are you Joe and Eileen Ferguson?"

"Yes we are."

"My name is Harry Long. I'm a detective with the Ottawa City Police Department. My partner, Al Nitti, is watching two men who have been following you."

Eileen stares at Harry.

"You can't be serious!"

"I'm positive. One person followed you to the funeral where the second man joined him. We have tailed them to your home, and from your home to this mall. We plan to arrest them, but if they are C.S.I.S. agents, we can't hold them. Follow me out keeping forty metres between us. Walk normally. Don't look suspicious. Keep well back until we have the suspects in custody. I want you to see them so you will be able to recognize them again."

Harry leaves the store, followed at a distance by the Fergusons. Stopping by the car's right fender, Harry raises his gun, pointing it at the passenger just as his partner, jerking the driver's door open, levels his weapon at the driver's head.

"Keep your hands in sight and get out of the car," orders Al Nitti.

The driver complies.

"Lean against the car."

When the driver obeys, Al searches him producing a gun. He then handcuffs the driver.

"We're agents of C.S.I.S."

"Shut up. Walk to the front of the car."

Al quickly moves to the passenger door and opens it.

"Keep your hands in sight and get out of the car."

After the passenger complies Al follows the same procedure as with the driver. He then searches the two men more thoroughly; producing two more weapons in ankle holsters, their C.S.I.S. badges and identification, and their vehicle operators' licences.

"I told you we're from C.S.I.S. Now get these cuffs off us."

Recognizing Joe and Eileen watching them, John Goullet stops his harangue of the police detectives.

"Did he say they're from that dreadful organization that shot Arthur?" Eileen asks. She stares at Cecil Mann "I saw you walk past our house on Friday. What are you doing here?"

"Following you," Al Nitti retorts.

Overcome by the events of the last few days and unable to control her emotions any longer, Eileen collapses into Joe's arms sobbing. Joe, his own feelings in turmoil, holds his wife close to comfort her.

Harry takes the C.S.I.S. agent's badges, C.S.I.S. identifications and operator licences to his own vehicle and phones the Greenbank Road Station.

"Ottawa City Police."

"Harry Long here, could I speak to Chief Montford please?"

"One moment please."

"Montford here Harry. What can I do for you?"

Harry quickly explains the day's events and then asks, "Is there anything we can charge them with?"

"Not really," replies the Chief of Police, "but you can harass them a bit more before releasing them. Make sure you obtain their names and badge numbers."

"There are already enough curious people gathered around. I don't think they need any more harassing for today."

Chief Montford is pleased... very pleased. His decision to place the Fergusons under friendly surveillance has proven C.S.I.S.

is continuing their secretive observation of the Ferguson family, C.S.I.S., knowing their every action is being monitored by the Ottawa Police Department, will have to be far more clandestine in their illegal investigation because any mistakes on their part will be investigated and recorded.

Harry cancels the call and records the information recovered from their C.S.I.S. badges and identifications, and their vehicle operators licences, first on the in car camera and then on a digital camera. Removing the memory chip from the digital camera, he places it in a small box, which he slips into his pocket. Picking up the licences and badges, he returns to the C.S.I.S. agents.

Eileen's grief overcomes her. She explodes at the agents. "Why are you following us? Why are you sneaking around our home? Why did you put those illegal listening devices in our house? Why did you kill Arthur?"

Eileen turns to Joe for comfort. She continues to ask him the same questions.

John Goullet listens intently to Eileen's harangue.

Cecil Mann continues to rant and holler attempting to bluster Alphonse, but only succeeds in drawing more attention to their predicament.

"Cecil. Shut up."

Harry Long returns to his prisoners. Having observed the threatening manner of Cecil Mann, he first uncuffs John Goullet and hands him his guns, badge and identification.

"Sorry about the inconvenience. Under the circumstances of the last few days I didn't know what the policy was at headquarters."

John grins at Detective Long, "That's a nice cover-up. I'll see you around sometime. Maybe we can have a coffee together."

John opens his car door and gets in, starting the engine.

Harry wonders why Goullet is no longer upset with the course of events.

Al Nitti uncuffs Mann, leaving him to get his own personal effects off the top of the car. The slight isn't lost on Cecil who begins to berate the two policemen again.

"Get in the car or walk!"

After Goullet drops Mann off at the church, he drives to the courthouse to check on some papers. After thoroughly researching the court documents, John is able to establish that no court order was ever granted to C.S.I.S., or any other law enforcement office, to install audio surveillance equipment in the Ferguson residence. John drives home. At six o'clock John Goullet is attending the Winston funeral. The absence of Jean Perrault is paramount in the minds of all the mourners paying their last respects to the memory of John Winston."

Harry Long writes up the report and gives Joe a copy along with the memory chip from the digital camera and his business card.

"Your lawyer may be able to use this information. I'll require the memory chip with the information on it as quickly as possible."

Eileen goes grocery shopping while Joe rushes over to the law offices of Jones, Smythe and Watson to give this latest information to his lawyer.

The Plan

Joe, after handing William Smythe the memory chip and the report from Harry Long, relates the events that have transpired over the last four days.

William installs the memory chip on the computer. Bringing the information up on the screen, he examines it very closely. From a safe under a wastebasket in the corner of his office, he removes a computer disk and records the information provided by the police detective. William replaces the disk in the safe, locks it and again hides the safe with the wastebasket.

"C.S.I.S. is paying an inordinate amount of attention to you. Their actions further clarify their involvement in the illegal immigration ring and shows their involvement is more involved than I first believed. Their actions also bear out the information you have regarding the Department of Immigration bringing terrorists into Canada. Do you have any idea whether you are being monitored at work because this certainly doesn't involve your private life?"

"I spoke to Alex Johansen about the possibility of surveillance devices in my office. He told me any video surveillance equipment would be installed in the fluorescent fixture and any audio surveillance would be in the telephone. The phone tap would enable them to record any conversation in the office and the conversations by both parties in all telephone calls."

"Have you given any thought as to who else from your office besides Pierre Montague could be involved?"

"I've given the matter some consideration since I discovered the documents," replies Joe. "I've noticed that certain immigration workers usually eat lunch with a few of the top civil servants in our office. They're just a bit too cozy and have me wondering. I'll give you a list if that will help."

"It might provide us with a lead as to who is most likely involved in the illegal activities inside the Department of Immigration. That will be a good place to start the investigation." William leans forward in his chair. "Do you have any other information that could provide us with leads Joe?"

"Nothing that comes to mind. Pierre Montague and the other fourteen top civil servants in our department are involved in a three-day golf tournament beginning a week from this Thursday at the Eagle Creek Golf Course. Included in the gathering are the Prime Minister, the Minister of Finance, the Minister of Foreign Affairs, the Solicitor General, the Minister of Immigration and the rest of Privy Council members. Also included are the mandarins from those departments and the top civil servants in each department. They leave for the Country Club at nine-thirty for social drinks, followed by a luncheon at eleven-thirty. If we could learn the foursomes and the luncheon arrangements we might possibly learn something from that information."

"Yes that information could provide us with some distinct possibilities."

"The tournament begins at one o'clock. I plan on discovering the surveillance equipment at one-thirty and I'm having Johansen Surveillance come in and remove the equipment at that time."

"No! You call Bob at the office. I'll be waiting for Bob's call to me near your office in the Immigration Department. We'll play it from there. The fewer outside people involved the safer it will be for all concerned. C.S.I.S. can remove their own damned equipment."

"We'll require a floor plan of the offices on your floor with the offices and cubicles of the civil servants most likely to be involved recorded on the drawing. I'll get you a pencil, ruler and paper because we'll need that information today. We have a spare office you can use. Keep the door closed. We need to keep the office staff oblivious of the diagram you are sketching. I'm going to set up a meeting with some people to see what ideas we can generate to facilitate the detection of the guilty parties and expose their crimes. We must also devise a plan to facilitate the removal of the terrorists from Canada. Come with me now and I'll get you settled. If you need a coffee the lunch room is beside your office."

William knocks on Bob's office door and then steps inside, closing the door.

"I'm setting up a meeting with Joe Ferguson at five-fifteen in the conference room. Will you inform Rae without alerting the office staff? I have some phone calls to make to complete the arrangements."

William dials.

"Johansen Surveillance Equipment, Alex speaking."

"William Smythe of the law offices of Jones, Smythe, and Watson. Alex, I need you to attend a meeting with Joe Ferguson, myself and some other people in my office at five-fifteen this afternoon. Can you make it?"

"Yes I can be there."

"Do you know a good private detective and a good computer hacker?"

"I know a very good private detective, Maurice Solinger of Confidential Investigations. Maurice, because of the nature of his work, is likely to know a computer hacker."

"Would you contact Maurice for me and have him come to the meeting and if he knows a computer hacker have him bring that person also? I can't begin to impress upon you how important this meeting will be.

William meets with his final client of the day and wraps up his business.

Alex dials Maurice.

"Confidential Investigations, Maurice speaking."

"Maurice who?"

Recognizing Alex's voice Maurice replies. "I'm sorry, that's confidential."

Alex chuckles. "Joe Ferguson's lawyer, William Smythe just phoned me. He's calling a meeting with Joe and some other people in his office at five-fifteen this afternoon. He wants you and me to be there. He said it's crucial. Can you come?"

"I'll phone my wife and tell her I'll be late for supper. Will you give me the address?"

"Do you know a good computer hacker?"

"I know an excellent hacker," replies Maurice. "He makes the computer sit up and listen. I've been using him for seven years now, since he was fifteen."

"Can you bring him with you?"

"I'll phone him right now and find out. Give me ten minutes and I'll phone you back."

Maurice dials.

"Hello."

"Hello Mrs. Roy. Is that son of yours behaving himself?"

"Hello Maurice. You know he always behaves himself. He's downstairs at the moment."

"Marcel, Maurice is on the phone."

"Hello Maurice."

"Marcel, I'm glad I could reach you, I have an important meeting that I was just contacted about and we need you there."

"When and where?"

Maurice gives him the time and address. "Wait for me in the parking lot if you're early and I'll wait for you if I'm early."

"I'll see you there. I'm going to grab a sandwich and I'll be on my way."

Maurice phones Alex Johansen "He'll be there. We've arranged to meet outside the lawyer's office."

"That's fine by me. I just received a phone call from the city police and I'll be a little late."

Eileen Ferguson, after parking her car in the driveway of her home, is called to by Marie St. Clair, the elderly widow living at 28 Rowanwood Avenue. Eileen crosses the street to talk.

"Good afternoon Mrs. St. Clair."

"Oh Eileen, I saw a man go into your house at twelve-thirty this afternoon. He came out and locked the door at ten to one. He talked to Tom Jackson for a few minutes before he drove away."

"Thank you Mrs. St. Clair. I'll talk to Tom and see what information he has."

Eileen feels the weight of the last few days returning, but is determined not to break down again. She meets Tom in her driveway.

"You had a visitor this afternoon. I believe C.S.I.S. has installed more surveillance equipment in your home."

Tom tells Eileen about the intruder that afternoon, omitting the information he had photographed the agent entering and leaving her home.

Eileen makes the phone call to Detective Rene Dubois from the Jackson residence.

"Ottawa City Police. Detective Dubois speaking."

"Hello Detective Dubois, this is Eileen Ferguson. Marie St. Clair, the elderly widow who lives at 28 Rowanwood Ave. just told me a stranger was in our house this afternoon. Could you come over here right now?"

"I'm on my way."

Rene makes his first of two phone calls.

"Johansen Surveillance Equipment, Alex speaking."

"Rene Dubois here. The Ferguson residence has been entered again. Would you meet me there?"

"I'm headed that direction. I'll meet you in twenty minutes."

Rene then contacts forensics to meet him at the site. The office will check to learn if the surveillance devices are legal.

Entering her own home via the garage entry door, Eileen begins putting the groceries away. She's had a terrible day and now this.

Cecil Mann retrieves his car from its location at the United Church – the site of the funeral. After a coffee, he searches for the Ferguson car, via the satellite-monitoring device. He locates it moving towards the Ferguson residence on Rowanwood Avenue. Parking in the alley behind the house, he begins monitoring the audio mikes in the residence. After the police detective arrives, he learns an elderly lady across the street observed him entering the house.

Tom directs Rene Dubois to the garage door. Rene accesses the door and enters the residence.

"Come in Detective Dubois. Would you care for a cup of coffee?"

"Thank you, I would. Just black please Eileen."

Rene takes out his notebook.

"You said that a neighbor witnessed a stranger entering your home at twelve thirty and leave about 20 minutes later. Who was the neighbor that witnessed the home invasion?"

"It was Mrs. St. Clair. Pardon me, Mrs. Marie St. Clair," Eileen replies. "She lives just across the street from us at 28 Rowanwood Ave. Mrs. St. Clair was on her knees weeding her flower bed when she saw the car stop and a man unlock the front door and go in the house. She went into her house and watched out the front window until he left. After he left the house, she saw the intruder talking to my neighbor, Tom Jackson. Tom never saw the man until he hollered, scaring the bird Tom was trying to photograph. The man did talk to Tom for a few minutes."

"I'll have to get statements from them afterwards. It looks like my friend has arrived.

"Hello Alex. Thanks for coming on such short notice."

"Hello Rene, I'm in a rush, you just managed to catch me."

Alex begins the search.

"Well they're not very original. There's one under this table again."

Removing the bug from under the dining room table, Alex Johansen shuts the equipment off. He finds the second bug in the living room. The bedrooms, located on the second floor, are clean. He conducts his search in the basement, finding a bug under the end table in the family room before arriving at the door to the office.

"I can't go in there," Eileen whispers. "I haven't been able to since Arthur was killed in that room."

"That's fine Eileen. You run upstairs and we'll join you in a minute."

Alex steps into the office and continues his search.

"There's a bug in the phone."

"We'll leave it there. Forensics can remove it while they're dusting for fingerprints. We'll see if the young smart-ass will remember what they look like. Send this bill to the station and I'll get it taken care of. That reminds me, I haven't seen your first bill."

"I'll get them out at the end of the month. I should check the cars while I'm here."

"My partner just walked into the back yard." Rene is looking out the office window. "Yes check the cars while I see what he's after."

While releasing Ralph into the back yard for some exercise, Tom spies a strange car parked in the alley just beyond Joe's fence. At the front door, he signals Marcel St. Croix, then meets him close to the lilac bushes.

"There's a strange car parked in the alley behind the Ferguson house. I can just see it over the fence. I know it wasn't there an hour ago. Could it be tied to the invasion of the Ferguson residence earlier today?"

Marcel strides past the Ferguson house towards the alley, but the car pulls out before he can identify it. On his return trip, he meets with Rene Dubois.

"What were you looking for?"

"There was a car in the alley, but it left before I got there."

"That was my big mouth. Lets see if Johansen found anything on the cars."

The C.S.I.S. agent, Cecil Mann, continues monitoring the transmitters in the Ferguson residence until he hears the policeman say, "My partner just walked into the back yard." Jamming the car into gear, Cecil races down the alley.

Eileen Ferguson just thinks she's had a bad day.

The two policemen find Alex with the trunk open, removing a tracking device from Joe's vehicle.

"You found one."

"Yes. The other car is clean and you can have this device. I'm late Rene, so I really must leave."

"Thanks for your assistance Alex."

Marcel St. Croix visits 28 Rowanwood Avenue to obtain a statement from Marie St. Clair, and then proceeds to 27 Rowanwood Avenue for a statement from Tom Jackson.

"I was attempting to photograph a bird when I heard a holler and the bird flew away," explained Tom. "The man was standing on the front doorstep of the Ferguson residence. I turned around to see where the bird was flying and the man came up behind me and spoke again, startling me a second time. He apologized for scaring the bird then looked at the pictures of birds I have in my camera. The man was about five foot five or six and weighed approximately 130 pounds."

The forensic police arrive and Rene takes them into the house to conduct their investigation. They remove the audio surveillance device from the phone and dust everything for prints. Tom, carrying his camera by its straps, places it on the dining room table in the Ferguson residence. The forensic unit photographs the only fingerprints they find at the site, which are on Tom Jackson's camera.

William enters the office where Joe is sketching, closes the door, and looks over Joe's shoulder at the diagram he is drafting.

"How did you make out with the floor plan?"

"I'm close."

William examines the drawing. "That will be fine for now. I'll photocopy this. I need you to go outside and keep two or three men away from the door until the office staff leaves. I don't want them to know anything about tonight. The one man you know, Alex Johansen. The second is Maurice Solinger."

"I've met Maurice. He's a member of the Elks Lodge I attend."

"Good. As you leave, tell the receptionist you'll phone in for an appointment. She'll think we're finished for the evening."

Joe exits the office. He takes a few steps and hears a horn beep lightly and sees headlights flashing. Joe walks over to the car, and Maurice Solinger rolls down his window.

"Have the conspirators all arrived?"

"Hello Maurice. We have to wait for the office staff to leave."

"Hop in the back. We can wait and watch from here."

Joe complies.

"Joe Ferguson, I want to introduce Marcel Roy. Marcel likes to play games 'with' computers. I've seen him make more than one computer snap to attention and say 'Yes Sir'. Do you happen to know the reason the meeting was called?"

"Not specifically. I do know the information on my computer screen at the Department of Immigration is involved."

The three men sit in the car and continue their conversation. Bob Watson opens the office door and looks out. The three men leave the car, heading for the lawyers offices, for their meeting.

"Alex Johansen isn't here yet."

"I think I just saw him parking the van," Maurice replies. "He flashed his lights at us as we were walking over here."

Bob waits for Alex as the other three enter the conference room. There are pens and writing pads set up at seven chairs and six of the sites have folded cardboard with six names on them. The seventh card is blank. Marcel Roy sits down and writes his name on the blank cardboard placard.

"I need to phone Eileen to tell her I'll be awhile." Joe rises to his feet.

"Don't phone home," Alex warns Joe "I just found some more bugs in the house and the one on the office phone is still active."

"I'll phone Tom and ask him to tell Eileen."

"Use the phone from the office you were in previously," Bob advises Joe. "There should be a directory in one of the drawers. While Joe's making the phone call the rest of you grab a coffee."

"Hello Tom. I was talking to Alex Johansen and he informed me there is an active bug on my office phone. Would you inform Eileen I'm going to be a couple of hours before I get home?"

"Yes. I'll go and tell her right now. Your friend from C.S.I.S. came to visit while you were out to the funeral today. The forensic police have just arrived to start their investigation and Rene's partner is interviewing Mrs. St. Clair.

While Joe is on the phone Alex takes the opportunity to speak to William.

"I take it this meeting entails information that will require secrecy."

"Yes. That's correct."

"It would be wise to check the office for bugs before we begin."

"That is an excellent idea. I'll let you out the door to pick up your equipment and we'll do a check of the conference room."

Alex returns and begins a complete search of the total office area finishing in the conference room. He sits down with the rest of the group.

William addresses the six men, apprising them of the situation.

"Joe Ferguson has uncovered an illegal Immigration Department operation bringing al Qaeda terrorists and likely other groups of terrorists into Canada. The terrorists are most likely using Canada as a base of operation to attack targets in the United States. The criminals operating this organization are the top members of the Department of

Immigration and the organization may extend into the top eulachon of our elected Members of Parliament. These criminals will place our country and our families' lives at risk of attack from these terrorists and when the rest of the world finds out, attack from other countries. Don't ever think that the United States will stand idly by and allow terrorists to operate with impunity in a country bordering them. We must accept the risk of destroying this organization ourselves to protect our own families."

"I require that that all of you must be willing to investigate every possible facet of this illegal operation. If any of you are not willing to help in this endeavor, you must leave this room immediately. The information I am going to present to you must not leave this room. The facts on the documents are tied directly to the criminal actions of the Federal Government. If the government learns we have this information it would jeopardize our whole operation and possibly our lives."

Everybody sits quietly waiting for William to enlighten them further.

Bob hands each person in attendance a file folder.

William begins his narration.

"This man, Ayman al-Zawahri, is second in control of the al Qaeda organization under Osama bin Laden. These documents show Ayman al-Zawahri has landed immigrant status in Canada. Although Joe Ferguson had never seen these documents before May 3rd of this year, the documents bear his signature. Joe took this information off his computer at the Department of Immigration. The next pages show the same man with the alias Mahmoud el-Hafnawi and again the documents bear the signature, Joseph P. Ferguson."

William pauses as the group examines the documents more closely. One by one, they lean back, reflecting on the information just passed on to them.

"Our first agenda will be to establish the identities of the people in the illegal operation and the identities of the terrorists that have been admitted into Canada. We must access the files of the Immigration Department to find the names of the terrorists. I am hoping those files will lead us to the workers and administrators in the Department of Immigration involved in the racket. Those leads in the Immigration Department should provide information on the people in Foreign Affairs who are involved. The illegal surveillance of Joe by C.S.I.S. points to the obvious conclusion that C.S.I.S. has links to the illegal activities in the Department of Immigration. The close affiliation between Pierre Montague, Jean Perrault and Guy Tremblay draws the R.C.M.P. into the equation. We can assume that some of the Members of Parliament and possibly even the Prime Minister himself are involved. This will be a complex operation but with the full co-operation of everybody in this room, we can succeed. I believe we must now, lay the groundwork towards achieving these goals. Marcel Roy, you're the computer hacker, what will be your requirements for accessing those files?"

"First of all I am not a computer hacker, I am a Computer Surveillance and Monitoring Specialist – illegal of course." Marcel becomes serious. "I will have to gain access to the main computers, which will be located in the basement of the Immigration Department. The safest way to gain entry will be as a janitor."

"Parliament Janitorial Service will only hire people to work in high security areas in the Department of Immigration who are unable to read or write either English or French." Joe continues to advise Marcel. "They prefer people who cannot speak or understand our two official languages."

"That's no problem. My mother grew up in what is now Bosnia. I am fluent in Serbian, Bosnian, Rumanian, Hungarian, Albanian, Turkish and

Greek, plus a few of the local dialects spoken in the Balkans. I am also proficient in Spanish and can handle Portuguese. Because of my proficiency in languages I've been studying in University to be a linguist."

"I will require a picture of you, the name you will be using, date of birth, place of birth, nationality and parents and grandparents names and I can provide all the paperwork you will require for the job."

Rae Jones interjects, "Early tomorrow morning I'll take Marcel to a man I know. He's a make-up artist for a couple of movie companies. We'll establish a disguise, so that he won't be recognized later."

"I still have uncles and aunts in Bosnia, I can use their names. I'll have it all worked out by tomorrow morning. After I access the main computers, I'll have to access some of the computers in the offices of workers in the Immigration Department. The more office computers I can access the less chance of discovery."

"We need to get that information to Joe as quickly as possible," Bob Watson advises the gathering. "We have no idea how long it will require for Marcel to be hired by the janitorial service."

Maurice then asks, "Joe, do you carry a lunch every day in a lunch box?"

"Yes, I use one of those foam insulated lunch boxes."

"Would it hold the documents you have to carry out?"

"Yes it would."

"Rae could you and Marcel have the pictures, names, and any other data required at your office by tomorrow morning?"

"I think so," Rae Jones responds. "I'll phone Andre right now and see how early we can set up the appointment."

Rae heads for his office to make the call.

"Don't do any of the papers on your own computer," Marcel warns Joe. "They will be monitoring every word you type and it will be on record even if you delete the document."

Maurice Solinger advises the group further. "Marcel should have a box number for an address and he will need a letter of release when he quits with a legitimate reason for quitting. Something like he's a machinist and has been offered a position with a company in Montreal at a specified time and date."

Joe interjects, "I can mark on the papers his occupation is machinist."

"I can set up a postal box at the Post Office close to my office." Maurice continues speaking. "They also send and receive faxes so we'll fax the letter to that station."

William smiles. "The good old paper trail. My brother in Montreal is a chartered accountant with a very large firm. They should have a machine shop as one of their accounts. I'll talk to him and explain what I need. I believe we have Marcel covered to that point. We'll cover the rest when Joe explains his plan. Alex, I plan to keep all of this business in the safe in my office. I need you to install audio and video surveillance equipment in the office to record anybody getting too curious about our actions."

"I can install the equipment tomorrow evening."

"I need to control it with a remote sensor. I don't require any record when I'm in the office and that would save me wasting time checking the information on the camera and tape."

"That's simple to do but I can set it up however you want."

Rae Jones enters the room and hands Marcel Roy a piece of paper. "We have to be there at five-thirty in the morning. Andre's also taking your photos for us. We should be back here before eight. Joe, leave your lunch in the trunk of the car and leave me a key. I will pack the information under your lunch, then meet you at coffee break outside the building. Write down the best time and place to meet so there will be no mistakes.

"I hope that you'll have time to complete the required documentation for Marcel before lunch. Marcel will be able to meet with you outside at lunchtime and you will give him the documents. Marcel can then apply for the job. That should give him a week to get hired and access the main computers in the Department of Immigration."

William addresses the gathering.

"I'm now going to ask Joe Ferguson to outline for us his plan to expose the audio and video surveillance equipment in his office."

"Pierre Montague and the other top fourteen civil servants in our department are involved in a golf tournament beginning June 21st, at the Eagle Creek Golf Course. They leave for the Golf Course at nine-thirty for social drinks, followed by a luncheon at eleven-thirty. The tournament will begin at one o'clock. I plan to discover the surveillance equipment at one-thirty."

Marcel Roy interrupts Joe's dissertation.

"Could you get me into the offices about ten? I would be well away from there long before any commotion in the office could draw attention to me."

"That won't be a problem," Joe explains. "Because of temporary hiring for the coming summer holidays, we have a lot of new faces in the department. Don't wear a suit but do wear a tie."

Marcel continues, "I plan on using the cover story that I'm installing anti-virus protection. There is always spam on the system and there are always specialists blocking the spam. Using that cover, even if I'm seen, I won't be noticed."

Joe continues with his dissertation.

"At one-thirty I contact Bob Watson in his office. Bob contacts William Smythe who will be waiting for the call near the Immigration Department. When he arrives, William will contact me with his cell phone. I'll go to the lobby and escort him back to my office. We want to get some of the other staff involved so we can put a scare into Pierre Montague."

"No we want to keep this very low key," William interjects. "When I enter the building I will have the receptionist contact you. You will then come to the reception area and take me back to your office. We will discuss the camera. I'll mention that it may not even be connected but I will contact the police detective to obtain the name of the person who found the surveillance equipment in your residence to learn if the camera is operating. We will discuss why the camera is there, probably used previously and forgotten. You will talk about the incident in your office and you have no idea why it happened. On Friday morning, I'll phone and tell you that Alex Johansen will be there on Monday to check the camera and ascertain if it is operating. It won't be by then and any other surveillance equipment will be gone. We want to quiet down their reconnaissance of Joe for our own purposes."

"I'll phone Pierre Montague and speak to him about the invasion of privacy, and Joe would probably feel better with the camera removed. We hope with the removal of the camera, the investigation of Joe will conclude. If we are to proceed successfully with our own investigation, we need all suspicion of Joe dropped."

Joe is upset. "I would like to expose them."

"So would I," William replies, "but it would put us at cross purposes with our prerogatives at this point. Maurice, we need you at the Eagle Creek Golf Course early Thursday morning. I need you to learn the names of all the contestants in the golf tournament. It will be very important to document the names of the individuals seated at each table, and the names of the people in each foursome. I also need you to keep an eye on Pierre Montague. We will need to know when or if he leaves the tournament after learning about our discovery of the surveillance camera. As soon as you find out, you'll need to contact me immediately on my cell phone."

"I'll take a look around the club Wednesday. Most golf clubs post their tournaments a day in advance. The security won't be there on Wednesday and that phase should be simpler a day in advance of the tournament."

"You should take Shannon with you," Alex Johansen adds. "She's a reporter for the Ottawa Citizen. Your task will be much simpler with press credentials."

"Who is Shannon?" William asks Alex.

"My daughter."

"Having a member of the press would legitimize the surveillance at the Golf and Country Club. We're almost finished here. Does anybody else have any other information or ideas?"

Maurice Solinger takes this opportunity to pass more information on for the group to digest.

"Adrian Montague has retained Confidential Investigations to uncover information regarding her husband's clandestine affair. I may be able to obtain information from Mrs. Montague that will aid our investigation."

Bob laughs at Maurice's information. "While Montague is trying to get information on Joe, Montague's wife may be helping us collect information on his illegal activities."

"We'll exchange cell phone numbers right now with the people who will need to access each other," William informs the group.

Joe and Alex leave together out the front door. Bob escorts Maurice to the back door and they both leave. Rae speaks to Marcel about their rendezvous tomorrow morning and the two leave, Marcel out the front door, Rae out the back. William smiles as he puts all the information away in the safe. By splitting up the men as they left, none of them should be conspicuous. Then he sobers up as he thinks about the momentous task ahead of them and hopes they will be up to the task with its inherent dangers.

William sets the alarms and leaves.

Disguise

Very early Tuesday morning Marcel and Rae are ringing the doorbell of the make-up artist. A young man opens the door. "Good Morning Rae. Is this the friend that requires a make-over?"

"Andre Prichard I want you to meet Marcel Roy. Marcel needs a disguise so good nobody will recognize him. Let's see what you can accomplish."

Andre Prichard begins to work. First, he cuts Marcel's hair short, and dyes it black. He deepens the facial lines, then stains the upper body, head, arms and legs a deeper brown color.

"For best effect we will have to re-do this every four days. The hair dye and the adhesive are both temporary and wash out readily with soap and water. When you wash your head, I will have to re-dye your hair and re-apply the beard and wig. The skin dye is user friendly and comes off readily with the proper solvent. What is Marcel supposed to do for a living in this production?"

"He's an machinist working temporarily as a janitor."

Andre clips Marcel's fingernails shorter, and then hands him dark brown contact lenses to insert. Marcel's eyes begin to run, but after half an hour, his eyes begin to adjust to the foreign objects. Inserts placed in his mouth, change the appearance of his cheekbones, and an adherent holds the curly, black beard in place. Andre carefully fits the matching wig.

"I've chosen a hairpiece and beard to match your new skin tone. You'll sleep with the beard attached. In four days, I'll remove it and reapply everything so you will be able to shave at that time. Put this stone in your sock and let's see you walk." Marcel complies and walks with a slight limp. Andre Prichard then hands him a pair of heavy glasses with plain lenses.

"I don't recognize Marcel and I brought him here. Can you change his fingerprints?"

Andre gives Rae a funny look and picks a few boxes from a desk drawer. He carefully adheres the fingerprints and thumbprints to Marcel's appendages.

"Those fingerprints will only work for a couple of days and I can't rematch them."

"That's fine. Will nine hundred dollars take care of this appointment and the products we have?" Rae takes out the money and hands it to Andre. "If it's not enough let me know and I'll reimburse you the remainder of the funds. There will also be subsequent visits to pay for. I almost forgot. The photographs."

Andre takes the pictures and develops them handing Rae the finished products.

"We may need another session on Monday but we will definitely need one for the following Wednesday." Ray continues, "I'll phone and confirm those appointments with you. Nobody is going to recognize Marcel in this disguise. We'll see you in a few days."

At the car, Rae collects the paper with the names of Marcel Roy's alias, Dragen Yankovich, born August 1, 1979, in Trstenik, Yugoslavia and all the other information pertinent to the alias. He puts them in a file folder with the pictures.

"My mother will be driving me to Immigration to pick up the information from Joe, then she will be driving me to Parliament Janitorial Services to make application for the job. Being a new immigrant I don't know my way around the city, so she will drive me to the job and pick me up after work."

"I see you've done a bit of clandestine work for Confidential Investigations."

Marcel drives home and rings the doorbell. Irena Roy opens the door, looks at Marcel and says, "Can I help you?" Spotting Marcel's car she starts to laugh. Marcel addresses his mother in Serbian; "May I come in?"

Irena, still laughing, opens the door wide and bows him in.

"I didn't recognize you until you spoke although I did know who you were when I saw the car. We'll have to make sure the neighbors don't see you. They'll think I have a new lover."

Marcel laughs, "I'm going to see if I can get some sleep. Morning came early."

Rae, in his office, is searching the pictures and information for mistakes. He changes year of birth from 1979 to 1971, the height from 176.1 cm. to 174.4 cm., his weight from 81.25 kilograms to 79.91 kilograms, hair color from blond to black and eye color from green to brown. For distinguishing marks, he fills in walks with a slight limp with his left leg. Joe can take it from there.

Problems

At eight o'clock, Cecil Mann enters the office of the Canadian Security and Intelligence Service and asks to speak to the Senior Director, Jean Perrault. Perrault is in a meeting with the Justice Minister, George Branch, and some of the top officials in C.S.I.S.

John Goullet enters the waiting room and speaks to the receptionist at ten-fifteen, then sits down beside Cecil. The two agents exchange small talk for a while, then sit back and wait. The meeting breaks up at ten-forty five. Cecil and John are kept waiting another hour before being called in to speak to the Senior Official. Perrault does this deliberately to better control his staff.

"Well, what do you two jackasses need?"

Cecil is upset and speaks first. "I thought that I should, that we should explain to you what happened with the Ferguson family yesterday. We figured you should know as soon as possible."

"So tell me."

Perrault addresses the agents in the same overbearing tone. His attitude makes Cecil even more agitated.

"After the Ferguson family left for the funeral I entered their premises using the key provided and planted the audio surveillance equipment.

I used rubber gloves and wiped off the bugs so no fingerprints will be found in the residence. When I left, I locked the door and met John Goullet at the funeral. (Cecil never mentioned speaking to the neighbor with the camera. He would be in enough trouble as it is). We followed Joseph and Eileen Ferguson home and then from their home to Carlingwood Plaza. We were waiting for them to return to the car when a man pulled a gun on us from the front of the car and another jerked the driver door open, holding a gun on John. John was ordered out of the car and handcuffed, and then I was ordered out and handcuffed. We both informed them we were from C.S.I.S. When they searched us and found our badges the one cop went to his car and contacted the police station. When he came back, they released us. They had noticed us tailing the Fergusons and that's why they stopped us, but they wanted to get clearance from their office before releasing us. I informed them that we were not going to stand for this treatment and they can expect trouble from the Justice Department for their interference in our investigation."

John noted Cecil never mentioned the Ferguson's seeing them, nor the fact Eileen had identified him. Another omission was the city detectives tailing them from the church building and probably having them under surveillance before that. John also decided not to mention Cecil was so busy hollering he drew a crowd and the detective spent much more time at his vehicle than he would require for a simple conversation.

"At that point our cover was blown," Cecil acknowledges to his supervisor, "so John drove me back to retrieve my vehicle and we split up. I drove to the Ferguson residence and parked in the alley. Eileen Ferguson entered the house and a short time later, a police detective came to the door. She told the detective a neighbor lady had seen a stranger enter her home. Then a man named Alex came and they started searching the house. They found the bugs in the dining room and in the living room. I couldn't hear anything for a while, and then they found the bug in the family room. I heard them enter the office. They were discussing the tap I installed in the phone when the policeman said his partner was walking into the back yard. I thought it was best to leave the site as quickly as possible so my identity wouldn't be compromised. There was nothing else I could do; therefore, I went home."

Perrault cursed the men out, venting his fury on the two C.S.I.S. agents. Cecil was cringing before the verbal onslaught from the Senior Official. John was sitting nonplussed. Jean Perrault, with his miserable attitude and uncontrollable temper had lost control of himself and the situation.

"**Do you have anything else to add to the fiasco,**" Jean explodes at John.

"Yes" John replies casually. "I'm off the case."

"**You're off the case when I tell you, you're off the case and not before.**"

"I stopped by the court house yesterday and I'm off the case."

Perrault is seething in anger. This smart-assed agent has figured out there is something more involved than a simple surveillance in the Ferguson case. Leaving him on the investigation could prove dangerous to the whole operation.

"**Fine,**" Perrault bellows, "**We don't require your incompetent efforts on the job. Now get your sorry asses the hell out of here and file your reports.**"

Cecil starts walking towards his office when John speaks to him.

"We need to go for lunch."

"Perrault ordered us to file our reports," is Cecil's reply.

"If there are as many discrepancies in the tape as there were in your speech about our arrest, you'll be fired," John responds.

"When he reads my report with the inclusion of your being identified by Eileen Ferguson you'll be fired for lying to the Senior Official. We'll go for lunch in your car."

John enters Cecil's car. "I need to hear your tape."

"Why?"

"To find out what you didn't tell Perrault to protect you," is John's exasperated answer. "If you want to stay with and rise in the ranks of the company you'd better learn to cover your ass."

John listens to the tape and then removes it from the machine. He finds a new tape in the glove box of the car and removes it from the container. Outside the car, John, using his lighter, heats the casing of the new tape. After placing the new tape in the recorder, he puts the Ferguson tape from the recorder into his coat pocket.

"Let's go for lunch."

"What are you going to do with the tape?" Cecil asks John

"I have a fire pit at home. It'll be in the next fire. I'll see if the other tape is seized up when we get back because you certainly don't want this one to be heard by your superiors."

The two men discuss the contents of their two reports, to synchronize them as much as possible. Back at the Canadian Security and Intelligence Service Headquarters, the two agents write up the reports and then speak to their superior officer, Marc Leblanc.

Marc addresses the two agents.

"I thought you two would be working your case right now."

Cecil hands Marc his report. "We would be but we ran into problems."

After reading the report, Marc ponders the situation for a few moments.

"This case has really been hit with a lot of disasters, and yet they are all problems that can happen on any case, but usually not this bad. We'll have to temporarily back up from our surveillance of Joseph Ferguson and pursue the investigation from a different angle. John, we need to gain access to the lawyer's files on Ferguson."

"I told Perrault this morning that I am off this case."

Marc ponders the situation for a moment, realizing John is suspicious. "That will work out fine. I have an agent, Philip Moore, coming in later this afternoon. When he arrives, I'll introduce you and you can work with him because his case requires two agents. Cecil can temporarily handle this case on his own. Now if you'll excuse us Cecil and I will discuss his next move.

John leaves the two agents discussing their options on the Ferguson investigation. He is relieved to be off the case. There is something illegal going on and John Goullet isn't going to be the patsy. He pats his coat pocket. Hello Cecil. If I ever need you, I have you.

Contact

At nine-thirty Rae Jones is handing Joe Ferguson his lunch box containing the Dragen Yankovich alias information. Re-entering the Department of Immigration Building Joe steps into the office of a co-worker he believes is involved in the illegal activities tied to the Immigration Department. Sitting down at the computer Joe brings up the IMM-1000 documents and fills them out from the information provided. He hits the print button and then deletes the screen. Joe places the original documents back in the envelope, then disposes of them at the shredder. He scans the photograph into the specialized photocopy machine and adheres the self-adhesive picture to the Landed Immigration Paper. After signing an alias, Joe folds the new Landed Immigration Papers and places the document into a government envelope. Joe hides the envelope under his lunch.

In the lunchroom, a co-worker jokingly addresses Joe. "Hey Fergie, if you didn't leave your lunch in the car you'd have time to eat it."

"That's a great idea Dave," is Joe's repartee, "I would never thought of that myself. Do you happen to have any other profound advice to share with me today?"

"Not at the moment but if you give me enough time I'm sure I can think of something. Can you give me until Friday?"

"Are you sure that won't crowd you too much?"

"I should be fine. I always work better under pressure."

Joe locks the lunch pail in his locker and the staff returns to their workstations.

At lunch, Joe picks up his lunch box, and meets Irena Roy outside the Immigration Department offices. He gives her the envelope containing the Landed Immigration document. Irena drives her son, disguised as Dragen Yankovich, to the offices of Parliamentary Janitorial Services. The receptionist photocopies the document. Marcel signs Dragen Yankovich, in Serbian, on the papers placed in front of him. She takes Marcel and his documents to the office manager. They fingerprint and photograph him for their records, and then issue him an identity card.

The manager asks Dragen Yankovich, "Can you work tonight?"

Marcel opens his hands and shrugs his shoulders.

The manager pokes Dragen Yankovich in the chest saying "You", he picks up a broom and makes a sweeping motion and says "Work", and then steps over to the wall clock and moves his finger from two o'clock to nine o'clock that evening in a sweeping motion and says, "Tonight."

Dragen Yankovich stands frowning, and then he grins. Nodding his head, he smiles and speaks quickly in Serbian. He points to himself, makes a sweeping motion, points to the wall clock and holds up nine fingers, all the time smiling and speaking in Serbian to indicate he understands the question. The manager takes a map of the worksite from a filing cabinet and marks an X where Marcel will enter the building. He writes the name of the contact worker, the door number, the name of the building and the starting time on the paper, then hands the map to Marcel. Dragen Yankovich smiles and limps from the office carrying his immigration document and the janitorial work documents with him. He starts tonight.

After John Goullet leaves the office, Cecil Mann and Marc Leblanc resume their discussion of the Joe Ferguson case.

"Do you have any problem continuing the Joseph Ferguson investigation?"

"None whatsoever."

Marc decides to fabricate a story regarding Joe.

"We have some proof that Joseph Ferguson is illegally aiding members of the terrorists organization known as al-Qaeda to obtain landed immigrant status in Canada. As the case stands right now, we may not have sufficient proof to obtain a conviction. All our information is strictly confidential and very hush – hush. You will be operating by yourself and if you require assistance that person will come in under you."

Cecil, buoyed up by his superiors' trust in him, begins to feel important. Forgotten is the humiliation of the meeting with the Senior Official.

"Marc continues his dissertation; "Joe Ferguson is under surveillance at his office in the Immigration Department. It would be advantageous to observe his lawyer for a period of time. We have information tying the law office to the illegal immigration operation run by Ferguson. You must obtain copies of everything his lawyer has recorded and you will be required to bug his office. You'll have to achieve those goals by every means at your disposal. It may be possible for you to recruit one of the staff of Jones Smythe and Watson by bribes, patriotism or love. Don't overlook any tool in your arsenal. Do you have any questions or qualms about the case?"

"Would I be able to examine the files on Joseph Ferguson to bring myself up to date on the case?"

Leblanc knows the surveillance is an office cover-up of illegal activities within the government. "Like I said the investigation is completely confidential. You will be given access to the files only if it is absolutely necessary. Make sure you file reports every day to keep the office up-to-date on your progress."

"Thank you very much for your confidence in me," is Mann's response, "I will do everything I can to break this illegal immigration ring."

"I know that you will. I was relieved when John Goullet requested to be removed from the case. Jean Perrault and I were concerned that he would hold you back. We have observed you have much more drive and ambition than John and believe you will rise more quickly in the organization not saddled with him as a partner."

Cecil leaves the office, buoyed up by the confidence Marc has in him, and anxious to prove Leblanc's trust in him is justified.

Cecil drives to the Carlingwood Plaza, the location of the law firm of Jones, Smythe and Watson. He parks in an inconspicuous site and sits waiting in his car, observing the front entrance to the firm. He sees a petite young lady, very chic in her appearance leave the law office and walk to Tim Hortons for a coffee. Deciding it could be in his best interest to meet her, Cecil follows the young lady into the restaurant.

Picking up his coffee, Cecil Mann proceeds to the table where she is seated.

"Will you allow me to join you for coffee?"

Marlene Moore watches Cecil enter the coffee shop and then advance towards her. She sees a young man, quite handsome and very well dressed standing before her. His fellow agents don't call him Dapper Dan for nothing.

"Why thank you, I would enjoy that."

"When I saw a lovely young lady, walking with such poise, enter this establishment, I knew my life would never be complete until I made her acquaintance. My name is Cecil Mann."

"Thank you for the lovely compliment. My name is Marlene Moore."

They talk for a short time about nothing – just making conversation. Then Cecil gets more serious. "I have enjoyed your company so much that I have hardly touched my coffee.

"I've enjoyed myself also."

"It would be a shame if I never saw you again. Would you allow me to take you dining tonight?"

"Why I would love that. Yes, I'd enjoy dinner with you."

"Will you give me your address or would you prefer to meet me?"

"Where were you planning on dining?"

"I always enjoy Wilfred's at the Chateau Laurier, say at seven thirty."

Marlene is flattered, "Could you pick me up?" She writes her address and phone number on the back of a business card and gives it to Cecil. "I really must run now. I'll see you at seven thirty this evening."

Security

After the office staff leaves, Alex Johansen enters the offices of Jones, Smythe and Watson carrying tools, power cords and a ladder. He returns to the car and carries the surveillance equipment into the premises. Wires connect a sensitive photoelectric cell to the camera located in the fluorescent light fixture. Wires from the camera connect to the industry special VHS recorder. The recording unit is located in the janitorial storage. Alex then installs a pencil mike through the ceiling tiles with cable running to the same recorder. In an hour and a half the audio/video, surveillance equipment is operational.

Alex Johansen installs a blank videotape into the recorder. He hands William Smythe a pencil light. "Go into your office and activate the system."

The unit begins recording.

"Shut off the office light."

William does. The recorder continues to operate.

"Close the door."

The recorder stops.

"Talk to me."

The recorder starts again.

"Quit talking and turn on the pencil light.

The recorder stops and starts.

"You can come out here. I'll show you the proper way to operate the equipment."

Cecil Mann arrives to escort Marlene Moore on their dinner engagement and presents her with a corsage, a lovely red rosebud. Marlene is pleasantly surprised and impressed by the thoughtfulness of the young man. Entering Wilfred's at the Chateau Laurier, a dining hostess escorts the couple to their table. Marlene smiles radiantly when she spies the centerpiece – a beautiful bouquet of roses, matching the corsage she is wearing. Cecil orders the Beef Neptune while Marlene prefers the Filet Mignon. To compliment their dinner he orders a bottle of Moet Dom Perignon. When they leave, the hostess presents Marlene with the lovely bouquet of roses that graced their table. As they stand talking in the doorway to her suite, Marlene embraces the bouquet lovingly to her breast.

"Would you join me for another glass of wine tonight Cecil?"

"I would enjoy that Marlene if I didn't have some important papers to finish for a meeting early tomorrow morning. I will have some spare time tomorrow at noon. Could you join me for a bite to eat at Tim Hortons?"

"Definitely. I have thoroughly enjoyed the time we spent together this evening."

Marlene steps close to Cecil, giving him a quick kiss.

Entering the elevator Cecil turns to see Marlene still standing in the doorway to her suite. He waves to her and she blows him a kiss as the elevator door slides shut. Cecil has made his second major step in recruiting an agent inside the law offices of Jones, Smythe and Watson. By working Marlene carefully, he will soon have the access he requires to the office of the Ferguson lawyer.

Marlene, completely enamored by the young man, is very impressed by the luxury car he drives. 'Cecil must have a very good income to drive a Lexus.' It has been a wonderful evening with promises of more to come.

On The Job

    Dragen Yankovich is waiting at the jobsite before the other cleaning staff arrive. The foreman posts him and five other men to work in the basement. Dragen Yankovich carries his lunch down with him. At the first break, he sits down on the floor and pours himself a coffee. When the elevator goes up, he enters the server room. Sitting down at a computer, he begins his search of the system very methodically. Locating a flaw, Marcel carefully installs a "Trojan Horse Program" over top of it. The Trojan horse program will allow him access the computer files, through the firewall, from an outside source and if security searches for bugs they will know there is a flaw at that location and will give it little consideration. He carefully removes all signs of ever entering the computer, then sits down to finish drinking his coffee. He is working when the five men return.

    At lunch, he installs three more "Trojan Horse Programs" over existing flaws and again removes all traces of his entry. Installing the fifth "Trojan Horse Program" during the last coffee break, he is lying on the floor pretending to be sleeping when the men return. He jerks awake and rolls to his feet, crouching, ready for an attack, then relaxes as he realizes he is no danger. The foreman exiting the elevator, startled by the sudden defensive posture of Dragen Yankovich, realizes the worker must have believed he was still in Bosnia. 'It will require some time for this immigrant from a war torn country to adjust to his new environment.'

He spends last hour and a half on the fifth floor, cleaning the offices of the Immigration Department bureaucracy. Marcel notices his foreman opening the doors to the private offices with keys on a ring that had been hanging on a hook near the computers. Just before quitting time, the foreman enters the elevator to return the keys to their basement location.

As the cleaning staff leaves the building, Dragen Yankovich, his limp more pronounced, quickly moves to the waiting car. At home, Marcel phones the office of Confidential Investigations and leaves the message, "I require some method of making fifteen key impressions," on the voice recorder.

Marcel recognizes that six "Trojan Horse programs" will be the minimum he will require to safely enter the Department of Immigration files from an outside location. He already has five safely installed in the system and hopefully will finish the project tomorrow night. He goes to bed satisfied in the knowledge his first night on the new job has been a success.

Spies and Counterspies

Marlene Moore leaves the law offices for her luncheon engagement with Cecil Mann. After taking a few steps, she notices Cecil hurrying towards her. Smiling radiantly, she waves to Cecil and changes direction, directly towards her handsome beau. She and Cecil hug passionately and kiss each other, and then Cecil holds her at arms length.

"I couldn't wait any longer to see you," Cecil tells Marlene. "I just had to meet you, and walk you to the restaurant."

Marlene pulls Cecil close and kisses him again. They turn and proceed, arm in arm, to enjoy their lunch together at Tim Hortons.

Tom Jackson has a coffee engagement with his cronies this afternoon. He decides to use the opportunity to deliver the floppy disk, containing the information he has acquired, to William Smythe before meeting with his friends. Driving to the Carlingwood Plaza parking lot early, he stops and picks up a newspaper. Tom is sitting in his vehicle reading when he glances at his watch and realizes the lawyers should be back from lunch.

As he looks towards the doorway of the law firm he spots the C.S.I.S. agent, whose picture he had previously taken leaving the Ferguson residence, walking arm in arm with one of the staff of the firm. Tom quickly raises the paper so as not to be seen, but the couple are so enamored with each other they are oblivious of their surroundings. He furtively watches as they enjoy a parting kiss before continuing on their respective ways.

Tom Jackson sits in his car thinking for another fifteen minutes before he decides to confront William Smythe.

William escorts Tom into his office and sits down. Observing Tom's serious visage William wonders what is on his mind.

"Do you have some new information for me?"

"Maybe yes, maybe no," is Tom's terse reply.

William is taken aback. 'What does he mean by that?'

Tom hands William the disk, which he inserts into his computer, bringing up the information. William looks at the pictures – then back at Tom – then back at the pictures.

"That's the man who installed the latest illegal surveillance equipment standing on Joe's front step."

"Yes. It's also the man I saw kissing one of your staff fifteen minutes ago."

William jerks around looking at Tom – his mouth ajar. He definitely was not prepared for this development. It takes him a moment to absorb the information.

William speaks softly "Which one Tom?"

"I don't know her name," Tom replies. "She's young, petite, reddish-brown hair and wearing a blue sweater and skirt."

William sits for a moment fully realizing the importance of this revelation.

"You've just described Marlene Moore. She's been with the firm about nine months. I wonder how long she's been seeing the man?"

Tom thinks for a minute. "Not too long."

"What makes you think that?"

"They were too passionate in public."

"Marlene takes lunch and coffee break every day over at Tim Hortons. Could you find out for us how long the man has been meeting her? I'll stop by your house tonight to talk to you. Under the present circumstances I don't want the staff seeing you in the office more than necessary and certainly not twice in one day."

"I understand your concerns."

William stands up and locks the door. Removing the garbage can from the corner and opening the safe, he reaches in and picks up a jewel case. After transferring a computer disk from the jewel case into the floppy drive, he signals Tom to come around the desk and look at the screen. Tom Jackson finds himself looking at the picture, identification and C.S.I.S. badge of the man he had photographed and subsequently seen with Marlene Moore.

"I thought it might be more of C.S.I.S. They're real busy little boys aren't they."

"Tom, I must really thank you for your information on our legal assistant. We now know where C.S.I.S. is making their next move and can prepare for it. Thanks to your diligence we won't be caught off guard."

"I'm already late for my regular visit with some friends. I'll have to leave now. Stop by my house on your way home and I'll try to have the information on the lady and the C.S.I.S. agent for you."

Tom leaves, William returns the disks to the office safe then sits, pondering his next move. If he fires Marlene, he could cast suspicion upon the whole operation. He takes small comfort from that old adage – keep your friends close and your enemies closer. He must warn everyone about the perceived danger.

At three o'clock, Tom and his friends are still sitting and talking while enjoying their coffee and donuts. Tom observes Marlene Moore come in for her coffee and then leave after finishing. It is action Jackson time. Tom walks up to the counter.

"I would really enjoy one of your blueberry muffins."

Tom pays for the muffin but stays at the counter talking to the young lady who served him.

"Doesn't the lady who left a couple of minutes ago work for the law firm of Jones, Smythe and Watson?"

"Yes that's Marlene Moore."

"I saw her leave here at noon with a young man." Tom continues, "but I've never seen that gentleman around here before."

"Yes, they had lunch together. He came in yesterday for the first time and asked to sit with her. I overheard him introducing himself."

"They seemed to be hitting it off pretty good for just having coffee together."

"When they were leaving I heard him ask her to join him for dinner last night and she accepted."

"He did better than me. Whenever I asked a young lady to have supper with me, she would tell me to 'get lost'. I better get back to my friends before they forget I'm here, and anyway, I wouldn't want you thinking I'm a garrulous old man."

"I would never think that."

"That's because you're a very nice young lady. Thank you again for the muffin."

Maurice Solinger is teaching Marcel Roy how to make key impressions using pliers and the pieces of small soft leather he brought with him. Maurice instructs Marcel to place the key on the leather then fold the other half of the leather over the key. Squeeze the pliers multiple times on the leather. Check the impression against the key.

Marcel is soon ready to tackle the keys at the Immigration Department.

After leaving the office William stops at the Jackson residence and rings the bell, then steps inside the front door.

"Were you able to learn anything?"

"Yes. They met yesterday afternoon."

William lets out a little sigh. "Good! There's been no harm done and we can watch her. Tell me everything you found out about them."

Tom relates the story as told to him by the clerk.

"Now I know where the potential problem lies," William responds, "I can take steps to control the situation."

"Are you going to fire her?"

"We can't under the Canadian Civil Rights Laws and even if we could it would cast suspicion on our company. However, I can use her to provide disinformation to C.S.I.S. A thank you seems hardly appropriate for everything you've done."

Tom smiles. "If that's the case maybe I can be reimbursed for my expenses – you know – two shotgun shells and one blueberry muffin."

William laughs. "Send in your bill. The firm will make a decision over coffee and donuts. Don't get your hopes up too high though, we're a bit of a tightwaddy company."

William is still smiling over the exchange of words as he rings the Ferguson doorbell.

"Come in Mr. Smythe. Mom and Dad are in the dining room."

"Thank you Jerry. Hello Eileen – Joe. I see you're doing what I hope to be doing in fifteen minutes. I dropped by to tell you we might have a mole in our office. Tom spotted our legal assistant with the smaller C.S.I.S. operative you met Monday afternoon. They had lunch together. Tom made inquiries and found out they met yesterday. We believe the agent made contact to groom her for their activities. If you must contact me do so on my cell phone and we will restrict visits to the office as much as possible. I plan on using her to plant disinformation in C.S.I.S. files."

"That's a good idea," Joe responds. "With the laws we have today you certainly can't fire her without ending up in a court battle and we don't need the publicity at this time."

"Tom has a very healthy sense of humor. I mentioned to him that a thank you seemed hardly appropriate for everything he has done for us. His repartee was in that case maybe he could be reimbursed for his expenses – you know – two shotgun shells and one blueberry muffin."

Joe and the boys laugh.

Eileen is offended; "I don't find the taking of human life funny."

"It's Tom's way of handling a very traumatic situation."

"It is just as traumatic for me."

William's frustration by her attitude comes to the fore.

"In no way is it just as traumatic for you as it is for Tom. It wasn't you who had to kill a man to save the lives of the boys. It wasn't you who went into the house to look for Art Condor knowing the boy was either dead or badly wounded. Don't pass judgment on Tom for the way he chooses to handle his trauma. It's much healthier to try to alleviate the situation by humor than by feeling morose and sulking about what happened. Now I must be getting home."

Eileen is not willing to drop the conversation. She continues her tirade to William.

"Tom had no business shooting that man."

"Tom's actions may have saved one of the boy's lives by deflecting his aim."

Jerry speaks up, "I didn't think of it at the time but when I heard the blast of the shotgun, I also heard a buzz past my head. Tom very likely saved my life."

Eileen is unwilling to drop the subject. "The bible says you shall not kill. Tom had no business killing that man."

Jerry, frustrated by his mother's attitude, will no longer hold back his feelings.

"I have heard you say on three separate occasions, Mr. Jackson had no right killing that killer. You should have thanked Mr. Jackson for saving either my life or my friends lives. I have never heard you condemn that killer for shooting Art or shooting at Andre, Sandy and me. It's as though our lives are less important than that killer's. I want you to know that I am glad Mr. Jackson killed that man. It's a small comfort after he killed Art."

Jerry turns and stalks out of the house. Keith hesitates for a moment and then he too leaves. William quickly excuses himself and leaves for home – upset over Eileen's attitude. Joe, disconcerted by Eileen's stance, heads downstairs to his office. Fifteen minutes later Eileen enters the office and speaks to him.

"We have to leave for bible study now."

"I'm not going."

"Why not?"

"I'm glad that my two sons are still alive. Unlike you I'm not willing to exchange their lives for the life of that asshole Tom shot."

The vehemence in her husband's voice stuns Eileen. She has never heard Joe swear before and he has never condemned her before.

Waiting at the church building after the congregation leaves, Eileen speaks to the minister relating to the conversation that had transpired at home.

"What can I do to show them they are wrong to think that way as Christians?"

"Nothing, because they are right and you are wrong."

"God says you shall not kill."

"God told the Israelites to conquer the land and kill every man, woman and child in the land they did conquer and God was angered because they did not kill all the inhabitants. Gideon took three hundred men and slew thousands, and God was pleased. I could speak of David, who was responsible for killing whole armies, yet was praised as a man dear to the heart of God."

"That's in the Old Testament."

"So is the scripture you just quoted. Eileen, I have seen you take the scriptures you want to accept, and reject the scriptures you don't like. A Christian accepts all scripture. A hypocrite accepts only what he wants."

"Are you calling me a hypocrite?"

"You are condemning the man whom everybody else considers a hero. You are condemning the man who may have saved your own sons' lives. Yes, I'm calling you a hypocrite."

Eileen storms out of the building and drives home. She watches TV by herself. When the boys are not home by bedtime, she phones the Dupree residence.

"Andre Here."

"Are Keith and Jerry there?"

"Oh it's you." Andre hangs up the phone."

Eileen is shocked. Andre Dupree had never spoken to her like that before. She phones the Hanger residence.

"Robert Hanger here."

"Are Keith and Jerry Ferguson there?"

"No."

"Do you know where they are?"

"No."

"Could I speak to Sandy?"

"No."

Eileen goes downstairs to the office to get Joe and go to bed. He isn't in the office. She finds him sleeping in the spare bedroom. Eileen sleeps alone that night, the first time since they've been married.

The following morning Eileen makes Joe's breakfast and packs his lunch while Joe is eating.

"I want to apologize for what I said yesterday."

"You don't need to apologize to me," Joe replies.

"I plan to apologize to the boys also."

"Yes they require an apology." Joe stands up and picks up his lunch box. "So does Tom Jackson."

New Job

The second evening on the job, Dragen Yankovich installs four more "Trojan Horse Programs" on the computers in the basement of the Immigration Department and makes the key impressions he requires. Before going to bed, he phones Maurice Solinger and leaves a prearranged message on his office phone. At seven thirty Thursday morning Maurice takes the message off his answering service. Maurice phones William Smythe at home and William phones his brother in Montreal. At eight fifteen, Maurice Solinger picks up the fax for Dragen Yankovich showing he has a job in Laval Quebec, and is driving to the Roy residence. Maurice picks up the pieces of leather with the key impressions and leaves the fax with Irena. At City Locksmith, he purchases the required key blanks. Back at his office, Maurice begins filing the keys close to the required cuts. Shortly thereafter, his wife Kathleen joins him in the task. She picks up a partially cut key blank and locking it in the vice, begins the intricate task of filing it to exactly duplicate the leather key impressions made by Marcel. Kathleen's phenomenal patience is exactly what this intricate job requires.

Irena Roy drives to the office of Parliament Janitorial Service where Dragen Yankovich shows the office manager his letter of acceptance. The letter reads, "Dragen Yankovich has been accepted for the position of machinist for Pelletier Welding and Machine Shop at 17 Boul. Industriel, Laval, Quebec. He is to begin working Friday, June 15th at 7:30 a.m. and his wages will begin at $17.65 per hour. From Parliamentary Janitorial, Irena drives to a movie production set for Andre Prichard to remove the disguise from her son.

"Did the disguise work?"

"I didn't recognize Marcel until he spoke. He didn't look like my son, he didn't walk like my son, and he even sounded a little different than my son. He was like a complete stranger."

"You did a great job Andre. I need another make-up job for a few hours next Thursday morning. Would Wednesday evening or early Thursday morning work best for you?"

"Thursday morning is best. I never know what time I'll get off the set. Be at my house at five thirty again. Did you want the same disguise or a different one? I have a beautiful red beard and wig that would look great on you."

"I would prefer something closer to my natural hair color."

Andre laughs. "You're missing the boat you know – you really are. That red hair and beard would make you stand out in a crowd like a peacock in a chicken house. You'd be the star attraction."

Marcel laughs. "Maybe next time. Say, do you have something to remove the dark coloration from my skin?"

Andre takes a small jar out of a box and hands it to Marcel. "This will do the job. Just follow the directions on the bottle. I'll see you next Thursday."

The Proof

At seven o'clock Thursday morning Cecil Mann is on the phone to Marlene Moore.

"Good Morning."

"Good morning Marlene."

"Cecil." Marlene is ecstatic. "It's great to hear your voice first thing in the morning."

"Thank you Marlene. I'm glad you think that way. I had to let you know I'll be out of town on business, but I'll be back Friday afternoon. Would you join me for an informal dinner after you leave work on Friday?"

"Yes, I'd really enjoy having dinner with you."

"Thank you Marlene. I'll look forward to seeing you Friday. We'll meet outside your office and go to dinner from there."

Cecil is bringing Marc Leblanc up to date on the case.

"I really need some proof I can show Marlene Moore and she'll do anything we need. I'll also require three telephone bugs to install in the lawyers' phones. When do you want me to pick up the necessary court orders?"

"You won't need to bother. I have a secretary who picks up all the court orders. It looks like you'll be free until tomorrow afternoon. I have another agent that requires some temporary help on his case. Speak to Matt Spence and he'll outline his case and explain your role. When you require aid, you will enlist Matt's help. Before you leave drop by and I'll give you any pertinent information I can glean from the Ferguson file."

Cecil leaves and Marc explains the situation to Jean Perrault. Jean phones Pierre Montague and ten minutes later Marc has the "evidence" he requires coming in on his fax machine. Cecil, upon returning to Marc's office, is present with a folder stamped "Highly Confidential" and the name on the folder is Joseph Ferguson. Cecil, opening the folder, recognizes the picture of Ayman al-Zawahri. Scrutinizing the file, Cecil learns that Ayman al-Zawahri has landed immigrant status in Canada. The documents bear the signature of Joseph Ferguson.

"This is a high profile case," Cecil notes. "If John Goullet realized the importance of this case he would never have asked for a transfer."

"John left because he already knew we were preparing to elevate you to the position of command on this investigation. I had previously recommended the change to Jean Perrault and he has accepted your promotion on this case."

Cecil leaves elated. He had been with C.S.I.S. for only two years and is already highly regarded by his superiors. By successfully handling this case, he will assure himself a rapid promotion inside the Canadian Security and Intelligence Service.

The Unwitting Assistant

Shortly before noon, Maurice leaves his shop to drive to Champaigne Apartments and begin the surveillance of Pierre Montague and his mistress. He has previously learned Montague owns the apartment and Caroline Tremblay is a dining room hostess at the trendy Empire Grill in the Byward Market.

Montague is enjoying his Thursday afternoon business luncheon with Henri Jolliette, the Minister of Immigration at the Rideau Club.

With their luncheon over, Henri Jolliette enters the lounge to visit with some of his contemporaries while Montague uses this opportunity to visit his mistress.

He pays no attention to the gentleman carrying a briefcase, arriving at the elevator before him and then holding the door for him. Montague enters the elevator giving the man a nod while punching the ninth floor button. The stranger steps to the back of the elevator, still carrying his briefcase as the elevator ascends to the ninth floor. Montague waits directly in front of the doors. The door opens and he exits the elevator, rushing towards a scantily dressed lady framed enticingly in the doorway of a suite. Maurice Solinger depresses the button to hold the door open and places the briefcase on the floor of the elevator, activating the digital movie camera which records the girl in the blue slippers and negligee standing in the doorway and then running to Pierre and throwing herself into his arms. She kisses him passionately, then the two lovers holding hands, race into the suite. Maurice smiles and picks up the briefcase. He had set the briefcase down momentarily on the main floor of the apartment building, obtaining pictures of Montague rushing towards the elevator. Knowing he will only draw suspicion to himself by loitering on the premises, Maurice leaves. The security cameras in the hallways of Champaigne apartments are going to make it hard to access the suite Caroline Tremblay occupies.

Maurice Solinger is driving back to his office when the buzz of his cell phone interrupts his thoughts.

"Confidential Investigations, Maurice here."

"Hello Maurice, it's Adrian Montague. I found a set of keys under the bed. One key fits the lock to Pierre's office. I don't know what the other keys are for."

"Did you enter the office?"

"No, I just came outside and called you on my cell phone."

"Good. The office could be bugged. Meet me at City Locksmith and we'll cut duplicate keys.

While waiting at City Locksmith Maurice phones Alex and Marcel, arranging to meet them Friday morning. Adrian is parking her car as Maurice hurries to her.

"I'll give Tom the keys," Maurice informs Adrian. "While he's cutting duplicate keys we can talk in your car."

Five minutes later Maurice opens the passenger door on Adrian's car and slips into the seat beside her. "He'll be twenty minutes cutting the keys. I've arranged for two people to meet me at your residence Friday morning at nine o'clock. One person, who deals in surveillance equipment, will check the office for surveillance devices before we enter. It might be wise to check the entire house while we're at it. The other gentleman is a computer expert. I hope three hours will give us sufficient time to accomplish our goal and find some information to help with your divorce. We'll concentrate on finding hidden bank accounts, stocks, bonds and other negotiables."

"Do you think you will find anything?"

"He keeps the office locked to keep you out for some reason. I assume he has documents in the office he needs to hide from you."

"Yes he's been secretive about that office for the past ten years," Adrian notes. "If nothing else we'll learn what he's been hiding in there. I know he has a safe."

"We'll have to see if we can find the combination to open it. Any secret bank records or other negotiables will be in the safe."

"I have the combination. When the company brought the safe, they left an envelope sitting on top of it. I opened the envelope, which wasn't sealed, and copied down the combination on the bottom of my jewelry case. I figured if he lost the combination I would have it for him."

"I was just leaving Champaigne Apartments when you phoned."

"Do you have pictures I can see?"

Maurice hands Adrian the digital movie camera and she views the pictures.

"There's not much question as to what is going on there."

"Tom should have the keys cut by now. I'll pick them up. Make sure you put the keys back exactly where you found them. I'll keep the duplicate keys. I want to check out some of the locks at Champaigne Apartment."

After Marcel receives the phone call from Maurice, he contacts Andre Prichard again, setting up another appointment for early the next morning. When he and Irena Roy arrive back at their residence Marcel heads straight for the bathroom and uses the cream provided by Andre to remove the dark coloration from his skin. Once the color is removed he has a shower and then to bed.

At 5:30 Friday morning Marcel is knocking on the door to Andre's residence.

"Good morning Andre."

"Come into the studio Marcel and I'll fix you up. Where's your wig and beard?"

"I have a part where I can use that red wig and beard."

Andre dyes his hair then takes out a kit and starts dabbing a brownish liquid on Marcel's cheeks, neck, chest and arms to give the appearance of freckles. He applies the adherent and fastens the beard to Marcel's face and then he carefully positions the red wig on his head. The last piece of the disguise is the green contact lenses.

"Put your shirt on and look at yourself in the mirror."

"It's hard to believe that handsome character is really me."

"I told you it would really look good on you. Roll up your sleeves."

Marcel rolls up his sleeves and looks in the mirror. "That's better still."

"You're ready to go."

"Not quite. One of the other actors, playing the part of a cowboy, wishes to wear my black beard and wig. Could I purchase some of the adhesive so we don't have to bother you all the time?"

"That's no problem, I'll add it to the bill. Say, what's his skin complexion?"

"About the same as mine – maybe slightly darker," Marcel replies.

Andre starts checking some boxes and comes back with a brown wig and brown handlebar mustache. "Have him try this first and see if he likes it. The black wig and beard will be too obvious."

"I'll do that and I'll see you next Thursday."

Marcel Roy, the first to arrive at the restaurant designated by Maurice Solinger as their rendezvous, purchases a coffee and sits at a corner table. Alex Johansen enters the restaurant, glances around, and then sits at a separate table. Maurice soon joins him. They order coffees, then put their heads together to covertly discuss Maurice's plan. While engrossed in their conversation, Marcel picks up his coffee and wanders over to their table.

"May I join you?"

Maurice looks up and almost drops his coffee.

"Marcel?"

It suddenly dawns on Alex who the man in the flaming red beard and hair is. He stares at Marcel and then speaks. "I didn't recognize you in that outfit. I don't believe anyone will know who you are."

Marcel sits down and the three Mr. Mumbles put their heads together, speaking quietly, not wanting anyone to overhear their conversation.

"I didn't want Mrs. Montague to identify me after I was at her house so I thought the disguise was in order."

"Adrian definitely won't be able to pick you out of a line-up," reflects Maurice.

"The disguise is a good idea," Alex muses. "I wish I'd thought of that."

"I have a fake mustache and wig in my car Alex. It will only take a minute to change your appearance."

"Let's go out to the van. I want to see how it looks. We'll let Maurice pay for our coffees."

Maurice arrives at the van to find Marcel has the mustache attached and is just finishing adjusting the wig.

Maurice begins to bug his friend. "You're much better looking with hair on your head. Maybe you should go there bald and wear the wig the rest of the time. Actually you should wear the disguise home, it could improve your sex life."

"Okay," Alex responds, playing along with Maurice. "Let's hear the rest of it. How will it improve my sex life?"

"Gloria might not recognize you."

Maurice ducks behind the seat.

The three men, laughing as they exit the van, climb into Maurice's car. Three blocks later, they are ringing the doorbell at the Montague residence.

Adrian opens the door and steps out. "The girls have left for school."

Maurice introduces his associates as Carlos and Eric.

Carlos enters the house and begins monitoring the premises with his equipment as Maurice and Eric put on latex gloves. Carlos pronounces the main floor clean, then proceeds downstairs, where he checks the office for audio and video surveillance equipment. He completes his check of the downstairs for surveillance equipment, checks upstairs and then leaves, walking back to his van.

Eric, carefully removing materials from the safe, finds jewel cases containing 22 computer disks. Using his own laptop computer he duplicates the information onto disks of his own, and then carefully removes the information from the original disk showing the last date and time that file was accessed thus reverting the file date and time on each disk back to the date and time previous to his accessing the file. He returns the original disks to their original jewel case, each into the compartment from which it was previously removed. Eric has been placing each duplicate disk into his own jewel cases, and when he is finished, places them in his briefcase. Eric removes seventeen pages of documents from the safe and scans them into his computer. He carefully replaces everything into its proper compartments. Checking under the desk and drawers, he finds 17 numbers recorded under the desktop. He writes the numbers in a notebook and then sits down to the computer, powering it up. The *enter password* security check appears. Adrian watches as "Eric" begins to carefully bypass the entry codes to access the files. Suddenly his hands are flying on the keyboard and then the computer begins to power up.

Eric searches the bank records, checking certain items and then printing them off. Adrian reaches for the paper as it exits the printer.

"Don't touch!"

"Why?" Adrian asks.

"If you touch anything I'm doing, I'm getting up and leaving. One fingerprint of yours could compromise the whole, damn operation. Now get out!"

Maurice is unable to glean much information from the files in the filing cabinet and desk but manages to find nine pages with minimal information on them. Marcel scans those pages into his computer.

Maurice leaves the office and sits down with Adrian.

"He's not very nice," Adrian complains

"No, but he's one of the top men in the business. Eric's prowess with a computer is legendary inside the F.B.I. Eric extracts information from computers that nobody else can ever hope to find. He was on one case when a C.I.A. agent tried to interfere. He got up and walked out. The agent was demoted and came close to losing his job because his actions compromised the case. He knows what he's doing and knows the risk involved. Eric is one man you never want to cross. It was just luck I learned he would be in town."

Eric finds more information of interest and prints it. He locks down the machine, leaving no trace of his presence in the computer.

Eric leaves the office, carefully locking the door and then handing Maurice the key.

"We'll leave now," Maurice informs Adrian. "We don't want your daughters or any of their friends to see us leaving. I'll get back to you on Monday and let you know what was on the computer disks. I'm going to have Eric working all weekend to find any information he can. Don't you ever, under any circumstances, enter that office again."

"There are no bugs in there."

"Every time you put a disk in a computer it shows the previous dates that disk was accessed. Every time you enter a program on the hard drive the computer shows the previous times and dates it was accessed. I'm one of only three people who can remove that information. We all live in the U.S. I have found $760 thousand on the files glancing through them and there will be more." "Eric" continues his tirade. "If you go into that office and touch anything there is an excellent chance you will lose that money and if I even suspect you have been in there I will not be passing this information on to Maurice. There is mention of a death made to look like an accident. His partner's name is Jean Perrault. Maurice you'd be smart to drop this case right now before this amateur detective gets you killed along with herself and her children."

"Eric the Red" walks out. Adrian is shocked. Jean Perrault has been in her home hundreds of times.... Jean and her husband golf together every Sunday....

"I had no idea that it could be dangerous. I'll stay away from that office."

"Life isn't like the movies," Maurice warns Adrian. "Amateur detectives are the first ones killed. Phone me from a pay phone on Monday and I'll give you the information Eric has gleaned from the computer disks."

The Mistress

Maurice and Marcel drive to the restaurant and order lunch. Maurice outlines a possible scenario to obtain pictures of the sexual liaison between Pierre Montague and his mistress, Caroline Tremblay.

Eric arrives at the Empire Grill at one forty and waits in the entrance. He recognizes Caroline Tremblay from her picture as he sees her walking towards the reception area of the restaurant. Caroline is talking to the other hostess when Eric walks up to them and speaks to Caroline.

"I was to meet a man here but he just called and cancelled. I hate to sit alone in a strange establishment so I was hoping you might accept my invitation and have a drink of wine with me."

Caroline views Eric, an exciting young man with flaming hair and beard. This could be interesting. Her body tingles.

"I have fifteen minutes until I begin working so I'm going to take you up on the offer."

The dining hostess escorts them to a table and they order a bottle of Grey MLH Ehrenfelse.

Marcel smiling, leans forward, placing both hands on the table he gazes directly into Caroline's eyes.

"My name is Eric. My friends call me Eric the Red."

"How do you do Eric the Red? My name is Caroline."

"I hope you don't think me forward, being so presumptuous and asking you to join me for a drink, but I do hate to sit alone.

"You are certainly no wallflower," Caroline jokingly replies, "but I don't blame you for not wanting to sit by yourself."

"Have you been working at this establishment long?"

"Yes. Ever since I graduated from high school."

"I get the impression you enjoy your work."

"I really do," Caroline agrees. "We meet so many interesting people here, like Eric the Red. Moreover, we meet politicians and a lot of young businessmen and ladies. Some of the conversations here are positively scintillating. I could never imagine myself working anywhere else."

Eric, still gazing into Caroline's eyes picks up his glass of wine and takes a sip. "You have a bubbling personality Caroline. I really enjoy being with people like you. You make everything around you come to life. Would you find me presumptuous if I asked if you had a current male friend, because if you don't I would like to come to know you better?"

"Yes I do have a gentleman friend and we plan to marry as soon as his children graduate and he gets his divorce."

"Do you realize you just broke my heart?" Eric replies with a ridiculously, sorrowful expression on his face. "I'm now going to have to go through life knowing that you love another man and not me."

Caroline laughs jovially, "I'm sure your heart will heal quite nicely."

"No it won't. My heart is completely shattered. I'm going to force myself to suffer for the next hour, maybe even longer." Eric brightens up. "There may be hope for me yet. How old are the children?"

Caroline laughingly replies, "No there is no hope for you. The girls are fourteen and sixteen."

"Three more years of school, four years of college, and two years to get the divorce through. Ahaa, there is time for me to change your mind; unless of course you do the same thing as my sister did to catch her husband. They were married within one year and she's been happily married now for five years."

Caroline feels her heart drop. Nine years is too long to wait, but she can't see herself living without Pierre. Then she looks at Eric. "What did your sister do?"

Eric checks his watch, "We don't really have time to discuss that right now. I have to meet with a local law firm on Monday. I can meet you here at one thirty and we can discuss your options. Also, it will give me a further opportunity to convince you how much better off you would be to go to dinner with me. Would you meet me on Monday?"

Caroline thinks for a minute, "Yes I will."

Caroline sits watching Eric leave the restaurant. If she could have Pierre all to herself within one year, **YYEEEEES!**

The Recruit

Keith and Jerry Ferguson arrive home from school Friday afternoon and make themselves a sandwich.

"I'm sorry for what I said yesterday," Eileen tells her sons. "I'm very glad that you're alive. I could never stand to lose you."

"Did you thank Tom for saving our lives?" Jerry asks his mother.

"I can't. He did kill a man."

Keith is frustrated. "You just don't get it do you mom."

The boys pick up their ball gloves and head out to the diamond for their baseball practice.

Cecil Mann waves to Marlene Moore as she is leaving the offices of Jones, Smythe and Watson. They rush towards each other, embrace, and kiss passionately. Walking back to his car, Cecil picks up a small box from the hood of the car, which he hands to Marlene. "I have a little present which I believe you will appreciate."

"What is it?" Marlene asks Cecil

"You'll have to open the package to find out."

Inside the package, Marlene discovers a petite, yellow, rosebud corsage. Holding it next to her pale green suit, it matches to perfection. Marlene embraces Cecil again, holding him close and kissing him repeatedly. They loosen their embrace and step back.

"Cecil, you're so thoughtful. Will you pin this on my jacket for me please?"

Dominico's Fine Italian Dining serves Marlene the baked Fettuccini Ala Fredo, while Cecil prefers the baked Chicken Fettuccini. With the meals, they choose a soft white wine. After the enjoyable meal at Dominico's they drive to Marlene's apartment to enjoy some quiet chamber music and another glass of wine. Sitting on the love seat, Marlene snuggles close to Cecil and relaxes. Cecil bends to kiss Marlene on the forehead. She lifts her face and they kiss on the lips. Snuggling closer, they continue to kiss. Marlene rises and taking Cecil's hand gently pulls him to his feet and leads him into her bedroom. They awaken the following morning to the sounds of the chamber music emanating from the living room. After more tender caressing and lovemaking, the couple shower and enjoy a bite to eat before leaving the apartment to spend the day and then that night together.

Sunday morning finds Montague playing a round of golf with his cohorts, Jean Perrault, Director of C.S.I.S., and Guy Trembley, Commissioner of the R.C.M.P. After the golf game, Montague drives to Champaigne apartments to visit with his mistress, Caroline Tremblay. His wife and daughters will have gone to church, and later to the home of her mother for lunch. He and his mistress will spend an enjoyable few of hours together before Caroline has to be at the Empire Grill. Montague is home by three o'clock and changes for dinner. A golf ball from his sweater pocket drops, hitting him on the foot and rolling under the bed. Kneeling down to retrieve the ball Montague discovers his missing keys. He is relieved to have the keys back in his possession again with no harm done.

Sunday morning Marlene and Cecil enjoy the beauty of the grass and flowers surrounding a tiny pond. Ducks leave the pond to relish pieces of bread thrown by little children who scurry laughing back to the safety provided by their parents. Tiny birds flit between the bushes around the pond. Graceful swallows flow over land and water picking off insects to feed their ravenous babies. Their undulating flights provide a living rhapsody to the eyes of all who enjoy beauty in motion. A squirrel carries on an incessant chatter, telling everybody present to move on. Peanuts placed on a bench mollify him momentarily, but once they're gone it's time again for everybody to leave.

A swallow, spying a cat a on a hunting expedition, poises in midflight then dive bombs, easily pulling out of his attack to elude the claws futilely lashing the air in a vain attempt to end the graceful flight of this tiny piece of poetry in motion flashing through the sunlit sky.

The talkative squirrel spying the feline, hurls a string of epithets that soon has the self-respecting cat on its way.

A lone dandelion shines like a beacon of sunlight, providing a welcome break in the green of the lawn. This lovely scourge, brought to Canada from France by a nun wanting a reminder of her beloved homeland, has proven to be a hardy adversary of homeowners everywhere.

As they relax together on the grass in the park soaking in the sunshine and the beauty that only nature can provide, Marlene and Cecil are attentively conversing.

"You've never told me what you do for a living," Marlene remonstrates her beau.

"I've always been proud of my work but the last two weeks has put a real damper on my career," Cecil explains. "I work for the Canadian Security and Intelligence Service."

Marlene is momentarily quiet as she forces herself to remain calm.

"Isn't that the same government agency the man who killed the boy at the Ferguson residence belonged to?"

"Yes it is," Cecil acknowledges. "I have no intention of trying to justify the events that took place because there is no excuse whatever for the agent killing that boy and shooting at the other boys. I don't know why the agency even kept him because he has always been a loose cannon. There is no place in any law enforcement agency for a rogue agent, certainly not in this country."

Marlene is relieved "You don't like what happened?"

"When I heard about the shooting I felt sick to my stomach." Cecil continues, "I felt so strongly about the boy's death I attended his funeral and not the funeral of the agent."

Cecil's explanation relieves Marlene's feelings of anxiety. "I'm glad you have such strong feelings about the death of the boy. I know you would never do anything like that."

Marlene snuggles closer to Cecil as they lay back on the grass. She feels a little shiver up her back. Later they drive to Cecil's apartment because he wishes to change his pants, having knelt in some bird droppings.

As Cecil enters the bathroom Marlene putters around the suite. Spotting some papers on the floor close to the fax machine, she picks them up and begins sorting them. Seeing the face and name of Ayman al-Zawahri on the documents and realizing the man in the picture is an al Qaeda terrorist, Marlene scrutinizes the papers, discovering Joseph Ferguson has approved this terrorist's acceptance into Canada as a landed immigrant. She sets the papers down stunned, fully comprehending the enormity of the crime committed by Joseph Ferguson as documented in the papers she has just examined.

Marlene sits down to think while Cecil changes his clothing. Cecil witnesses Marlene's expression as she pores through the papers and knows he has successfully recruited a member of the law firm Jones,

Smythe and Watson. Finished changing, Cecil joins Marlene on the sofa where she sits, slowly digesting the facts she has just seen on the immigration documents.

"What's bothering you Marlene?"

"I started tidying up some papers I found on the floor and recognized the name and the face of the man on the documents. Mr. Ferguson signed his immigration papers. He really is a criminal isn't he?"

Marlene begins to sob. Her body is shaking with the wretchedness she is feeling. Cecil, feeling compassion for his lover, puts his arm around her and holds her close.

"Yes he is," is Cecil's quiet response.

"Hehehe's responsible for the death of that boy."

"Not completely, but his actions and callousness contributed to the boy's death."

"Www… we have to catch him Cecil. We just have to catch him."

"Will you help me put him in jail?"

"Yes. Yes, I will. What can I do to help?"

Marlene and Cecil enter the law offices of Jones, Smythe and Watson. Cecil memorizes the code as she disarms the security system. After he installs audio surveillance devices in the phones of the three lawyers, Marlene helps him photocopy the documents in the Ferguson file. They leave, resetting the burglar alarm.

Marlene and Cecil return to the park to reflect on their actions, and to enjoy the remainder of their evening together.

As the sun begins to set the normally azure sky, beginning as a red glow in the far off western horizon begins a radiant dance towards them in brilliant hues of red. Mesmerized as she lies on the grass, Marlene is entranced by the splendor of the moment. As the magic slowly disappears, she continues to lie on the grass, still spellbound by the fading glory. Cecil, his eyes closed, can still behold the feeling of standing on a promontory in the coastal mountains, overlooking the magnificent cedars of his native British Columbia and watching the sun setting in all its glory, its brilliance radiating towards him from the sky and the dancing waves before the blazing globe drops, disappearing into an ever darkening western sea. The two lovers slowly return to the present time but their minds still hold the image that has dominated their feelings as the sun displayed its fiery image of farewell to them.

Early Monday morning William Smythe is checking the video surveillance tape. He observes Marlene and Cecil enter his office to install an audio surveillance device in his telephone. Listening to the videotape, he hears Marlene say, "Are you sure three surveillance devices are sufficient?"

The C.S.I.S. agent replied, "Yes, I only require the lawyers' conversations and I only have court orders for these three phones. We'll photocopy the Ferguson files now."

William steps outside the back door of the company office and places a phone call to Bob Watson, explaining the recent developments. Bob phones Rae Jones and then they break up the calls to Tom Jackson, Maurice Solinger, and Marcel Roy. William phones Alex Johansen to warn him. "One of my staff helped a C.S.I.S. agent place audio surveillance equipment on the phones in our offices. We need to know which phones, and I need a bug placed on her phone to record her telephone conversations."

"I'll be there at seven o'clock this evening."

Tom Jackson will inform Joe about the latest development in the law offices at the first opportunity.

Early Monday morning Cecil Mann has filed his report and requisitioned a van outfitted with an audio surveillance monitoring system to park close to the offices of Jones, Smythe and Watson. Cecil will pick up the tapes each evening to examine the following day. Events are finally progressing favorably for Cecil in the Joe Ferguson investigation.

Two Ladies – One Divorce

Monday morning, Marcel visits Andre to re-establish his Eric the Red disguise then drives to the office of Confidential Investigations to discuss the results of his research of the computer disks obtained at the Montague residence. They work on a tentative plan to gain access to the assets.

When Adrian Montague phones, Maurice Solinger arranges a meeting with her in his office.

"What did the other man find out?" Adrian inquires of Maurice.

Maurice explains the plan he and Marcel have formulated.

"Eric has not finished searching the files yet but he calculates that he has found close to $1,290,000 in cash and receivables and a further $1.84 million in securities and investments. It will be hard to access but he has a plan to transfer the funds into new accounts in your name that will not involve any risk to you. We will be able to introduce the other $1.84 million in securities during the divorce proceedings and you will receive 50% of those assets. Eric will continue to search the files to find other assets."

"Do you have any relatives living close to the U.S. border?"

"I have a brother who has a business in Syracuse, New York. My father is an American and I was born in the U.S. and still hold U.S.

citizenship. When my parents' marriage failed, my brother stayed with him in Syracuse, New York and my mother returned with me to Ottawa. My father is retired and now lives in Rochester, New York."

"Visit your brother and father and open five bank accounts in each city, using your brother's and father's addresses as your own," explains Maurice. "When you return to Ottawa you will turn the account information over to me and I will pass it on to Eric. The tentative time frame until you have the money will be approximately three months from the time we receive the records because Eric will have to go to another country to access the funds."

"You'll have to change the address for bill delivery on the cell phone to this box number at this address." He hands her a piece of paper. "That way the phone records will not appear at your home while you are away. Destroy any cell phone bills if you have any with calls to me. I can get a second cell phone for you if you really need one but you will be far safer using pay phones to contact me, and for God's sake don't use a neighbor's or relative's phone. If your husband gets suspicious, they'll be the easiest to trace."

"I don't see the need for all this secrecy," Adrian exclaims. "I think your paranoid."

"Eric sure has you figured out," Maurice reiterates. "He says your stupid enough to get killed."

Adrian is mortified. "Pierre wouldn't kill me."

"Eric says there are five murders in those documents. One by your husband was a mistress who four years ago got herself pregnant deliberately. One by a person named Guy Trembley of a man who accidentally learned of an illegal operation the three of them are involved in and three by a person named Jean Perrault and your husband of people who owed them money. All the amounts owed were under $20,000. You are responsible for the compromising of their files on their illegal activities. You are taking not $20,000 but $1,290,000, plus 50% of $1.84 million in assets, plus the house, plus alimony payments and you are spying on Maurice to divorce him. Now please explain to me why you feel I have misplaced paranoia?"

Adrian is shocked. Guy, Jean and Pierre have all killed people who were a threat, and would kill her if they felt she was a threat to them. Pierre had been playing golf with them yesterday and sees them constantly. She could never afford to be complacent about her husband again.

"I'm waiting."

Adrian begins to feel her world closing in. She almost shudders in fear as her body tightens and her mind begins to churn.

"I want the disks back. I'm going to drop the divorce."

"You're too late," Maurice responds. "Eric has the disks in Washington and Caroline Tremblay has agreed for us to install a video camera in her suite to get the evidence. She wants Pierre to herself and will tell him about the investigation if we attempt to back out. If she tells Pierre, he will begin to wonder about the missing keys. A search of the house will turn up the safe combination on the bottom of your jewelry case."

"I'm trapped."

"We both are. You'll have to act as though nothing is wrong. We'll get the divorce and the money and by being careful and moving slowly, your husband will be none the wiser. Give me the keys to the office. If Pierre find them in your possession you won't last ten minutes."

Eric the Red enters the Empire Grill and finds Caroline Tremblay waiting for him. The dining hostess seats him with Caroline and takes his order for a coffee and a glass of wine for the young lady.

"I thought you would join me in another bottle of ice wine."

"I would but I have an appointment with a lawyer. It's not wise to show up with the smell of alcohol on your breath when you wish to impress a law firm."

"What did your sister do to catch her husband?"

"I haven't even had an opportunity to ask you out for supper yet."

"If your plan works I'll treat you to supper and an evening you'll never forget," Caroline promises Eric the Red.

"My sister had a private detective install a hidden camera in the suite," explains Eric. "She turned it on when he was coming into the suite. It recorded for 10 minutes as they made love. The private detective also took pictures of the man coming to see my sister a few times to show it was not a one-night affair. The detective took the pictures to his wife and she kicked her husband out of the house. He moved in with my sister and they were married within a year."

"I'll do it. Pierre is coming to see me Wednesday afternoon so we'll have to work quickly."

"Go to a locksmith and cut spare keys to your suite and the apartment entry doors. Write your address down so I'll know the apartment and unit. I'll see you tomorrow afternoon to pick up the keys and help a detective install the equipment. I can pick up the camera Thursday afternoon. I fully intend to hold you to your promise of an evening together."

Caroline watches Eric leave. She is already looking forward to an evening with the young man with the flaming red hair and beard. Pierre has kept her on the hook for two years and planned for another nine years. Caroline feels no chagrin about her decision to spend an evening with Eric the Red. She may even decide keep a lover of her own if the evening is as exciting as she fantasizes.

Alex Johansen arrives at the office of the lawyers early Tuesday morning, entering through the back door. He locates the remaining surveillance bugs on the phones of Bob Watson and Rae Jones. Alex installs a surveillance device on the phone of Marlene Moore, wiring it to activate by lifting the phone receiver.

Caroline Tremblay smiles as she watches Eric the Red enter the Empire Grill. Yes that head with the flaming red hair and beard would make a beautiful trophy hanging on her wall. She walks up to him smiling and hands him the envelope. "Don't forget my promise."

Eric looks admiringly at the beautiful young lady smiling at him. "There's absolutely no chance of that Caroline. I only wish it could last longer than one evening."

"I'm beginning to find you very tantalizing. I could quite easily develop the same feelings myself."

Maurice Solinger and Eric the Red install the video surveillance equipment inside the closet of Caroline Tremblay. Unbeknown to Caroline they fasten a "C.S.I.S." audio surveillance device to the back of the headboard. Eric then phones Caroline with specific instructions on the method of using the remote video/audio activator.

On Wednesday afternoon, a reporter and a cameraman from the Ottawa Citizen are visiting the scenic Eagle Creek Golf Course, taking photographs of the proceedings for the government golf tournament the following day. Shannon Johansen is pleased that the staff at the club notices her because they will recognize her tomorrow, making her task easier. Thursday morning there will be a beautiful picture of the club with a write up on the Eagle Creek Golf Course and their hosting of the prestigious government golf tournament.

In the Champagne Apartments Maurice Solinger follows Pierre Montague into the elevator. Montague exits at the ninth floor and the private detective again sets down his briefcase, presses the button to keep the elevator door open, and waits in anticipation of Montague's mistress putting in an appearance. Caroline doesn't disappoint him. She steps eagerly from the suite into Pierre's arms, hugging and kissing him passionately, wearing nothing but a radiant smile. Pierre hugs and kisses her in return. Lifting her into his arms, Pierre carries Caroline into the suite. The young lady has played her part far better than Maurice expected.

The Trojan Horse Program

Early Thursday morning Andre Prichard is working on a new disguise for Marcel Roy. "How did you do as a red head?"

"Great!" Marcel responds. "They liked it so much they expanded the role of the character. I had a ball with the part. The other mustache and wig were also great. It sure changed the look of the other actor, especially since he is as bald as a cue ball. I'm playing a private detective who dons different disguises to spy out information for an industrial client."

Andre is carefully adhering the beard to Marcel's face.

"Since this beard and wig are shorter and more revealing than the others I'll do a little work to make your face and hands look older."

When Andre is finished, Marcel carefully examines himself in the mirror.

"Man you do good work."

"It's been a real pleasure working with you," Andre replies. "On the sets you rarely have a chance to use the full extent of your expertise. Most of the work is quick disguises and touch ups. It's very gratifying to actually do complicated disguises."

Today is June 21st, 2001, the first day of the golf tournament planned for the members of parliament and their staff. Marcel Roy proceeds directly to the Department of Immigration Building. Before entering the building, he sprays liquid band-aid on his hands to hide his fingerprints. Inside the Immigration Building, Marcel proceeds directly towards the security door entering into the staff office area. Seated in a chair he listens intently while scrutinizing a manual. Hearing people advancing towards him from inside the office area he moves towards the closed door. As a group of men and ladies exit the door, Marcel holds it open for them, and then enters the forbidden office area. In the elevator, he presses the fifth floor button. The door opens, he presses the main floor button and steps out of the elevator. Not taking a chance on a returning secretary hearing him, Marcel quickly unlocks the doors to all the offices, entering the last unit. One key doesn't work. The thirteen unlocked doors are a testament to the care and diligence Kathleen Solinger has put into filing the keys to match their leather impressions. Marcel sets at the first computer and enters it carefully. He installs the "Trojan Horse Program." and then, as he exits the computer, removes all traces of ever entering the computer programs. He is at the second computer when he hears the elevator door open and a lady walking to the private secretary's desk beside the office of Pierre Montague. Working quietly, he continues to install "Trojan Horse Programs" on the computers in the offices.

At ten twenty-five, the secretary opens and closes a filing cabinet drawer, then walks click, click, click, click towards the elevator. Glancing out the office door, he notices she is carrying her purse and sweater. She is either taking a very long lunch break or is leaving the building, most likely the latter carrying her sweater.

Marcel unlocks Pierre Montague's door and carefully enters his computer, installing a "Trojan Horse Program." He sees electronic wires dropping from the ceiling to a new cabinet. Opening the door to the cabinet, he discovers a combination audio/video receiver with Joe Ferguson's head in the video display. Marcel, to contact Joe, presses the memory dial. Joe, feeling the phone vibrate twice, rises from his chair and begins walking towards the security door to let Marcel in, believing he is very late. When the phone starts vibrating a second time Joe pushes the on button and listens.

"I've found the surveillance equipment. The camera is in the light fixture. Pick up your office phone, start to dial home, and then change your mind and hang up."

Joe re-enters his office, starts to dial, and then hangs up. The audio surveillance receptor starts to record and stops. Marcel takes a small camera from his briefcase and snaps pictures of the equipment, then locks the door as he leaves Montague's office. Marcel locks the doors to the offices in which his work is finished, and continues installing "Trojan Horse Programs" in the remaining offices. Finished, he tries once more to enter the remaining office – to no avail. Marcel finishes early and takes his time, using the stairs to descend to the main floor. He times his entrance as the staff head to the lunchrooms. Marcel moves around the office accessing computers designated by Joe Ferguson, installing "Trojan Horse Programs" on six of them. There is no need for secrecy here because the computers are all operating. He leaves the offices of the Immigration Building just as the staff are returning to their desks. As Marcel unlocks the door to his car, he feels the tension leaving his body and his breathing is more relaxed. He looks around, observing the beauty of the day and breathes a sigh of relief.

Discovering the Camera

Maurice and Shannon arrive early at the Eagle Creek Golf Course. They wander around the grounds and buildings once again admiring the prestigious Country Club with its glorious scenery. The grounds are immaculate with flowerbeds and shrubs interspersed along winding paths leading through vistas of bucolic scenery. Magnificent oak trees dominate the view – lifting their mighty arms in prayer. Marigolds flash their sensuous yellow and orange eyes at the flow of traffic wending its way past the beds of flowers. Roses, hanging like giant rubies from emerald bushes, cast their own magic spell on the panorama.

The two reporters tear their eyes away from the magnificent scenery surrounding them – they have a mission to accomplish. They once again begin taking pictures and talking to staff. The name card groupings on the dining tables are recorded. When the members of parliament and civil servants arrive Shannon approaches the Prime Minister.

"Mr. Prime Minister would you allow me to photograph you and would you say a few words on this auspicious occasion?"

Prime Minister Patrick Champlain poses for the camera. Any opportunity to get his face before the public is a bonus.

"I wasn't really planning to make a speech but I will say this. This golf tournament provides an excellent opportunity for the elected members of parliament and the civil servants working for our great country to get to know each other as individuals in a social gathering as well as on the professional basis they now know each other."

"That was beautiful," Shannon gushes. "You always speak so eloquently Mr. Prime Minister. Thank you."

Shannon and Maurice stay in the background and carefully observe the people involved in the tournament and specifically Pierre Montague and Jean Perrault.

Joe Ferguson stands up and stares at the light fixture. Standing on the desk, he removes the lens from the fluorescent fixture. Staring at the camera and then glaring at it he steps down off the desk, closes his office door, then makes a phone call.

"Offices of Jones, Smythe and Watson. How may I direct your call?"

"I need to speak to William Smythe."

"Mr. Smythe is out at the moment, could I take a message."

"Is Bob Watson in?"

"Yes he is. Whom shall I say is calling?"

"Joe Ferguson."

The receptionist tries to reach Bob in his office and then pages him. "Mr. Watson, Mr. Joseph Ferguson is on the line for you."

Bob is deliberately waiting in the meeting room for the call knowing Marlene Moore will hear the page on the intercom system.

Speaking loudly and jovially, Bob answers his phone.

"Hello Joe Ferguson. What can I do for you today?"

"I found a surveillance camera in my office."

"**What!** Did say you say you found a surveillance camera in your office? Just a minute while I close my door." Tlyk. "Listen Joe, William is meeting an associate close to your office. I'll contact him and get him over to you immediately. Don't do anything until he arrives."

"Okay. I'll wait for him."

Marlene Moore takes the bait. When Bob Watson closes his office door, she is instantly on the phone to her lover.

"Cecil Mann"

Marlene bends over the phone and speaks into it in a whisper. "Mr. Ferguson just called Mr. Watson. He found a surveillance camera in his office. You need to come to your van right now and listen to what he said."

Cecil caught in the conspiratorial moment, whispers back, "I'll be there in about half an hour. If you hear anything else let me know."

Bob sits and reflects for a moment. The plan is beginning to unfold. He dials William's cell phone number.

"William Smythe."

"Bob here. Joseph Ferguson just called. He found a surveillance camera in his office at the Department of Immigration. I told him to wait for you."

"Good God! I hope he doesn't do something drastic. I can be at his office quickly. That surveillance equipment person that the policeman called left us a card. Do you remember where we put it?"

"Yes. It's in Tom Jackson's file."

"Call him and have him meet us in Joe's office."

"I'll phone him right now."

Bob places the call that Alex Johansen's receptionist is expecting.

"Johansen Surveillance Equipment. How may I help you?"

"I'm Bob Watson attorney at law, could I speak to Alex Johansen please?"

"I'm sorry, Mr. Johansen is out of town until tomorrow afternoon. Could I take a message?"

"I'll have to talk to my partner. We'll call back later."

Bob calls William back.

"William Smythe"

"I just talked to Alex Johansen's secretary. He's going to be out of town until tomorrow afternoon. Do you want me to contact a different surveillance specialist?"

"Not now. We'll make a decision when I'm back in the office. I'm pulling into the government parking area now."

When Rae Jones hears the announcement on the intercom he leaves the office and drives to the Court of Queens bench to learn if the surveillance equipment in Joe Ferguson's and their own law offices are legal or illegal. He learns no court order granting authority to install the equipment in either building is on record.

William enters the Department of Immigration Building and speaks to a receptionist.

"I'm William Smythe, Attorney at Law, could I speak to Joseph Ferguson please?"

"I'll contact him for you."

The receptionist dials a number.

"Joe Ferguson here."

"Hello Joe. There is a Mr. William Smythe here to see you."

"I'll be right out."

The receptionist informs William, "He's coming to see you, and will only be a moment."

"Which door he will be coming out?"

The receptionist turns and points. "That door."

William moves towards the designated door and waits for Joe. When he arrives, they talk until the receptionist is busy again, and then proceed to Joe's office.

"How did you happen to find the camera?"

"I thought I heard a noise come from the light. When I checked I found the camera. I'm so mad I could hit somebody."

William photographs the surveillance camera.

"Put the lens back in the light fixture. I assume with the surveillance camera in your office, you are also being monitored by audio surveillance equipment. We can talk more openly in my office."

As Joe and William leave the Immigration Department, William contacts Bob Watson at their office.

A blast of hot air greets Cecil Mann as he opens the van door. He opens the back and side doors to dissipate the heat, then closes the doors and starts the engine to run the air conditioning. Cecil switches the Bob Watson taped recording to a different machine. Listening to the Watson tape, he brings himself up to date on the telephone messages made and received by the lawyer.

Cecil Mann places a phone call to C.S.I.S.

"Canadian Security and Intelligence Service. How may I direct your call?"

"Marc Leblanc please."

"One moment please."

A phone rings and a female voice answers. "Mr. Leblanc's office, how may I help you?"

"This is agent Cecil Mann. I have pertinent information for Mr. Leblanc."

Marc Leblanc's secretary informs Cecil, "Mr. Leblanc is out of his office, do you wish to leave a message?"

"Yes. Joseph Ferguson has found the surveillance camera one of our operatives installed in his office at the Canadian Department of Immigration Offices."

"I will convey this message to him. He will call you back if he deems it necessary."

A few minutes later Cecil's phone buzzes.

"Cecil Mann here."

"Marc Leblanc. You have a message for me."

Cecil, overcome by enthusiasm, speaks more quickly than normal, conveying his excitement to Leblanc.

"Yes. Joseph Ferguson found the surveillance camera in his office. Ferguson and his lawyer are now returning to the lawyer's office to talk. I am monitoring the equipment at the present time and I will contact you again once I learn more from their conversation."

"Without your diligence we wouldn't have found this information until too late," Leblanc responds. "When you have more information phone my secretary and she will contact me."

William is pulling into the rear of his office when his cell phone buzzes.

"William Smythe."

"Maurice Solinger here. Montague just heard the good news. Perrault received a phone call. At eighty metres, I could almost hear him cussing. He told Montague and Montague missed a three-foot putt… Then a six foot putt…."

"Joe and I are at the office. Watch for another phone call in about half an hour and then you can leave. I'll call you back later. Thanks for watching Montague and Perrault for us."

Cecil's phone buzzes.

"Cecil Mann."

He listens as Marlene whispers excitedly into her phone.

"Mr. Smythe and Mr. Ferguson are in Mr. Smythe's office."

He taps into the Smythe machine.

"Sit down Joe while I talk to Bob Watson."

"Bob Watson."

"William here. Would you contact the surveillance company again and inform them we will be contacting them Monday morning to set up a surveillance check?"

William sets down the phone. Activating an office recorder, he turns to Joe.

"Do you have any clue why this invasion of your privacy in your home and at the office is taking place?"

"I have no idea," Joe replies, "unless it is somehow tied to an incident that took place in the office about seven weeks ago."

"Tell me about it, starting at the beginning."

Joe had his story memorized.

"On May 3, 2001, I found the files I required on the computer and printed them. Picking up my material at the office printer, I realized there were a couple of pages in the papers that were unrelated to my work. I shredded them and returned to my office to begin my days work."

"How did you know they weren't part of your work Joe?"

"They were landed immigrant documents with photographs on them."

"Do you remember the pictures?"

"No, I only glanced at them. He may have been Middle Eastern or North African from the clothing but that's all I remember. The only reason I remember that information is the badgering I received from Montague and the C.S.I.S. agent. Those printing glitches have happened to me before so I didn't give it any thought at the time. Later I left my desk. When I returned there was a man going through my work. I said, 'What do you think your doing?' I surprised him. When he turned around, I recognized Pierre Montague, the Senior Official in the Immigration Department. He said, 'Who do you think you are, speaking to me like that?' I said, 'I didn't recognize you with your back turned to me rifling through my papers.' He asked me if I'd seen anything unusual on my computer that morning. I said, 'No. Was I supposed to?' He paged through the work on my computer and left."

"What about the pictures Joe?"

Joe responds to the query with, "I never saw them on the monitor."

"It may have been what he was referring to."

"I didn't see the connection at the time. I wish I'd paid more attention to the pictures after I left to go home. At quitting time, Montague and a stranger accosted me as I was leaving my office. Montague said, 'We'll talk in your office'. I asked, 'Why.' Montague said, 'Get back in your office.' They practically forced me back into my own office. Montague said, 'Give me your coat.' When I did, he searched the pockets then threw it on the chair. Then Montague ordered me to take off my pants and shirt. I told him, 'You must be kidding!' I couldn't believe what I was hearing. The stranger produced a badge and said 'I'm from C.S.I.S. Do as your told.' I picked up the phone. The man from C.S.I.S. hollered at me saying, 'Put down the phone and take off your pants and shirt.' He was extremely threatening and frightened me. I complied and he searched the articles and threw them on the chair. The two men left. I got dressed and opened the door to leave. The man from C.S.I.S. was standing there. He said, 'don't tell anybody about this! Have you got that straight?' His words and manner were again extremely threatening. I walked past him and went home. I was scared but I was also mad."

"It looks like you stumbled into something crooked Joe and they're trying to find out if you know anything." Even if you did know something the top eulachon of the government and civil service has so much power and protection you could never bring them to justice. Because they are so powerful and corrupt, they pose a real threat to you and your family. It should be obvious to them after more than a month and a half of surveillance and finding no evidence to the contrary, that you have no evidence about their schemes. Their greatest danger to being exposed is their paranoia. When I bring in the specialist to examine the camera and possibly find an audio unit they will realize they could be found out through their obsession and quit their surveillance. If they remove the camera, we will know that they also have you under audio surveillance. There is also an outside chance that the camera was installed a long time ago and is no longer in service. I hope to have some resolution to the problem on Monday."

"I hope you do too. This continual harassment is really affecting me. I'm finding it hard to concentrate on my work and discovering the camera can only deteriorate the situation further."

"Did you ever learn the name of the C.S.I.S. operative who forced you to undress?"

"I saw his picture in the paper a couple of weeks later. His name is Jean Perrault. He's the Senior Official in C.S.I.S.

"You do realize that you can sue Montague and Perrault for their actions Joe."

"I've always known that but I don't believe in suing. If this harassment keeps up I could easily change my mind."

"I have a question for you Joe. If your signature is on a document, did you have to sign it?"

"Theoretically yes, but everybody's signature is on file to be accessed from their own computer. I use it all the time on documents retained in the computer. Since the top civil servants on the fifth floor have access, to all the documents I have finished or am processing, they also have access to my signature and of course, the signatures of everybody working under them. So, in reality, the people above me can put my name on any document. Because of the nature of my work, most of the workers in the Department of Immigration would never have access to my signature. Most of my research passes on to Foreign Affairs to guide them in their selection of potential immigrants. If another worker did have access to my research he could file my name and use it"

"When do you have your holidays booked?"

"The first three weeks in August. We're going to Disney World."

"Good, you need to get away from all this harassment for a while."

Marcel Roy's first stop after leaving The Canadian Immigration Department is Champaigne Apartments. He removes the surveillance equipment from the suite of Caroline Tremblay and returns it to Confidential Investigations.

Marcel goes home to change and remove his disguise. He then starts searching for a place he learned about eight years previously. It was a small foundry located at the end of a gravel road just off Bexley Point in the Bells Corner Industrial Area. The foundry was located behind a metal fabrication shop. There is a very steep hill beside and behind the buildings covered in maple trees. If the upstairs rooms were still for rent, it would be perfect for his plan. He finds the building. Leaving his car, Marcel sees a man step out of a half-ton and advance towards him.

"My name is Marcel Roy. I wish to find the owner of this fine establishment."

The stranger laughs, "It's been many a moon since this building was called a fine establishment. My name is Don McFarland. How may I help you?"

"You had an upstairs room to rent at one time and I was hoping it is available."

"Yes it is. I'll get the key."

They climb the outside staircase to enter the unit. There is a small washroom, a small office and a larger room.

"This will work just fine Don. What will you need for rent?"

"You realize it can get pretty loud in here during the day. The clamor has always deterred potential renters."

"That shouldn't pose a problem for us. We're planning to use it probably once a week in the evenings. My friends and I need a place where we can hang out and play music or play bridge or just sit around and talk. We don't enjoy the bar scene and our music disturbs the neighbors because it's more loud than good. I remembered this place from the days I used to run along that hill. I started wondering if it was still for rent."

"Your need is social rather than business Marcel. How does $400.00 per month sound to you and I cover the utilities?"

"I believe that will be fine. I will still have to check with the others and let you know tomorrow."

Cecil Mann, watching Joe Ferguson leave the office of William Smythe, phones the office at Canadian Security and Intelligence Service. Marc Leblanc returns the call.

"Cecil Mann"

"You have some more information for me?"

Cecil explains the information he has gained since they last spoke.

"You had better cut the wires to the camera and remove the audio surveillance hardware from his phone," Marc decides. "We'll remove the camera next Monday evening. I'll have Guy Trembley arrange with the R.C.M.P. on duty to let you in tonight.

Cecil waits for the office staff of Jones, Smythe and Watson to leave for the day. Rae Jones, waiting inconspicuously in the parking lot, photographs Marlene Moore entering the C.S.I.S. van.

Marcel phones Alex Johansen and Maurice Solinger, arranging to meet them at the Nepean Creative Arts Centre. He shows them the building and they agree the location will provide a safe haven for the group with the offices of Jones, Smythe and Watson compromised by C.S.IS.

Putting the Horse to Work

Friday morning Alex arrives at Maurice's residence with 1x4's butt hinges and 1½" screws to build 24"x18" and 36"x30" sawhorses. Loading the sawhorses and the table and chairs from the yard sale onto Alex's half-ton truck they drive to the foundry and speak to Don McFarland.

"I'm Maurice Solinger. I have some money for you and I need to collect a key."

Don hands Maurice the key. "If you will wait a minute I'll get you a receipt."

"Unless you really need to give us a receipt we don't need one. Is it okay to move some things upstairs?"

"It's your place now Maurice."

"I was afraid the noise we made might pose a problem."

Don is laughing as Maurice walks away. Maurice and Alex put their belongings in the building and then drive to a lumberyard to pick up two sheets of 4'x8'x¾" K-3 board which they have cut into four 2'x8' pieces to set on the 18" high sawhorses for benches and two sheets of ¾" MDF board to set on the 30" high sawhorses for tabletops. The next stop is again the Solinger residence to collect the articles from the garage sale and transport everything to the new office. On the way to the office, they stop at a locksmith and cut seven keys.

Friday afternoon Alex phones William.

"Jones, Smythe and Watson, attorneys at law."

"Johansen Surveillance Equipment returning a call to William Smythe."

"William Smythe here. Is this Alex Johansen?"

"Yes it is. How can I help you?"

"We met when the police called you to the Joe Ferguson residence to search for audio surveillance equipment." William reminds Alex.

"Yes I remember you William."

"Joe Ferguson found a surveillance camera in his office yesterday afternoon. We need to learn if the camera is active and if there is any audio surveillance equipment located in his office at the Canadian Immigration Service."

"I'm going to be busy early Monday morning, but should be able to check Joe's office at the Immigration Department around ten thirty. Would that be fine with you?"

"Joe Ferguson is going to check for the camera early in the morning. He will phone me as soon as he learns if the camera is still in the light fixture. I'll phone your office as soon as I hear from Joe."

"I'll be expecting your call."

Marcel has been in cyber cafes, Internet cafes and is now in a library searching for any information that will lead him into the location of the files he requires. By logging onto "Trojan Horse", running the program to "spoof" (fake) real computer address he accesses the Immigration Department and begins to search the files. At the present time he is observing Sharon Johnston completing an IMM-1000 Document. She calls up the name of a co-worker, Gerald Stone, puts the papers in a file folder and sends the file to its proper destination. As he follows the file Marcel realizes this is the breakthrough he is searching for. Accessing the files, Marcel begins at a set point pulling up files and downloading the information onto his I-Pod. Realizing his safe time is coming to an end Marcel backs out of the system erasing his presence as he leaves. Again accessing the "Trojan Horse Program" from a different cyber café, he tries to re-enter the files again, but through an alternative computer in the Immigration Department and finds himself in a different file. As Marcel downloads files, he realizes that each worker has his own file cabinet in the system. He will have to access the missed office on the fifth floor and as many computers of suspect lower caseworkers in the Immigration Department as possible. He continues moving to a different cyber café, library, or Internet café every fifteen minutes, downloading the files as quickly as possible. He has to stop at four thirty – security staff will immediately spot any action on the files after the staff leave.

Marcel has begun a dossier on all the terrorists in the Ottawa area. Over the weekend, he visits the streets where they live. Using his Wi-Fi-equipped laptop and the highly directional antennae he built, he begins searching for and detecting Wi-Fi wireless computers in the homes and apartments of some of the terrorists. Accessing the "Trojan Horse Program" through the terrorist computers will be much safer, because any tracers will dead end at their computers. He will also glean pertinent information about their affiliates through those same computers.

Another Ally

Adrian Montague and her two girls are driving to the U.S. to see Adrian's brother first, in Syracuse, New York and then her father in Rochester, New York. Pierre Montague is back at the golf course for the last day of the tournament and Maurice Solinger and Alex Johansen are installing audio surveillance equipment in both the home phone and the office phone in the Montague residence. They both believe that William has badly underestimated Pierre Montague's reaction to Joe discovering the surveillance camera.

The golf tournament at the Eagle Creek Golf Course, winds down Saturday afternoon. All except the Montague foursome have enjoyed themselves.

School is out for Keith and Jerry Ferguson. They leave by bus Saturday morning for a visit to their grandparents' farm at Belle River, Ontario. Joe, wishing to hide the destination of the boys from C.S.I.S, buys tickets to Toronto paying cash. In Toronto, the boys will buy tickets to Windsor, again paying cash.

Saturday afternoon Joe is mowing his lawn when Tom Jackson speaks to him.

"The government has been giving you a lot of attention lately. Would you mind telling me why their intense scrutiny of your every move?"

Joe thinks for a moment... "I'll get the computer disk and show you what I found in the files at the Department of Immigration."

Joe locates the computer disk in the attic of his garage, and then enters the Jackson residence. Tom inserts the disk into the floppy disk drive and brings up the incriminating evidence on the monitor.

Tom scrutinizes the documents. "If you were really involved in bringing terrorists into Canada you wouldn't be showing me these documents. What is going on?"

Joe relates the whole story to Tom excluding the information concerning the efforts to learn more about the government officials involved and the search for the terrorists granted landed immigrant status in Canada.

"I can certainly believe you," Tom replies. "I was in the Canadian military and high enough up to see all the corruption at the top. The way they act is a disgrace to the country. Patriotism is just a meaningless word to the politicians and government mandarins although they use the word plenty to keep the ordinary citizen in line. I always found it surprising how many people actually bought their crap. If you can use my help in any way let me know."

"We have a plan we're working on," Joe responds. "If it will work we'll definitely need your help."

Sunday afternoon Pierre Montague phones Jean Perrault from his home office.

"Jean Perrault."

"Pierre here."

"I have company. I'll phone you from my office."

Montague's phone rings.

"We need to get rid of that ass-hole Jean."

"I presume you have a reason for needing him dead."

"I checked the security tape and the video. There's no way the discovery of the camera was an accident. That smart-ass figured out the camera is in the light. He also figured out we have audio surveillance on him. Let's take care of the problem and be done with him."

"If you want Ferguson eliminated we'll take care of it."

"Good. What do you have in mind?"

"I'll call in a favor from an Iraqi family to eliminate him. The whole Abu Zubaydah family are members of al-Qaeda. They owe me big time for my help in getting the old man out of jail in Pakistan and into Canada. I have an agent, Matt Spence, who can handle the operation and a wannabe agent, a runt named Mann we can kill and blame the death on Ferguson. Mann doesn't have the guts for the killing of innocents and he's involved in the case. We can't have any witnesses but he'll make a good martyr. We'll hit them early Wednesday morning. As soon as we get the all clear from Spence, I'll have our forensic agents move in and process the crime scene before the cops get there. Leblanc can start on the operation first thing in the morning.

In the late afternoon, Maurice Solinger films Pierre Montague unlocking the suite of Caroline Tremblay and entering the unit. He exits Champaigne Apartment and drives to Montague's residence to change the tapes in the surveillance equipment. Listening to the recordings while driving home, he hears Montague and Perrault discussing Joe Ferguson. Phoning Alex Johansen, they decide to meet at the Fergusons' home.

"Can we talk privately?" Maurice inquires of Joe.

"No problem. Eileen is attending evening worship."

Alex checks the house for audio receptors, while Joe listens to the tape.

"I was afraid it might come to this. Can I count on some help from you?"

"That's why we're here," Alex informs Joe. "The Ottawa City Police can't help you against C.S.I.S. and the Mounties definitely won't."

Joe phones Tom Jackson and invites him over. He then phones his mother-in-law, Angie Marks, in Toronto.

"Hello."

"Hello Angie. It's Joe. I need you to do me a favor."

"Sure Joe. What is it?"

"The boys are visiting my parents on the farm for a few weeks so Eileen is in the house alone all day. She's having a real problem coping with the death of the boy in our basement. I found a surveillance camera in my office at the Immigration Department Thursday and I'm expecting more trouble on Monday. I'm hoping you can find some excuse to get Eileen to visit you for a couple of weeks. I need her to leave the house tomorrow morning and not get further involved in the problems here."

"I can do that for you Joe. I've been wanting to see her for some time now."

"When she gets back from church I'll tell her you called and to phone you back."

"That will be fine," Angie responds. "I'll be waiting for the call."

When Joe hangs up the phone Tom is already listening to the recording.

"They talk as though it will be a simple operation. Are you two planning to be here for the excitement?"

Both Alex and Maurice are hard faced as they nod assent.

"They'll plan on using knives to do the killing," Tom notes, "because guns attract too much attention. When they enter the house they will be very quiet, very careful, and ready for any eventuality. Once outside the bedroom doors their only thoughts will be the job at hand. We'll put stuffing in the bed to make it look like someone is sleeping there and put a recorder under Fergie's bed with a person snoring on the tape. They will concentrate on killing the people in the beds. When they charge in and drop down on the beds, shoot. That will be your best opportunity for the shot and you'll only get two seconds maximum. After that time they will be moving fast and searching for you. There will be between two and four assassins. Most likely three, but if there are four, two will enter the master bedroom. How many guns do you have Fergie?"

"We have three 12 gauge, double barrel, Mossberg shotguns. The boys and I enjoy skeet shooting and duck hunting."

"How about you two?"

"I have a 12 gauge shotgun, single shot," Alex replies, a 9mm. automatic and an older 38 caliber revolver."

"I have a 22 caliber automatic, a 9 mm. automatic and a 45 caliber handgun," adds Maurice.

"Bring all the handguns loaded and also bring rubber gloves. The best place to pick up the gloves is a paint shop because they'll be larger. We don't want your fingerprints on the shotguns or in the house. Fergie, you wipe down the tables and chairs after we leave. Tomorrow I'm going to pick up those foam heads they use to display wigs and paint them to represent hair. I believe that covers everything until Tuesday evening, so we'll leave before Eileen gets home."

While driving home, Maurice phones Marcel Roy.

"Hello."

"Maurice here. I need all the information you can find on the Abu Zubaydah family, including pictures. I will need it by tomorrow evening if possible."

"Just a minute. Give me the name again slowly."

"A-bu Zu-bay-dah."

"Got it. I'll see what I can do tomorrow."

Marcel has spent the weekend accessing the disks he copied from the Montague safe. He finds they contain Swiss numbered bank accounts for the civil servants and Cabinet Ministers involved in the immigration fraud. The information includes access codes, deposits and account balances.

First thing Monday morning, Joe phones William confirming the presence of the video surveillance camera in his office. William phones Johansen Surveillance Equipment. By eight o'clock, Alex is removing the camera and checking for audio surveillance equipment. By nine o'clock, he is in the law office of William Smythe with the camera.

"You're early."

"I had an important call close by so decided to re-arrange my schedule. This camera was manufactured in December 1999. Probably purchased within the year. The wires were cut within the last week to deactivate it. The ends of the copper wire are too bright to be cut any longer ago than that. The telephone receiver had been dismantled and something removed, again within the last week. Because he was under video surveillance, the most likely object removed from the phone is audio surveillance equipment."

"We can assume Joe has been under surveillance in the office since the shooting took place in his home and possibly since he found those stray immigration papers in with his documents." William concurs.

He dials the Canadian Immigration Department.

"Department of Immigration. How may I direct your call?"

"Pierre Montague."

"Office of Pierre Montague."

"This is William Smythe, attorney at law. Could I speak to Pierre Montague?"

"What is the nature of your call?"

"It's of a personal note and I don't wish to divulge it to another source."

"I'm sorry, I cannot put you through without that information."

"It concerns the illegal surveillance camera Montague had installed in Joseph Ferguson's office."

Secretary, speaking very softly, "I'll put you through."

"Pierre Montague."

"My name is William Smythe. I am the attorney for Joe Ferguson. We have found video surveillance equipment in Joe Ferguson's office that has been active until recently and other evidence showing that he had audio surveillance equipment recently removed from his phone."

"This is the first I've heard about this. I'll have the R.C.M.P. remove the camera and do an investigation as to when and how this atrocity occurred."

"You know how it happened. Don't try to pull that bullshit with me. If this doesn't stop we'll be starting legal action."

"I've already told you I'll look into it."

William hangs up and looks at the note Alex Johansen has put on his desk. The two men walk out the back door. Once away from the building Alex hands William the tape recorder.

"They're planning to kill Joe."

"We're having a meeting tonight. Meet me at the liquor store at the shopping mall between Larkspur Drive and Lynhar Road off Robertson Road at 7:30 this evening. Bring Bob Watson and Rae Jones. Make sure you're not followed."

Alex checks the cars of the lawyers for tracking devices and leaves.

By noon, Marcel Roy has learned that only five of the computers on the fifth floor, in which he installed "Trojan Horse Programs" are involved in criminal activities. Those five are constantly in and out of all the files on the terrorists making it simpler for Marcel to access the material he requires. He no longer needs to install a "Trojan Horse Program" on the remaining computer on the fifth floor of the Canadian Department of Immigration Building, nor will he need to access additional workers' computers.

After finishing for the day on the Immigration files, Marcel begins carefully accessing the only Ottawa bank account on the tapes obtained from the safe in the Montague Residence. He discovers this is an account controlled by C.S.I.S. Most of the transactions have been cash withdrawals although there has been a large transfer of money within the last week to an account in Ottawa. Following the electronic transfers to the financial institution containing the deposit he learns the account is in the Royal Bank at 2121 Carling Avenue. The account, in the name of Joseph Peter Ferguson, contains $526,000. Marcel begins to formulate plans to access the funds from both accounts. Two and one-half million dollars would provide them with operating capital to access the Swiss bank accounts of the MPs and civil servants. Marcel places a call to Andre Prichard to arrange for another disguise.

At seven o'clock a car belonging to Maurice Solinger and containing the three passengers, Joe Ferguson, Tom Jackson and

Shannon Johansen leave the office of Confidential Investigations, heading for the "hideout". At 7:30, Alex Johansen pulls up beside a car driven by Bob Watson and signals the three lawyers to ride with him. Alex and his three companions drive to the "hideout". Alex previously waited down the street watching for Bob and his partners to arrive, making certain nobody was following their car, before picking them up. Marcel Roy is the last conspirator to arrive at the hideout. He observed both the Solinger car and the Johansen car pass his place of concealment without being followed. He places a box on the table in front of Tom containing two wigs. With the wigs already in Tom's car from Kathleen Solinger, Tom Jackson has the full complement of hairpieces needed for tomorrow night.

"Maurice, I have obtained the documentation on the Abu Zubaydah family." Marcel informs his friend.

"Good. What are the ages of the boys?"

"Omar is 19, Shaukat is 16 and Pervez is 7," Marcel replies.

Shannon Johansen then speaks up.

"Abu Zubaydah was spotted in Toronto over a year ago. The family was supposed to be deported at that time. Omar and Shaukat have both received training in Afghanistan in the al-Qaeda terrorist schools. The father, Abu Zubaydah, is a known terrorist with a price on his head. The U.S. government wants him in connection with the embassy bombing in Somalia and they really don't care if he's dead or alive."

Marcel adds some more information on the terrorist.

"In the immigration papers he is also given the alias Muqtada Musharrof. Their place of residency is on 154 Street in Surrey, British Columbia."

This is the information Tom Jackson requires.

"It looks like we can expect five visitors. The two C.S.I.S. agents will remain in the hallway and light out down the stairs when the shotguns cut loose. They're not likely prepared for that kind of firepower. We'll go over any final strategies tomorrow evening in the house."

Bob has been giving a lot of thought to the events about to transpire in the Ferguson residence.

"We have to arrange for the police and lawyers to arrive at the Ferguson home as quickly as possible after the shooting to combat the arrival of the C.S.I.S. forensic agents. Somebody from the scene will have to phone William when C.S.I.S. and the terrorists arrive. We need Rene there if we can arrange it. Rene doesn't like C.S.I.S. and he's been in the force long enough they won't run over him. After the police are finished at Joe's house we'll have to find some way to discover the surveillance equipment C.S.I.S. installed in our offices."

"We can contact Pierre Montague and let him know we have learned of their plan to kill Joe Ferguson," Rae Jones interjects, "That will put an end to the murder attempt."

Marcel realizes that act would only postpone the execution until some future date when they wouldn't be able to counteract the actions of C.S.I.S. It would also alert Montague and Perrault to the fact Joe has allies working with him, and those allies are a major threat to their operation.

"We'll look at that aspect later," Marcel says. "Right now, we have a few question to address. One problem we have is phone calls. We will have to purchase U.S. satellite phones and contact each other using only those satellite phones. They may eventually learn of our communications via the cell phones and land line phones but once it ends there will no longer be a trace. Tomorrow morning Rae and I will enter the U.S. consulate and begin negotiations on the terrorists. We will also have to see about the American Government protecting

Joe as soon as is necessary. When this operation is over and the U.S. government has the files on the terrorists, we may all require U.S. citizenship."

"We may need to set up a computer in here and we may need more computers. I have the names of all the people involved in these illegal immigrations starting with the Prime Minister and the Leader of the Opposition, and at this point the names of over eight hundred terrorists from twenty-three different countries."

"Another phase will require every one of our families for a full month, maybe more. I have sufficient information to access the money deposited in Swiss Bank accounts by the individuals involved in this conspiracy. I believe we can hinder their criminal actions more by removing the money from the Swiss bank accounts than by any other approach to the problem. The techniques we will employ to remove the funds will prove more damaging to the illegal immigration operation than will the actual removal of the funds."

"We will also require the aid of Andre Prichard in the disguises for our operation. He will also be aiding us in acquiring the funds in the Swiss bank accounts. My parents, who will be aiding us, and Andre's family, will share equally in our ill-gotten gains."

"Why do we need that many people to get a few million dollars?" William asks.

"We need them because the sum of money we are after is not a few million dollars," Marcel interjects, "but in the vicinity of $1.92 billion Euro. After all expenses, we will each receive over $85 million Euro. Every person involved will have one share in the funds except for myself who will be acquiring two shares."

Everybody is staring at Marcel. Silence descends over everyone in the room. Mouths previously hanging open now begin to close as the full impact of Marcel's statement begins to registers in their minds.

William is the first to respond to the information presented by Marcel, "My share will be over $85 million Euros."

"So is your wife's share," Marcel interjects, "but only if we manage to acquire all the funds."

Rae starts to laugh. "It's surprising how easily one can progress from the altruism of destroying the illegal immigration ring to the greed of acquiring $1.92 billion Euro, but if we do succeed in acquiring the money the criminal immigration ring will be destroyed."

"If any of you can come up with ideas to help we'll go over them here on Friday night. Nothing said in this room will be spoken of outside that door," Marcel cautions everyone present.

Maurice Solinger addresses the group. "We need a name for this place for easy identification. The hill beside us is loaded with maple trees so I believe the name Maple Hill would be a fitting name for the location and a good name for our group."

Tom glances around the makeshift table at the rest of the gathering. With a knowing smirk on his face, he christens them. "Yeah, the Maple Hill Mob".

Maple Hill it is.

"We need to decide on the question Rae Jones posed," Marcel advises the group. "At the present time we know when C.S.I.S plans to kill Joe Ferguson, where they plan to kill Joe Ferguson and the number of individuals involved in the plot to kill Joe Ferguson. With this knowledge, we have the advantage. Pierre Montague and Jean Perrault both have close to 30 million Euro dollars each in their Swiss bank accounts. They will let no one stand in the way of their criminal actions. Any person phoning Montague to inform him we know of the murder attempt is only postponing the inevitable attempt on Joe Ferguson's life and signing his own death warrant. Do any of you have questions you require answers to, or information we can use? If not I wish to speak to Rae and the young lady alone."

Marcel picks up the kitchen table and carries it to the back of the room. Rae and Shannon join him, carrying the chairs.

Marcel addresses the lady, "I presume you are Alex's daughter."

"Yes, I'm Shannon Johansen."

"Do you have a current boyfriend?"

"No I don't."

"Good. It will be much safer if you keep it that way until after this business is over. I will have a fair amount of work for you and it could get dangerous. Anyways, I don't think you can find a boyfriend worth compromising $85 million Euro."

"I'm willing to help in any way I can."

"You'll have help. Whatever we do we'll always have backup and contingency plans." Marcel hands Shannon a folder. "Here's the information on the Abu Zubaydah family. Disguise the pictures if you use them so nobody can tell they came from immigration papers and shred the immigration documents as soon as you are finished with them. I have the information on file if you need it later."

Marcel looks at Rae. "I've discovered a C.S.I.S. bank account with over $2 million in it. They've transferred $526,000 to an account with Joe Ferguson's name on it. I'll require help to acquire those funds. Tomorrow morning meet me in front of the American Legation at exactly eight forty-five. If one of us isn't there at that time, we'll rendezvous there exactly twenty minutes later. If there's a problem phone me from a pay phone."

Enlisting Powerful Allies

Marcel Roy turns the corner to the U.S. Embassy and sees Rae Jones reading a newspaper at the bus stop in front of him. Rae, spotting Marcel, drops the paper onto a bench and begins walking towards the gate of the embassy. At the gate of the American Legation, they both turn and walk up to the marines on guard duty.

"Would there be any F.B.I. or C.I.A. agents in the embassy?" asks Marcel.

"Do you have an appointment?" a marine asks the two men.

"The information I am carrying in my briefcase would get us an immediate audience with your president, let alone the ambassador or a member of your justice department."

"I doubt that," is the marine's scornful reply.

"Don't doubt it unless you wish to be demoted. Will you open my briefcase or shall I?"

"I'll open it."

Taking out the folder the marine removes the immigration papers for Ayman al-Zawahri. Looking at the papers he suddenly realizes whose picture is on the document.

The marine hands the briefcase back to Marcel.

"Thank you, we'll take it from here."

"In other words we can go."

"Yes. You got that right."

"Lets go Rae." Marcel and Rae walk outside the gate, and then Marcel turns around.

"By the way we have the alias and the new address of the of the terrorist in those documents."

Marcel Roy and Rae Jones continue walking down the street. The marine races up behind them. Grabbing Marcel by the shoulder, he suddenly finds himself lying on the ground. Scrambling the marine grabs his rifle and rises to his feet.

Marcel's voice is as hard as granite.

"You laid your hands on me!"

"I was only trying to get you to stop."

"That is no excuse. You laid your hands on me!"

"I'm sorry. I won't touch you again."

"You're carrying a weapon on Canadian soil."

The marine, seeing a policeman walking towards them, orders Marcel and Rae, "Wait here! I'll be right back."

The marine runs back to the embassy compound and hands his weapon to his partner. He turns, to see Marcel and Rae walking away from him. Dignity suffers as he races after the pair. The policeman stops in front of Rae and Marcel.

"That marine is running to catch up to you."

"Let him run," is Marcel's response.

"Is there a problem?"

"Nothing I can't handle."

The policeman smiles, having witnessed the previous confrontation between Marcel and the marine, and continues on his way. Marcel and Rae continue walking. The marine races up.

"I told you to wait."

Marcel and Rae continue walking.

"We heard you," is Marcel's answer to the marine.

"Why don't you stop?"

Marcel, still walking, "I don't take orders from marines."

"Please stop."

Marcel and Rae stop. Then Marcel asks, "Did he say please?"

Rae, taking the cue, "I believe he did."

"I need the rest of the information."

Marcel is adamant. "You're not getting it."

"If you come back to the embassy I will arrange for one of the embassy staff to meet with you."

"We will come back to the gate of the embassy and we will enter only if invited to do so by the Ambassador himself," Marcel informs the marine, "and you can tell the Ambassador that we also have the names, addresses and aliases of another 800 terrorists located throughout Canada." We have also located 59 of their affiliates located in the States, complete with names, addresses, phone numbers and E-mail addresses."

The marine runs back the embassy. Shortly after Rae and Marcel arrive at the gate, a gentleman exits the door of the embassy and strides up to them.

"Good morning gentlemen. My name is Henry Kilmer, the U.S. Ambassador to Canada."

"Good morning. My friend is Rae Jones, Canadian Attorney at Law, and I'm Marcel Roy, Canadian student at large."

The Ambassador smiles, "Will you please come with me? It always gives me great pleasure to converse with gentlemen of title. I believe you gentlemen have documents that could prove of great value to my country."

"The information is also of great value to our own country," Marcel informs the Ambassador. "The problem we are facing is the elected heads of the Canadian Government, the R.C.M.P. Commissioner and the Senior Official of C.S.I.S. are some of the individuals responsible for bringing these terrorists into Canada. Up to the present time we have found eight hundred terrorists that have paid money to the top civil servants and elected members of parliament to receive landed immigrant status in Canada. I believe in the next month we could possibly obtain information concerning another twenty thousand terrorists and possibly more."

"I presume you require something for this information?" the Ambassador asks.

"There are some things we will require on a temporary basis," Marcel responds. "Others we may be forced to adopt on a permanent basis. First on our agenda, we will need help concerning our safety. C.S.I.S. is already planning the murder of one of our members. They previously had illegal surveillance equipment in his home when one of their agents, illegally in the house, killed a sixteen-year old boy. He was shooting at some other boys when shot by a neighbor. After that, they again installed illegal surveillance equipment in the home. When that equipment was discovered, C.S.I.S. illegally installed audio surveillance in the law firm, of which Rae Jones is a partner. Four days ago Joe Ferguson discovered illegal audio and video equipment in his office."

"How do you mean illegal?"

"They never applied for permission from the courts to install the devices," Rae explains to the American Ambassador. "The laws in both our countries are the same in that respect."

Rae hands the Ambassador the tape recorder with the information obtained at the Montague residence.

The Ambassador carefully listens to the tape.

"Who are Jean and Pierre and the other men on the tape?"

Rae enlightens the American Ambassador.

"Jean Perrault is the Senior Official of the Canadian Security and Intelligence Service. Pierre Montague is the Senior Official in charge of the Canadian Department of Immigration. Joe Ferguson is the man from the Immigration Department who found proof the Federal Government is bringing terrorists into Canada."

"Those two are right at the top. Who else is involved?"

"The Prime Minister, Minister of Immigration, Minister of Finance, Minister of Justice, Minister of Foreign Affairs and the top bureaucrats in those departments and the Privy Council members including the Leader of the Opposition. There are 473 government officials involved in the illegal immigration operation in Canada and in Canadian Legations located throughout Europe, Africa and Asia.

"What do you need to safely provide us with the information on the terrorists?"

"The first item of business is satellite phones with American accounts, for which we are willing to pay." Marcel continues to explain, "We need to communicate without fear of being overheard or the calls being traced to each other. We require 22 phones at this time because husbands and wives need to be able to communicate for safety but we may require up to thirty phones."

"That is no problem," the Ambassador replies, "I should have them for you by tomorrow afternoon."

"Second," Marcel states, "We will require instant protection in the United States for any of us fleeing the R.C.M.P. or C.S.I.S. no matter how close they are." He continues, "We should have an easily remembered, immediately recognizable password to cross the border into your country."

"I perceive no problem in fulfilling that need and I believe that goal can be quickly achieved."

"Third, we must have U.S. citizenship with passports, identifications, drivers licences, green cards and anything else your security feels we will require for our needs. We will need this for our real identities and for at least one false identity each. We will only need these for a maximum of two years and then only periodically, the false identities for only three months. If we receive this help we should be able to destroy the illegal immigration ring."

"I will let you know if we can do that," the Ambassador replies. "I feel, under the present circumstances it will be possible. I know the information you can give us and the elimination of the illegal immigration ring will be a top priority with our government. We should be able to work together to achieve this common goal."

"If we find our lives in jeopardy in Canada and we wish to apply for U.S. citizenship we will be given proper consideration."

"I can take this up in Washington and get back to you within a few days. What are you planning for the terrorists and C.S.I.S. tonight?"

"They'll be taken care of," Marcel replies. "Rae give the Ambassador the disks with the terrorist information and we'll have to be leaving."

The American Ambassador is pleased with the outcome of the meeting. "I wish to thank you for this information. Any information you can give us will increase the security of our country and all of North America."

While walking away from the Embassy, Rae speaks to Marcel.

"From the way you handled that marine you must have taken some training from one of the city martial arts schools."

"Yes and no," Marcel replies to the query from Rae. "My Uncle spent twenty years with the British Special Forces. He retired back to Ottawa and trained me in all phases of hand-to-hand combat. We train at least twice a week and I run three miles a day."

"Don't they teach you how to kill?"

"Yes. His weapon of choice is the garrote. He fought in the Falklands war."

Rae decides not to upset Marcel.

Hamed Ahmidam

From the embassy Marcel Roy and Rae Jones drive to the make-up trailer of Andre Prichard, sitting at a movie set location in an older residential area of Ottawa. Producing a picture of an Arab, bearing a striking resemblance to himself, Marcel hands it to Andre. When Andre is finished applying the disguise Marcel looks identical to the man in the picture, a Saudi Arabian terrorist by the name of Hamed Ahmidam. Marcel and Rae then proceed to the Ontario Department of Motor Vehicles where Marcel Roy obtains an operators licence to replace the licence "Hamed Ahmidam" has lost. They have no problem obtaining the licence with immigration papers supplied through the "Trojan Horse Program", a sworn declaration that Marcel Roy is Hamed Ahmidam and the driver licence number Marcel has previously obtained from the files of the Ontario Department of Transport.

Marcel begins to open bank accounts under the alias of Hamed Ahmidam in seven different banks beginning with the Royal Bank on Carling Avenue. At each bank, he informs the bank personnel setting up the account he will be receiving the sum of $75,140 and will be making a major withdrawal when it arrives. The next stop is 96 Powell Avenue – the house Hamed Ahmidam shares with two of his accomplices. Sitting in his car, and using his Wi-Fi-equipped laptop, he surreptitiously enters the Wi-Fi-equipped computer belonging to the three men renting the home. Quickly accessing the account through the Internet, he transfers the $526,000 from the Joe Ferguson account to the seven bank accounts of Hamed Ahmidam. Still parked outside the house he uses his "Trojan Horse Program" to access the Department of Immigration computers and download terrorist files. Fifteen minutes later, he is moving on to another terrorist Wi-Fi-equipped computer.

Rae Jones drives back to Andre Prichard's movie location. He explains the situation with the terrorists buying Landed Immigrant Status from the Canadian Government and the government's plan to sell those terrorists to the American Government. He informs Andre Prichard about the money in the Swiss bank accounts and asks if Andre would aid them in destroying the illegal immigration ring by helping them to steal those funds from the bank in Switzerland.

"Are you absolutely certain it will work Rae?"

"Marcel has already placed "Trojan Horse Programs" within the computers of the Department of Immigration to access the files on the terrorists and has already accessed eight hundred names and addresses of terrorists who have paid money to obtain Canadian landed immigrant status."

"You mean there are eight hundred terrorists in Canada brought in by the Federal Government?"

"Marcel believes there are over twenty thousand names he hasn't accessed yet."

"Mon Dieu!" Andre curses. "Oui! I'll do it! My wife will help too."

Ambush

Marcel drives home for a quick lunch and a change to dark clothing, and then drives within one block of the Ferguson residence. In the residence, Tom Jackson has been busy installing a night-light in the ceiling of the hallway to the upstairs bedrooms. This light will cause momentary night blindness to the assassins when they charge into the bedrooms. Joe Ferguson first loads the three shotguns, then places one in each bedroom. The tape recorder with the snoring tape is in place, under the edge of the bed. The three beds are stuffed to resemble sleeping people and are placed with the foam heads straight in from the doorway. Marcel Roy will be in the master bedroom, Joe Ferguson across the hall in Keith's bedroom and Maurice Solinger in Jerry's bedroom across the hall from the bathroom. Alex Johansen and Tom Jackson walk back to the Jackson residence. Both houses leave the lights on with Joe leaving the front outside light on waiting for someone to return. Everybody sleeps until eleven o'clock, then all the lights in both residences are switched off. The men in each house take turns sleeping and keeping watch for any sign of the expected visitors.

At eleven o'clock that evening Cecil Mann receives a phone call from Marc Leblanc telling him to be at the office in one hour for a briefing on the Joe Ferguson case. Matt Spence, a swarthy man, introduced as Muqtada Musharrof, and two boys, introduced as his sons Omar and Shaukat are waiting in the office with Marc Leblanc when Cecil arrives.

Marc Leblanc presents Cecil Mann with a document signed by Jean Perrault authorizing the immediate arrest of Joseph Ferguson. Leblanc begins outlining the procedure for tonight's action.

"We are arresting Joseph Ferguson and his family tonight and charging them with aiding terrorists to immigrate to Canada. The Immigration Department has found two more terrorist families Joseph Ferguson has just supplied with landed immigration papers and with the Ayman al-Zawahri file, we have sufficient evidence to arrest him. Once he is incarcerated, it will be a simple matter to gain any extra evidence we will require to secure his conviction on the illegal immigration operation. I believe you have the search warrant to enter the Ferguson residence Matt."

Matt Spence pats an attaché case lying on the table.

"I also have the arrest warrants."

Marc Leblanc continues his dissertation to the five men present.

"After you finish at the Ferguson residence phone this office. I'll have two forensic agents waiting here to do a search of the house, looking for more evidence of Joseph Ferguson's illegal activities. I believe that is all."

"Why are Muqtada Musharrof and his two sons involved in a C.S.I.S. arrest," Cecil asks Leblanc, "and why are only two C.S.I.S. agents involved?"

"Muqtada Musharrof is a C.S.I.S. agent. His two sons are special agents. They are working undercover on a case in Montreal. While they were in town reporting to Jean Perrault, he asked them to help in the arrests."

At one thirty-five Tom Jackson spots a van driving down Rowanwood Avenue with no headlights. He shakes Alex Johansen telling him, "They're here!" Picking up his hunting rifle and a white towel, Tom leaves via the back door.

Alex quickly phones Joe.

"We've seen them."

Cecil Mann quietly unlocks the front door of the Ferguson residence and slips inside, followed by the other four men. Matt Spence, touching Cecil on the arm, stops him. The three terrorists move towards the stairs, followed by Matt Spence, with Cecil Mann bringing up the rear. The three Arabs leading the entourage slip eerily up the stairs towards the dim light on the second floor, making no sound with their passage. A stair squeaks as Spence steps on it, then the quiet returns to flood over the group. Cecil moves as quietly as the lead members of the arrest party. A gentle snore emanates from one bedroom and flows peacefully into the hallway. Spence stops on the second last step. Cecil stops on the landing, still trying to deduce why the three Arabs are in the lead – still not satisfied with the answer given by his superior.

Vigilantly watching Shaukat Musharrof ever so quietly begin to open the bedroom door, Cecil suddenly realizes the boy has a knife in his hand. He shouts as the boy explodes through the doorway. Cecil, alerted by the knife in the hand of the young terrorist, watches Spence whirling around awkwardly on the stair to face him. In his hand, as he frantically searches the shadows for his target, is a gun with a silencer. Cecil, moving instinctively, his reflexes honed by years of martial arts training, leaps to the side even as he hears the angry roars of the shotguns. Revolver shells, on their mission of death, slam harmlessly into the wall where he had just been standing. Matt Spence spins back to the blast of the shotguns, a shocked expression on his face. They have walked into a trap. With the roar of the shotguns still ringing in his ears Spence watches in disbelief as a man with dark skin steps from a bedroom with a shotgun just as the Musharrof boy darts from the bedroom in front of him, charging the man with the shotgun. Spence, feeling as though he is moving in slow motion, dives down the stairs and rolls to protection on the stairwell landing. The shotgun sends another angry roar flooding over Spence and down the stairwell, forcing him to momentarily cringe. Rising quickly to his feet, he charges down the stairs. At the doorway, Spence catches sight of the obscure figure of Cecil racing across the lawn. Raising the gun, he fires again, knocking Cecil to the ground. Spence lopes from the house towards his partner lying prostrate on the ground. A voice barks at him out of the blackness of the night.

"Halt! Raise your hands!"

Joe Ferguson, Marcel Roy and Maurice Solinger watch the three terrorists streaking towards their respective beds, and then plunging their knives into the bedding. The blasts from the shotguns held by Marcel and Joe drives the life from two assassins. Maurice squeezes the trigger on his weapon, and to his chagrin, realizes he hasn't cocked the gun. He is fumbling for the hammers as the boy spins and streaks towards the light in the hallway, turning in the direction from which the blasts of the shotguns had emanated. Marcel steps into the hallway raising his shotgun. He sees Matt Spence diving down the stairs. The young terrorist suddenly appears to Marcel, charging him with the knife in his hand. Marcel fires the second round at point blank range. The blast stops the terrorist in mid stride, crumbling him lifeless to the floor.

Tom Jackson watches the last terrorist enter the house. Creeping to the lilac bush, Tom hangs the towel on the bush, and then retreats to the corner of the Ferguson residence. Lying on the ground with his rifle ready, Tom waits for the drama to unfold in the house. Hearing the blasts of the shotguns, Tom is primed for the exit of the C.S.I.S. agents. Cecil Mann flies from the house towards the protection of the van. Tom is lining up his sights when a muffled shot crumbles Cecil to the ground. Matt Spence exits the house, loping towards his helpless partner to execute the coup-de-grace.

Tom Jackson swings his weapon to cover the shadowy figure making its ghostly passage through the night.

"Halt! Raise your hands!"

Matt Spence stops and slowly raises his hands still holding the gun. He begins to turn slowly towards the voice. Seeing an object shift in the light breeze, he drops to one knee and places two shots into the towel. Tom follows Matt Spence as he drops to one knee. The crack of the rifle sends its deadly missile directly into the chest of the agent, leaving him sprawled and lifeless on the grass. Tom lays there waiting, then sees light spilling from the upstairs windows and shining on the lawn.

Rushing up to Spence, Alex Johansen kicks the revolver away. He checks Cecil Mann, finding the C.S.I.S. agent still alive, his kevlar vest having stopped the shell from the 32-calibre revolver. He disarms the agent and puts his own cuffs on him. Alex retreats behind the lilac bushes and waits.

Upstairs Joe feels nauseous over the bloody carnage wreaked by their weapons. Marcel tells Maurice to wait on the stairs to limit the tracks in the blood spatters. Scrutinizing the scene, Marcel tells Joe to release the hammer and lay his shotgun on the floor in the master bedroom. Handing Joe the shotgun he had fired, Marcel has Joe aim the weapon to place fingerprints in the proper locations then lean that shotgun against the end wall in the hallway. Marcel removes his shirt and pants, throwing them in the shower and turning on the cold water. After wiping his shoes with a damp cloth, he hands Joe the cloth to smear some blood and water stains onto his own shoes. Joe gives Marcel a shirt and pants to wear. Collecting the four wigs and the nine-millimeter revolver Joe is carrying, Maurice and Marcel carefully leave the house by the back door where Alex Johansen joins them. The trio enters the Jackson residence via the back door. The towel with the bullet holes is folded and placed neatly in a drawer in the bathroom vanity. Alex phones his daughter Shannon, who is waiting for the call in a nearby coffee shop. Moving silently down the alley, the three shadows covertly leave the scene of the shootings, leaving no evidence they were ever present.

Joe shuts off the tape recorder, removes the tape from the machine, and then carries it to Jerry's room placing it on the dresser. He phones his lawyer, and then the police, requesting that Rene Dubois be present. William also phones the police precinct to guarantee that Rene Dubois would be conducting the investigation.

By walking past the body in the hallway a few times, Joe's shoes will pick up more blood while obliterating any footprints left by Marcel. Retrieving the third shotgun, Joe walks into the front yard where Tom Jackson is quietly waiting in the shadows. The night air and the action help to relieve the churning feelings in the mind and stomach of Joe Ferguson.

Alex Johansen and Maurice Solinger drive to the Montague residence and retrieve their audio surveillance equipment without incident.

Shannon Johansen arrives on the crime scene just as the first neighbors begin to make an appearance. She begins taking photographs, first in the yard and then upstairs. Tom removes badges, identities and operator licences from the two C.S.I.S. agents and then the identification papers and operators licences from the terrorists, laying them out by each person for Shannon to photograph.

Shannon is interviewing Tom Jackson and Joe Ferguson in the yard when the police arrive.

"I was watching a movie. When it finished, I let Ralph into the back yard. I was standing in the living room waiting for him to return when I saw a van with no lights pull up in front of the Ferguson house. I phoned Joe, and then got my rifle from my gun case. Rushing upstairs, I saw the men entering Joe's house. I ran outside and lay down in the grass by the corner of the house. I knew this wasn't a police operation because three of the five people were wearing Arabic clothing and nobody was in uniform."

"I heard a shotgun blast, a second shotgun blast, and then a third shotgun blast. One man sprinted from the house towards the van. I heard a pop and I saw the man crumble to the ground. The second man ran towards the first holding his gun to shoot him again when I hollered 'halt! Raise your hands!' He stopped and raised his hands head high and then started to turn. He dropped to one knee and fired two shots at me. I returned the fire."

"I fell asleep on a chair," Joe begins his statement, "and woke when Tom phoned me. I was home alone because my wife is visiting her mother in Toronto and the boys are holidaying at a summer camp. Believing there could be trouble after finding a surveillance camera in my office in the Immigration Department last Thursday, I had made the beds up to look like people were sleeping in them. I loaded the shotguns, and placed them in the master bedroom, hoping I wouldn't need them."

I was standing in a corner when the bedroom door crashed open and a man in Arabic attire leaped into the room and began stabbing the bed with a knife. I fired at him. Grabbing a second shotgun and stepping to the open door, I saw another person in Arabic clothing stabbing Keith's bed. I shot at him. I stepped into the hallway to see another person on the stairs holding a revolver. Before I could fire he dove down the stairs and another person in Arabic clothing charged from Jerry's bedroom, running towards me with a knife in his hand. I fired at him. I heard a light popping noise in the house. Then I heard Tom Jackson holler, 'Halt. Raise your hands.' I heard a double pop outside. Then I heard the blast of the rifle firing. I phoned the police and my lawyer, then went outside to find Tom with the two C.S.I.S. agents lying on the ground. One was still alive but unconscious. He must have been in shock from the shot in the back by his partner.

Cecil Mann is still lying on the grass handcuffed. Listening groggily, 'he blearily realizes he owes his life to the man with the rifle. In the house, he heard two shotguns fire simultaneously.... Then a third shot.... It had to have been two guns firing.... It was too loud for one shot.... even in an enclosed space.... His mind is hazy.... It's hard to think clearly.... Where's the man who took his gun and handcuffed him...? Maybe he will remember everything more clearly later.... Yes, think about this later....'

Rene Dubois and Marcel St. Croix arrive on the scene. Joe calls them over for Shannon to speak to Rene.

"The identification on the man in the master bedroom claims his name is Muqtada Musharrof, but I have seen his picture recently and that wasn't his name. I'm going to the newspaper office right now and if you wish I can phone you with his true identity?"

From the office of the Ottawa Citizen, Shannon contacts Rene Dubois.

"The man with the alias Muqtada Musharrof is actually a terrorist named Abu Zubaydah. U.S. authorities are looking him for his part in the bombing of the U.S. Embassy in Somalia. The American Government has placed a reward of $500,000 on Abu Zubaydah. His two sons, Omar and Shaukat, have both received training in the al-Qaeda camps in Afghanistan. Refugees discovered Abu Zubaydah in Toronto a few months ago and he was supposed to be deported to Afghanistan. I have no idea how he managed to move to Vancouver and obtain false immigration papers but C.S.I.S. seemed to know how to find him when they needed him."

Marcel St. Croix rides to the hospital in the ambulance with Cecil Mann. From the hospital they proceed to the police station to book Cecil and to obtain a statement from him showing his involvement in the crime.

In his statement, Cecil begins with the phone call by Marc Leblanc and proceeds to tell of the evening's events. When he states that the attaché case containing the arrest warrants is on the dashboard of the van, Marcel St. Croix stops the interrogation and places a call to his partner.

"Rene Dubois."

"Marcel here. There should be an attaché case on the dash of the van with arrest warrants in it for all four Ferguson family members and also two C.S.I.S. forensic specialists are coming to the crime scene."

Opening the van door and retrieving the attaché case, Rene is not surprised to discover it is empty of any documents.

"There are no warrants in the case but our forensic specialists have found packages of drugs in the pocket of Matt Spence and the C.S.I.S. forensic specialists arrived a few minutes ago."

Marcel St. Croix speaks to Cecil Mann, "There are no arrest warrants in the attaché case."

"I've come to that conclusion myself." Cecil hands Marcel St. Croix the arrest document signed by Jean Perrault. "I was alerted and hollered when I saw a knife in the hands of the Arab entering the bedroom. Matt Spence turned around on the stairs with a gun in his hand to shoot me. I leapt to the other side of the landing and raced down the stairs and out the door. I was almost to the van when everything went blank. I recovered my senses to discover I was in handcuffs." Cecil decides to remain silent about his still hazy recollections of events that unfolded at the Ferguson residence. His recollections of the events he did document are still not completely clear in his mind.

"I believe that covers everything. I'll type your statement and have you sign it."

"Not really. I have some more pertinent information I need to pass on to you." Cecil informs Marcel.

"I was ordered by Marc Leblanc to find any information I could from the law office representing Joseph Ferguson. I entered the office believing that C.S.I.S. had obtained proper court documentation for me to enter and place bugs on their telephones. In light of this evenings developments, I have reason to believe the listening devices are illegal. I have a blue C.S.I.S. van parked in front of their law office to record their conversations.

After signing his statement, Marcel St. Croix places Cecil in a holding cell.

More C.S.I.S.

Failing to receive a phone call from Matt Spence by three o'clock, the C.S.I.S. forensic agents waiting in their office decide to investigate. To their chagrin, they find the Ottawa City Police Forensic Unit already working the crime scene.

"Get your men out of here we're taking over the investigation," orders the Senior C.S.I.S. agent, Donald Prince.

"You leave right now or you'll find yourselves arrested for obstruction of justice," counters the Detective, Rene Dubois.

They are arguing heatedly when Rene, receiving the phone call from Marcel St. Croix, walks over to the van to remove an attaché case. After examining the interior of the attaché case, he carries it over to the C.S.I.S. agents. Opening wide the empty attaché case he growls, "Here are the arrest warrants for the Ferguson family. Drugs to be planted were found in the dead agent's pocket. The three dead men upstairs, who used knives in an attempt to kill the Ferguson family, are al-Qaeda terrorists. The agent, Matt Spence, who shot his partner in the back, did so with a street gun that has the serial number removed and is equipped with a silencer. You are under arrest for attempted obstruction of justice and conspiracy in the attempted murder of the Ferguson family."

Donald Prince blusters at Rene, "If you don't have your men out of here in…" He spots Joe Ferguson and Tom Jackson angrily stalking up to them – Joe menacingly brandishing his shotgun. Joe and Tom have heard as much of this argument as they can tolerate. Observing the look on Joe's face, the agent realizes that his life could be over in seconds. Joe is barely holding on to his sanity and any sudden action could see him explode. Prince, wanting nothing to do with a half-crazed Joseph Ferguson wielding a shotgun, raises his hands saying, "We surrender." They are cuffed, searched and each one placed in the back of a separate police cruiser to be removed to jail for booking and incarceration. The city police will not allow the pair to make a phone call until Leblanc and Perrault are in custody.

Joe replaces the shotgun inside the front door of his home and he and Tom again sit on the front step.

Returning to the crime scene, Marcel St. Croix informs Rene Dubois about the audio surveillance equipment in the law offices of Jones, Smythe and Watson. The two policemen speak to William. Rene calls Alex Johansen, arranging to meet him at the lawyers' offices. Alex is immediately on the phone informing his daughter Shannon, about the latest developments.

William and the two detectives are waiting in the lawyers' offices when Shannon arrives, followed shortly by her father. Alex finds the three bugs on the lawyers' phones. The phones of the office staff appear to be clean. Checking the van, they find the surveillance recording system. A tow truck will haul the van to the impound yard for a more complete forensic examination.

Before returning to the Ferguson crime scene Rene speaks to Shannon.

"Thank you for the information you provided on the terrorists. I believe we'll never be able to bring these criminals to justice because they have too much power. If we are to stop this criminal activity, the surest way is through the press. With all the flack we have received from the Department of Justice and the lack of co-operation from that department somebody in authority in the Justice Department has to be involved, behind the scenes, in the illegal surveillance of Joseph Ferguson, and indirectly the death of the boy in the Ferguson residence."

"We found drugs, which we believe were to be planted at the crime scene, in the pocket of the dead C.S.I.S. agent, Matt Spence. The C.S.I.S. agent, Cecil Mann, whom the dead agent Matt Spence, tried unsuccessfully to eliminate, knows too much and has incriminated the Senior Official, Jean Perrault, and his immediate subordinate in the C.S.I.S. organization, Marc Leblanc. Mann is now in jail, although we believe he had no knowledge of the attempt to murder Joe Ferguson. The gun used in the attempted murder of Mann was not registered and the serial number was previously removed. The crime has all the markings of an assassination attempt. There were supposed to be arrest warrants in an empty attaché case. Two C.S.I.S. agents, forensic specialists, were arrested at the scene and charged with conspiracy to commit murder and attempting to disrupt the evidence investigation. Their names are Donald Prince and Roger Dugan. Forensic specialists are always summoned to investigate a crime scene, so we know they are part of the conspiracy. How did they know of the crime unless informed in advance there would be a crime committed? In his confession Cecil Mann admitted the C.S.I.S. forensic specialists were waiting in their office for a phone call from Matt Spence to process the house after Joe Ferguson was arrested." Rene hands Shannon a folder. "This folder contains a copy of the confession of the C.S.I.S. agent, Cecil Mann and a copy of the document signed by Jean Perrault authorizing the arrest of the Ferguson family. We will be arresting Jean Perrault, the Senior Official in the Canadian Security and Intelligence Service and Marc Leblanc, a senior C.S.I.S. official tied directly to Jean Perrault, as conspirators in the attempted murder of Joe Ferguson."

Shannon shuts off her tape recorder and thanks Rene for the information. After Rene leaves, William gives Shannon a folder containing more information on C.S.I.S. involvement with Joe Ferguson.

The Argument

Shannon Johansen returns to her desk at the Ottawa Citizen to file her story on the attempted murder of Joe Ferguson by the federal government.

At eight fifteen Shannon receives confirmation of the arrest of Marc Leblanc and the search for Jean Perrault. A few minutes later she has the faxed photograph of Marc Leblanc, taken by an Ottawa Citizen photographer, on her desk. Gathering up her photos and story, she presents it to the editor.

"Leave your article in the IN file. I'll check it later and see if we can use it," responds the Editor.

"If you want to miss the biggest story to hit the city this year, it will be your own fault," Shannon retorts irately. "This newspaper could be the first to publish the story of the attempted murder of a citizen by C.S.I.S. using al Qaeda terrorists, but if your time is too important it's definitely too important."

The editor angrily picks up the paper and begins scanning it. His countenance changes as he gives the article his full attention. With an inquiring look on his face he asks Shannon, "Have you verified all the facts?"

"All my sources were directly or indirectly involved in the case."

The editor returns to the article, scrutinizing it diligently. "I owe you an apology. You have done a great job on this story. This is feature material and I'll have it on the presses and on the Canadian Press web site immediately."

Jean Perrault leaves his office at seven forty-five in the morning. Stopping at the desk of Erin Henley, they converse for a minute, then he leaves, stopping on the front step to light a cigarette. Erin joins him a few minutes later and after lighting up, they walk arm in arm to a local hotel to engage in their adulterous behavior. An hour later, they are lying naked on the bed smoking when the ringing of Perrault's cell phone interrupts their conversation.

"Jean Perrault here."

"Marc here. The Ottawa police arrested me for conspiracy to murder Joe Ferguson. They arrested Mann, Prince, and Dugan at the Ferguson residence. Matt Spence died at the scene. Three alleged terrorists were killed inside the Ferguson house. The police have warrants for your arrest."

Jean Perrault storms to his feet. He is livid as he hurls his cell phone against the wall. Screaming and cursing at the police, Joe Ferguson, and his own incompetent staff, Perrault charges around the room. The tirade continues. He squeals in agony as he doubles over clutching his chest. Erin supports him back to the bed and lying down, trying to make her lover comfortable. After removing the burning cigarette from the floor and placing it in an ashtray, Erin picks up the phone to dial 911, and summon an ambulance to the aid of her companion. Realizing her name will come out, and her husband will learn of her adulterous behavior, she replaces the phone in the cradle. Erin dresses quickly, then leaves with Jean Perrault collapsed on the bed, his helpless gaze imploring her for the assistance he would never extend to any fellow human being.

Erin Henley returns to the office, works until noon, then leaves to pick up her daughter and go home. She sits in the living room staring at a blank wall, conscience stricken about leaving her lover suffering and alone in the cold hotel room. Twice she picks up the phone to dial 911 and twice she puts it down again – torn by the desire to aid her lover but unwilling to compromise her marriage.

The hotel staff discovers Jean Perrault in a coma that afternoon. An ambulance rushes him to the hospital where doctors place him on life support. Six weeks later Perrault will keep his appointment with his maker.

Marcel Roy, accessing his "Trojan Horse Program" in the Department of Immigration computer through "Wi-Fi-equipped" terrorist computers is again downloading terrorist files into his I-pod. By nine o'clock, he has accessed the illegal Joe Ferguson account in the Carling Avenue Royal Bank, and found the money transferred to his Hamed Ahmidam accounts. Working carefully, he removes all trace of the account moving from the illegal Ferguson account into the illegal Hamed Ahmidam accounts. Visiting all the banks, he withdraws $3,000 from each account and informs the institutions he will be withdrawing $68,000 from the account the following morning. The next step for Marcel is another transfer. He moves $2.213 million from the C.S.I.S. account to the Joe Ferguson account knowing if the funds are traced, C.S.I.S. will believe it was transferred in error. From there it's back to the "Trojan Horse Program."

"Why Joe Ferguson?"

At nine-thirty that same morning, Jerry McIntyre, wife of the Alliance Party Justice Critic, Terry McIntyre, receives a phone call from her sister, Vicky Thompson, in Calgary, Alberta.

"Have you read the news article on the Canadian Press web site this morning?"

"No I haven't Vicky. I don't usually pay too much attention to the news."

"You'd better make sure that Terry sees that article immediately. It says that C.S.I.S. was involved in the attempted murder of an Immigration Department worker and they hired known al-Qaeda terrorists to kill him. It just appeared on their web site under the caption 'Why Joe Ferguson?' This is going to be big."

As they are talking on the phone Jerry walks over to her computer and brings up the Canadian Press web site and begins to read:

Why Joe Ferguson? by Shannon Johansen

This morning at 1:30 A.M., June 27, 2001 a neighbor, Tom Jackson, spotted a van drive slowly down the street without any headlights and stop in front of the Ferguson residence. He immediately phoned Joe Ferguson.

Five men – two C.S.I.S. agents – three al Qaeda terrorists – entered the front door with a key and stole quietly upstairs. Three terrorists raced into the three bedrooms and began stabbing the beds with knives. Then Joe started shooting, killing three members of the Abu Zubaydah family. One of the assassins, the father is wanted by the US government for his part in the U.S. Embassy bombing in Somalia. His two sons, Omar and Shaukat, are known to have trained in the al-Qaeda camps in Afghanistan. Tom Jackson watched as one C.S.I.S. agent, Cecil Mann, raced from the house only to be shot in the back by his partner. His partner Matt Spence, another C.S.I.S. agent, then rushed up to the first C.S.I.S. agent, Cecil Mann, in an attempt to kill him. Tom Jackson ordered the second C.S.I.S. agent to halt and raise his hands. Instead, the agent fired twice at Tom Jackson before Tom Jackson returning the fire, shot and killed him. Two C.S.I.S. forensic agents, Donald Prince and Roger Dugan, arrived at the scene later and were arrested, charged with conspiracy to commit murder, and hindering an ongoing investigation. At eight-fifteen this morning, Marc Leblanc, a senior agent of C.S.I.S. was arrested and charged with attempted murder and the Director of the Canadian Security and Intelligence Service, Jean Perrault, has warrants out for his arrest. The C.S.I.S. agent shot by his partner gave a full confession, telling of his part in the plot and the involvement of Donald Prince, Abu Zubaydah, Omar Zubaydah, Shaukat Zubaydah, Marc Leblanc and Jean Perrault in the murder attempt of the Ferguson Family. The C.S.I.S. agent, Cecil Mann owes his life to the kevlar vest he was wearing when shot in the assassination attempt by Matt Spence at the Ferguson Residence.

This attempt on Joseph Ferguson's life is part of an ongoing saga that began on May 3, 2001. On that date, Joe Ferguson returned to his desk to find the Senior Official, Pierre Montague, of the Canadian Immigration Department rifling through the papers on his desk. Joseph Ferguson was asked if he had seen anything unusual on his screen that morning. He remembered later when he had printed off some papers there were two pages mixed in with his work that didn't belong. He had shredded the papers without really looking at them. When leaving his office at the finish of the workday, Joe Ferguson was forced to return to his office and was strip-searched by Pierre Montague, Senior Official in charge of the Department of Immigration and Jean Perrault, the Senior Official of the Canadian Security and Intelligence Service. When Joe Ferguson attempted to phone a lawyer he was threatened by the C.S.I.S. agent. They examined his clothing and then left. Joe Ferguson dressed and opened the door to leave only to have the doorway blocked by Jean Perrault. The C.S.I.S. agent again threatened him. **"Don't tell anybody about this. Have you got that straight!"**

Five weeks later, C.S.I.S. technician John Winston, in the basement of the Ferguson residence, killed a boy. The C.S.I.S. technician was killed while trying to shoot the other teenagers fleeing the house. Police found surveillance equipment belonging to the Canadian Security and Intelligence Service in the house. C.S.I.S. never applied for a court order to install the equipment – making the investigation a criminal act. On the Monday of the boy's funeral, a neighbor spotted, C.S.I.S. agent, Cecil Mann, entering the Ferguson residence. Again, the police found illegal surveillance equipment. Last Thursday Joseph Ferguson found surveillance equipment in his office at the Canadian Department of Immigration. The equipment was again illegally installed. This morning, C.S.I.S. surveillance equipment, discovered in the law office of the firm Joe Ferguson retained to defend him. Again – no authorization from the courts.

What is on those two pieces of paper that the Canadian Immigration Department and the Canadian Security and Intelligence Service find so threatening? Why did they attempt to kill this citizen? What type of criminal action is the Canadian Department of Immigration and the Canadian Justice Department trying to cover up?

Jerry McIntyre prints the article and thanks her sister for the information.

In the lobby of the House of Parliament, Jerry McIntyre speaks to a Page.

"Please contact my husband, Terry McIntyre, the Justice Critic for the Alliance Party. It's urgent that I speak with him immediately."

"I'll try to locate him for you."

The Page enters the floor of the House of Parliament, and spotting the Alliance Party Justice Critic, speaks to him.

"Mrs. McIntyre is in the lobby and says that it is urgent that you speak to her immediately. I'll take you to her."

"Do you have something for me?" Terry asks his wife.

"I've just downloaded this article from the Canadian Press web site."

Terry McIntyre begins reading the news article, and then addresses the page. "Will you get Tom Jones, the Alliance leader, for me? Tell him that it's urgent."

The Page leaves on his mission. Seeing a reporter entering the House of Commons, the Page speaks to him.

"Talk to Terry McIntyre in the lobby. There's something happening."

The Page conveys the message from Terry McIntyre to the Leader of the Opposition.

"What's so important that it can't wait?"

"Read this."

Tom Jones reads the article. He reads it again searching carefully for the full implication of the information on the document. His face clouds in anger. Jones forces his demeanor to change and speaking with the full authority of his position informs Terry, "We'll call a caucus meeting and make a decision as to what course to take on this information."

"Why do you want to wait?" is Terry McIntyre's incredulous reply. "This material will have the greatest impact right now. If we wait the Liberals will have their answers ready and we will learn nothing."

"We will wait," snaps the Leader of the Opposition. He is angry again.

"We can't wait. A Canadian citizen is being prosecuted by the very agency that is supposed to protect him."

"You will say nothing until I tell you." Tom Jones orders his Justice Critic.

Tom Jones sees the reporter taking notes and growls, "This is a private conversation."

"Your statements will make interesting copy in tomorrow's newspaper," the reporter replies "It will probably make the front page. Leader of the Opposition refuses to allow his Justice Critic to confront the government on illegal activities within the Justice Department. The Senior Official of the Canadian Security and Intelligence Service charged with conspiracy to commit murder. Why is he procrastinating? Is the Leader of the Opposition involved in illegal activities within the Justice Department and the Immigration Department? This will make excellent copy."

"If you print that," storms the Leader of the Opposition, "I'll sue you and your newspaper."

"Why, is it the truth? Your looking worried."

Tom Jones is facing a dilemma. To argue further could expose his involvement. The reporter is already getting too close to the truth. He finally relents.

"Ok McIntyre, do what you want. But you accept the responsibility."

Tom Jones stalks back to his seat in the House of Commons.

The reporter sits down with Terry McIntyre to confer with him.

"Jean Perrault is a good friend of the Prime Minister. I have seen him at many private functions at the Prime Minister's official residence at 24 Sussex Drive.

"Thank you," Terry replies. "That is pertinent information. Thank you Jerry for bringing me this article. I need to ask the Prime Minister some questions before he is advised about this development and can prepare his answers."

Terry McIntyre returns to his seat in the House of Commons where he continues to plan the questions he will ask the Prime Minister during Question Period.

"Speaker of the House."

"The House of Commons begins Question Period."

Terry rises to stand by his chair.

"The House now recognizes the Honorable Member from Calgary West."

"Mr. Speaker. I have some questions I wish to direct to the Honorable Prime Minister and the Honorable Minister of Justice."

"Mr. Speaker. I wish to hear from the Justice Minister how the investigation into the murder of a boy by an agent of the Canadian Security and Intelligence Service in the home of Joseph Ferguson is progressing?"

"Mr. Speaker. I wish to know how the discovery of audio surveillance equipment, illegally installed by C.S.I.S. in the same home, is progressing at this time?"

"Mr. Speaker. I also wish to know which division of the Justice department is conducting this investigation?"

"The House recognizes the Honorable Minister of Justice."

"Mr. Speaker. We have an ongoing investigation conducted by C.S.I.S. into the terrible incident at the Ferguson residence. The Official Secrecy Act prevents me from commenting further at this time."

The Liberal Members of Parliament express their admiration for the profound answer, given by the Justice Minister, to the question posed by the Justice Critic by clapping their hands, stomping their feet and thumping their desks.

"The House now recognizes the Honorable Member from Calgary West."

"Mr. Speaker. Would Mr. Prime Minister please explain to me why he believes the Canadian Security and Intelligence Service can impartially investigate a crime in which it is so deeply implicated?"

"The House now recognizes the Honorable Prime Minister."

"Mr. Speaker. Jean Perrault, head of the Canadian Security and Intelligence Service is a very honorable man and has very high moral standards."

"Mr. Speaker. His presence guarantees an honest and non-prejudicial investigation into the case."

The foot stomping, clapping and desk thumping by the Liberal Party faithful rises to a crescendo, filling the House of Commons.

"The House now recognizes the Honorable Member from Calgary West."

"Mr. Speaker. I take it then the Honorable Prime Minister knows Jean Perrault personally to speak so highly of the Senior Official of C.S.I.S."

"The House now recognizes the Honorable Prime Minister."

"Mr. Speaker. I have met with Jean Perrault regularly in his capacity as the head of the Canadian Security and Intelligence Service."

" Mr. Speaker. He has attended many social functions my wife and I have hosted at our official residence at 24 Sussex."

"Mr. Speaker. This last weekend I am happy to say we enjoyed the company of each other and other cherished friends in the same foursome in the Federal Government sponsored Golf Tournament at the Eagle Creek Golf Course."

"Mr. Speaker. I find he is an admirable man whom I greatly respect."

The air reverberates with the applause of the Liberal Members of Parliament.

"The House now recognizes the Honorable Member from Calgary West."

"Mr. Speaker. Jean Perrault, the man of honor and integrity, along with another friend the Prime Minister enjoyed the company of at the Eagle Creek Golf Course, Pierre Montague, Senior Official of the Department of Immigration, strip searched Joe Ferguson in the offices in the Immigration Department and threatened him when he tried to phone an attorney."

"Mr. Speaker. When Mr. Ferguson was allowed to leave he was again threatened by Jean Perrault who said, 'Don't tell anybody about this! Have you got that straight'!"

"The House now recognizes the Honorable Prime Minister."

"Mr. Speaker. I know nothing of that situation but I will have the office of the Minister of Justice investigate the alleged accusation and report back to the house on the validity of the claim."

Clapping and desk thumping.

"The House now recognizes The Honorable Member from Calgary West."

"Mr. Speaker. Since that fateful day in June, illegally installed surveillance equipment has been found twice in the residence of Joseph Ferguson, illegally installed surveillance equipment has been found in the office of Joseph Ferguson in the Department of Immigration, and illegally installed surveillance equipment has been found in the law offices of Joseph Ferguson's solicitors." "Mr. Speaker. All the illegal surveillance equipment was previously installed by, and belongs to the Canadian Security and Intelligence Service."

"Mr. Speaker. At one-thirty this morning, three known al-Qaeda terrorists and two agents of the Canadian Security and Intelligence Service invaded the home of Joseph Ferguson in an attempt to kill him. Joseph Ferguson managed to kill the three terrorists, a neighbor managed to kill one C.S.I.S. agent, another C.S.I.S. agent was shot in the back by his partner. He and two other C.S.I.S. agents were arrested at the site."

"Mr. Speaker. One of the agents confessed implicating Marc Leblanc, the head of the Ottawa division of C.S.I.S. who was arrested in his office this morning and charged with conspiracy to commit murder. Also implicated was Jean Perrault, who has yet to be found. The Senior Official of C.S.I.S. has outstanding warrants for his arrest, charging him with conspiracy to commit murder."

"Mr. Speaker. My questions to the Honorable Prime Minister are these. Why is the Justice Department using paid assassins in an attempt to murder a man they are supposed to be protecting?"

"Mr. Speaker. Does Joseph Ferguson have knowledge of criminal activity within the Department of Immigration or the Canadian Security and Intelligence Service and does this information pose such a serious threat to the people involved in the conspiracy they have to kill Joseph Ferguson in order to silence him from exposing their criminal activities?"

"The House recognizes the Honorable Prime Minister."

"Why did you ask me those questions? I have done nothing wrong." The Prime Minister pauses for a moment. "Mr. Speaker. I have official business elsewhere and cannot answer any more questions at this time."

The Prime Minister picks up his papers and leaves amid loud clapping and desk thumping by his colleagues. Members shake his hand and congratulate him on the ease with which he answered the questions posed by the Justice critic.

Disguises

Heather Smythe and Mary Watson pick up Marie Prichard and drive to Montreal to open bank accounts in the names of the Arabic terrorists' wives they represent in their disguises. The Muslim ladies dress code of wearing the abaya, hijab, and niqab simplifies the makeup artistry Andre Prichard must perform on each lady to hide her true identity.

Joe Ferguson and Marcel Roy have provided proper documentation for everybody involved in the bank caper.

The men are disguised in the Muslim beard and hairstyle and wearing the disha dasha and either the juba or men's abaya. Their headgear consists of the traditional turban cloth, the kufi, or the shora held in place with the egal. The men and ladies both wear brown contact lenses and their exposed skin is the brownish coloration of natives from the Middle East. Joe Ferguson and Tom Jackson meet Irena and Henri Roy while Andre Prichard is applying their disguises and decide to join the Roys' in their van for the excursion to Montreal. Shannon Johansen rides with Rae and Andrea Jones. Maurice and Kathleen Solinger ride with Gloria and Alex Johansen. Before entering any of the banks, the fake terrorists spray liquid band-aid on their fingers and thumbs. They will establish 56 bank accounts in the greater Montreal area before returning home.

Henri Roy waits patiently at the government weigh scale along Ontario highway 417. The other vehicles belonging to members of the Maple Hill Mob stop, leaving with him the necessary documentation for Marcel to make the money transfers to each account. When Henri Roy has received all the transcripts, he phones his son. Marcel is running his "Trojan Horse Program" but soon extricates himself and phones back. An hour later Marcel has the information needed to transfer the funds waiting in the illegal Joe Ferguson bank account.

Arriving back in Ottawa, Rae Jones proceeds directly to the U.S. Embassy. Proceeding to the marines on duty, he addresses them. "Would you inform Ambassador Henry Kilmer, Rae Jones is here on his appointment to meet with the Ambassador?"

Marine, looking hard at Rae in his disguise, "Do you have identification?"

"Weren't you here yesterday?" inquires the second marine.

"Yes I was."

"The Ambassador is expecting you. Follow me please."

The marine takes Rae to Henry Kilmer's secretary and announces, "Mr. Rae Jones to see Ambassador Kilmer."

The secretary checks and then shows Rae into the Ambassador's office.

"Are you certain you're the Rae Jones who was here yesterday?" asks the Ambassador, "because you certainly don't look like the same man."

"I'm not absolutely positive myself."

The American Ambassador continues to look at Rae in his disguise. "I would not have known you had I met you on the street. The biggest surprise to me is the brown eyes. Your eyes are blue if I remember correctly."

"You have good observation, because they are blue."

"The F.B.I. has procured 30 satellite phones for your use. I'm instructed to keep the phones you do not require at this time. The phone numbers are consecutive, the phones are numbered, and the speed dialing is set. If you wish to call a number using the speed dial just hit star, star and the number of the phone such as * * 0 8 and you will reach the party who has phone number 8." The American Ambassador continues with his dissertation, "Before you leave I'll have my secretary help to record the name of each party, the speed dial number and phone number for each phone. He will activate each phone. The code to enter the States on instant notice is United States Ambassador to Canada. It should prove simple to remember."

Rae Jones is relieved that the American government is willing to aid them in their endeavor to expose the terrorists, and the criminals within the government, bringing those terrorists into Canada

"Thank you for your help Mr. Ambassador. It will certainly make our efforts both safer and easier. It is also a relief to know we have an ally in our endeavor to destroy this Federal Government criminal organization"

"The F.B.I. have taken the fingerprints from the dead terrorists and once the identity is confirmed we will be issuing a $500,000 US cheque to Joe Ferguson. I'll leave you with my secretary now."

Rae Jones gives the secretary the list of twenty-one names to record. The Ambassador's secretary had previously activated twenty satellite phones. After recording the information on the computer, the secretary runs twenty-one photocopies. He activates the last phone and programs in the codes. The secretary gives twenty-one satellite phones and twenty-one photocopies to Rae.

The closest stop is the trailer of Andre Prichard where Rae leaves two satellite phones, warning him about the danger of being traced if they phone anyone not on the list and to make all calls only between the satellite phones. The three have their disguises removed. Shannon Johansen retrieves her vehicle and drives home with five satellite phones. Alex Johansen will give Maurice and Kathleen Solinger their phones tomorrow.

Shannon changes then places a phone call.

"Rene Dubois."

"Shannon Johansen here. Would you have more information on the Joe Ferguson case I could use?"

"Yes I do. Jean Perrault had a heart attack this morning shortly after Marc Leblanc phoned him. He's in intensive care right now but the prognosis is that he will not recover. He was discovered in the Sheraton Hotel this afternoon by one of the staff. The investigation turned up four cigarettes, two with lipstick on them. We found body fluids on the sheets and on some tissues in the wastebasket. I would hazard a guess that his girl friend left him when he had the heart attack, although she may have left sooner. The Federal Government posted bail of a quarter of a million dollars each for three of the C.S.I.S. agents charged with conspiracy to commit murder. The fourth C.S.I.S. agent, Cecil Mann, although his bail is only ten thousand dollars, the government refused to post his bail. Cecil Mann is not charged with attempted murder but is charged with illegal entry and attempting a false arrest. The arrest document, signed by Jean Perrault weighed heavily in favor of Cecil Mann. I'm afraid C.S.I.S. will be putting somebody into the jail to kill him tonight and that will end the cases against Leblanc and Perrault."

"That would be a travesty of justice. I'll see if we can help him. Thank you for the information. I'll talk to you tomorrow."

Shannon quickly writes the article for the newspaper, faxes it to the Ottawa Citizen, and then phones the news editor. A few minutes later, she's on the phone to Rae Jones.

"Hello, Rae here."

"It's Shannon. The C.S.I.S. agent that confessed implicating Jean Perrault and Marc Leblanc is still in jail. The policeman handling the case, Rene Dubois, believes that C.S.I.S. will plant somebody in the jail tonight to kill him and that will end the case against Perrault and Leblanc. Is there anything we can do to help him?"

"I'd like to see the confession before I do anything. Would the policeman let me look at it tonight?"

"I have a copy of the confession."

"I won't ask how you got it. Can you bring it to the Roy residence at 12 Java Street? I'll be waiting there for Marcel to arrive."

Rae proceeds to the Jackson residence to drop off five phones. He will deliver three phones to the Roy residence and the last four to his partners at the office tomorrow morning.

Arriving home, Joe Ferguson contacts his wife in Toronto, informing Eileen of the developments early that morning.

"You killed three men!"

"Three terrorists. The father has a $500,000 price tag on his head. The other two were his sons. They were probably paid by C.S.I.S. to kill us, or they could have been there because they like the work they were trained to do."

"I'm coming home!"

"You'll be alone," Joe replies coolly. "I've booked off for a week and I need some time alone. If you do come home, you can start cleaning up the blood of the dead terrorist and his two sons in the bedrooms and hallway. We'll probably receive the reward money that the American Government has offered for the terrorist.

"That's blood money! We're not touching it!"

"Speak for yourself. I'm going to pay off the mortgage and replace the blood soaked and slashed mattresses, bedding and carpeting upstairs."

"You had no business resisting them like that. I should have been at home. I would have given them what they wanted and they would have left."

"Yes I know you would have. They wanted us dead and you would have delivered us to the killers. It's time you grew up. Put your mother on."

"They didn't want us dead!"

"I have to talk to Angie. Put her on the phone."

"They didn't want us dead!"

"Either put Angie on the phone or I'm hanging up."

Joe informs Angie about the latest developments and asks, "Do you still have that 32 caliber revolver?"

"Yes I do."

"Keep it loaded and close. Only Eileen doesn't believe they're playing for keeps. She just told me I had no business killing the terrorists who were trying to kill me. I'm afraid, with her attitude, she will be instrumental in getting the boys and me killed, and I'm not going to allow that. Previously she condemned the man for shooting the C.S.I.S. agent who was firing his gun at Jerry."

"I heard her. I can't believe how stupid she's acting. Right now she's the best friend your enemies have."

"I have to talk to the boys now Angie. I'll phone you back in a few days."

Joe talks to his parents and the boys in Belle River, Ontario, assuring them he is fine. While talking to his father, Joe warns Peter to be very observant. He's extremely worried C.S.I.S. will find out where the boys are and make an attempt to kill them, but realizes at the present time they're safer in Belle River than they would be in Ottawa.

Posting Bail

Marcel Roy accesses, from his car, the Wi-Fi-equipped computers of the terrorists. Using the "Trojan Horse Program", he downloads information from the Immigration Department files to his I-Pod. After taking delivery of the bank records on the Montreal accounts Marcel stops outside the home of Hamed Ahmidam. With his computer, he transfers the $2.213 million from the illegal Joe Ferguson account in the Carling Avenue Royal Bank. Marcel transfers $31,500 to each of the fifty-six terrorist accounts in Montreal and then transfers the last $449,000 in the Ferguson account to the seven Hamed Ahmidam accounts in Ottawa.

Rae Jones and Marcel Roy, after perusing the confession, decide it could be in their best interest to post the bond for Cecil Mann. Phoning Rene Dubois, Rae arranges to meet the detective at the City Police Headquarters located at 474 Elgin Street. Marcel removes the bond money from his safe, located in the basement of the Roy residence, and gives Rae the funds necessary to post the bond to extricate Cecil Mann from the dilemma he now faces.

"I don't want the policemen or the C.S.I.S. agent to see me like this," Marcel explains. "I'll have to miss the fun. Can you find a secure place for the C.S.I.S. agent for the night and we will make further plans for his safety tomorrow?"

"He can stay with us tonight." Rae decides. "Andrea and I have a spare bedroom."

Detective Dubois helps Rae Jones with the paperwork to release the prisoner while Detective Marcel St. Croix brings Cecil to the desk Rene is using. Rene activates the recorder to tape phone conversations from this desk.

"Anybody curious about the prisoner leaving?" Rene asks his partner, Marcel St. Croix.

"Yes. The two bikers. The one asked where he was going. I said 'home'. The second one asked 'how come he got to leave'. I said 'he posted bail'. They didn't look too pleased when we left."

Rene speaks to Rae and Shannon, "I figured they had a hit on for tonight. Take Mann and meet us at his apartment. Marcel and I will be planning a surprise if they show up tonight. Make sure Mann leaves his car at the apartment. Shannon, I need you to stay here for a few minutes to tie up the wall phone."

Rae and Andrea Jones and Cecil Mann leave the Elgin Street Police Station while Rene Dubois and Marcel St. Croix requisition a pair of 12-gauge pump shotguns. Marcel places them in the police car and waits while Rene visits with the dispatcher. Soon a guard speaks to Rene.

"There's a prisoner that wants to speak to his lawyer. He's starting to raise quite a fuss."

"Lets go back there and I'll bring him out to make his phone call."

Rene escorts the prisoner into the office area of the lockup only to find the pay phone in use.

"Stay in that chair until you can use the pay phone or you can use the phone on that desk if you don't want to wait."

Rene again walks over to the dispatcher to continue his conversation. The prisoner waits for a few minutes, watching Shannon Johansen, but the lady shows no inclination to stop talking, so he picks up the phone on Rene's desk and dials.

"Marc Leblanc."

"Bob here. Mann just made bail. The pig said he was going home. We couldn't do anything so I figured we better let you know."

"Okay. Thanks for the information. We'll take care of the problem."

The prisoner is again locked in his cell for the night.

Rene listens to the tape, plays it a second time for Shannon and the dispatcher, then locks it in the desk.

Marc Leblanc places a phone call to one of his C.S.I.S. agents.

"Hello. Donald Prince here."

"Marc Leblanc here. Mann just made bail. Can you take care of him tonight?"

"Consider it done. I'll give Dugan a call."

"Get rid of the body. I don't want it found."

"There's a cot in the sick bay if you want to sleep for a few hours," Rene informs Shannon. "I'll wake you when we return and give you the story."

At the apartment, Cecil Mann shows Rene Dubois to his suite. Marcel St. Croix parks the police car in a different apartment block and Rae Jones drives him back to Cecil's apartment. Rae and Andrea, along with Cecil Mann, leave for the Jones residence while Rene and Marcel prepare the suite for their visitors' arrival.

Two more constables arrive and are dispatched to the suite next door. The apartment dwellers from that unit had been previously located in a motel.

Rene lies down behind the chesterfield and sleeps for an hour then Marcel sleeps for the next hour. The time is approaching two o'clock when they hear a light scratching noise at the door. The door opens quietly and the two C.S.I.S. agents creep silently down the hall and enter the bedroom. There are two pops of a silenced 22 and then cursing. Marcel pushes the entrance door making it slam shut. With the shotguns pointed down the hallway, Rene addresses the two C.S.I.S. agents.

"Good morning Roger Dugan and Donald Prince. This is your friendly Ottawa Police Detectives making their morning wake up call." Rene's voice becomes authoritive. "Throw your weapons into the hallway and exit the room with your hands raised."

"Go to hell," is the epithet Prince hollers at the policemen.

Rene speaks into his cell phone. "Bang on the wall."

Prince and Dugan hear a muffled thumping on the party wall in the bedroom.

"What's that noise?"

"Bang three more times."

Thump, thump, thump.

More cursing from the bedroom.

The door to the suite opens and a voice says, "Can we come in Rene?"

"Yes, come ahead."

The closing of the door has the sound of finality to the C.S.I.S. agents.

"How is everyone positioned?"

"Willy's in the bedroom next door in case they try to exit via the party wall, two more cops (non-existent) are stationed in the hallway, and we're in here. Everybody is wearing kevlar vests and armed with shotguns."

There is whispering. The C.S.I.S. agents realize the firepower of their handguns is no match against the firepower of the shotguns held by the Ottawa City Police. A 45 calibre Glock automatic is thrown into the hallway followed by another 45 Glock, then a 22 automatic with a silencer still attached is slid into the hallway. A moment later two hands extend from the doorway and an agent exits the bedroom with his hands raised. He is searched and handcuffed.

Rene addresses the second C.S.I.S. agent. "Your turn Prince."

Prince leaves the bedroom cursing the police and the dilemma he finds himself in. The police search and handcuff him.

"Marcel, you and Willy bring up the cars while we read these two their rights. Bring the camera from the glove box when you return. The two constables in the hallway can leave once you return."

Rene takes pictures of the guns, and then takes a picture of the powder burns and holes in Tom Jackson's foam head, leaving all the evidence for the forensic specialists to collect.

At the station, the prisoners are booked and incarcerated. Shannon photographs the C.S.I.S. agents, and then Rene gives her the information on the arrest.

"If you follow us Shannon you can take photographs of the arrest of Marc Leblanc for his part in the conspiracy to kill Cecil Mann. I'll be taking him into custody as soon as the warrants arrive."

Shannon Johansen, not taking any chances on missing the arrest, is the first to arrive at the Leblanc residence, stopping a short distance from the house. Two police cars pull up in front of the Leblanc residence with their lights out. As Shannon walks towards the house, Rene steps out of the car and places a phone call, using the cell phone belonging to Donald Prince.

"How did you make out Don?"

No answer.

"Well?" Leblanc growls, "Did you get rid of Mann?"

"This is constable Rene Dubois of the Ottawa Police Force. You are under arrest for conspiracy to murder Cecil Mann. We are waiting outside your front door. Come quietly or we will use force."

The Ottawa Police turn on their wigwags and headlights.

Leblanc answers after a minutes hesitation. "I'll get dressed and will be right out."

Shannon Johansen takes the photographs of Marc Leblanc's arrest. At her desk in the Ottawa Citizen, she completes her news article and presents it to the editor.

June 28, 2001.

Yesterday three Canadian Security and Intelligence Service agents, Marc Leblanc, Roger Dugan and Donald Prince were arrested for the conspiracy to kill Joe Ferguson. A C.S.I.S. agent, Cecil Mann, admitted to his part in the plot and implicated Marc Leblanc, The head of the Ottawa division of the Canadian Security and Intelligence Service, and Jean Perrault, Senior Official of the Canadian Security and Intelligence Service, as the instigators of the plot. The three agents were held on $250,000 bail each, which was paid by the Federal Government. This morning Roger Dugan and Donald Prince were arrested while attempting to kill Cecil Mann in his own apartment. A short time later Marc Leblanc was arrested for ordering the attempted murder of Cecil Mann. What right does the Federal Government have to spend taxpayers' money to pay the bail of agents charged with conspiracy to commit murder? Will the Federal Government be paying the bail on the second attempted *murder by these same members of the Federal Justice System? Why do the agents of the Canadian Security and Intelligence Service believe they are above the very law they are supposed to uphold and protect?*

Shannon Johansen

"I believe we'll be transferring you to police reporter Shannon. This news reporting is excellent. You seem to have the inside track on everything important happening at the Ottawa Police Department. I'll take care of this article immediately."

The House of Parliament

Shannon Johansen takes a copy of her news article and drives home for a couple of hours sleep. After a quick shower, she heads for the House of Parliament. Inside the building, she speaks to a Page.

"I wish to speak to the Justice Critic for the Alliance Party, Terry McIntyre."

"I believe he will be in his office at the present time. Will you come with me please?"

The Page leads Shannon through a maze of corridors and into an office. Speaking to the secretary Shannon learns the Justice Critic is in. Shannon thanks the Page who leaves to attend to other duties. The name on the desk of the secretary is Thomas Jones Jr.

"My name is Shannon Johansen. I'm a reporter for the Ottawa citizen. Could I please speak to Terry McIntyre? I have pertinent information for the Justice Critic to use during question period today."

The son of the Leader of the Alliance Party knows whom Shannon is and has orders to keep all reporters away from the Justice Critic at this time. 'This nosy reporter won't be giving McIntyre any material for today's Question Period.'

"You don't have an appointment. You won't be able to see him today,"

"It's imperative that I speak to him."

"In your mind it's imperative that you see him. He's too busy to see you."

"Your attitude is atrocious," Shannon admonishes the secretary. "I will talk to him."

"I told you he's too busy. Now get the hell out of my office right now."

Shannon is angry. She stalks over to the door of the Justice Critic and begins to open it. The secretary grabs her from behind and slams her into the doorjamb, ripping her blouse. Falling to the floor, she rolls and rises to her feet. The angry secretary grabs her again. Stepping close, Shannon drives her knee into his groin. As he releases her, she drives her fist into his nose. Blood flies from the smashed appendage.

Terry McIntyre, witnessing the event, hollers, "**Stop that!**" and rises from his chair.

Shannon drops her guard and glances at Terry McIntyre, then catches a glimpse of the secretary stepping in and swinging. Stepping to the side and blocking the blow with her arm, she drives the toe of her shoe into her aggressor's throat. The secretary crumbles. Justice Critic secretary Thomas Jones Jr. never expected this kind of response from any lady, but Shannon Johansen has proven to be the solid 5'7", 170-pound adversary this 220-pound bully couldn't handle.

A call to the infirmary and the secretary is removed for treatment.

Terry McIntyre removes a shirt from a cabinet drawer and hands it to Shannon. "Would you step into my office? I will require a record of what transpired. I wish to apologize for the conduct of my secretary. He will be gone from my office today."

Activating an office recorder Terry McIntyre begins dictating, "My door started to open and then slammed open wide as I observed Thomas Jones Jr. smash a young lady against the door jamb of my office, knocking her to the floor, and tearing her blouse."

Terry continues with his dissertation telling the story as it had unfolded.

Terry McIntyre holds the mike out for Shannon to speak. "My name is Shannon Johansen. I informed the secretary of the Alliance Justice Critic I had pertinent information for the Justice Critic to use during Question Period today."

She relates the entire episode into the office recorder.

"Your pretty good at defending yourself," Terry tells Shannon. "Did you take martial arts?"

"Yes. It was fun in my early teen years. I could wup all the boys, but they ruined it by growing up. I still train a couple of times a week when I'm not playing softball or basketball. It helps to keep me in condition and control my weight."

"I enjoyed watching you handle Jones but he'll probably beat his wife again tonight. He's a real bully if the other person is small enough."

Presenting her news article to the Justice Critic, Shannon Johansen informs him, "This is the information I wanted you to have for today."

Terry McIntyre reads the report very carefully, then reads it again. "I will be addressing this information on the floor of the House of Commons during Question Period. There is an excellent chance I will be losing the Justice Critic Portfolio over this."

"Why would that happen?"

"Tom Jones was livid over my accusations yesterday during question period. He contends we have no business hitting the Liberal party with those questions. He informed me if I ever humiliate the Liberal party again, without the Alliance Caucus first scrutinizing the questions he would remove me from the position of Justice Critic. Yesterday he attempted to stop me from acting on your article. I'm not going to give him a chance to veto this exposé.

Shannon sits in the Visitors' Gallery.

"Speaker of the House."

"The House of Commons begins Question Period."

Terry McIntyre rises and stands by his desk.

"The House now recognizes the Honorable Member from Calgary West."

"Mr. Speaker. I have a short newspaper article I wish to read to the house and then I wish to ask three questions posed by the author and one question of my own."

"Mr. Speaker. Yesterday three Canadian Security and Intelligence Service agents, Marc Leblanc, Roger Dugan and Donald Prince were arrested and charged with conspiracy to kill Joseph Ferguson. A fourth C.S.I.S. agent, Cecil Mann, admitted his part in the plot and implicated Marc Leblanc, The head of the Ottawa Division of the Canadian Security and Intelligence Service, and Jean Perrault, Senior Official of the Canadian Security and Intelligence Service, as the instigators of the plot. Three agents, Marc Leblanc, Roger Dugan and Donald Prince were held on $250,000 bail each, which the Federal Government paid."

"Mr. Speaker. This morning Roger Dugan and Donald Prince were arrested while attempting to kill Cecil Mann, the witness who implicated Marc Leblanc and Jean Perrault in the attempted murder of Joe Ferguson. A short time later Marc Leblanc was arrested for ordering the attempted murder of Cecil Mann."

"Mr. Speaker. The first question posed by Shannon Johansen is directed to the Honorable Prime Minister. By what right does the Federal Government spend taxpayers' money to pay the bail of agents charged with conspiracy to commit murder?"

"The House now recognizes the Honorable Prime Minister."

"Mr. Speaker. I did not know their bail was paid by the Federal Government."

"Mr. Speaker. I will have the Honorable Minister of Finance look into the matter and report back to the house on his findings."

Foot stomping, clapping and applause from the Liberal bench for the profound answer by their honorable leader.

"The House now recognizes the Honorable Member from Calgary West."

"Mr. Speaker. The second question asked by Shannon Johansen is directed to the Honorable Prime Minister. Will the Federal Government be paying the bail on the second attempted murder by these same members of the Justice Department?"

"The House now recognizes the Honorable Prime Minister."

"Mr. Speaker. I will pass this information on to the Honorable Minister of Justice and ask him to make a ruling on this matter."

More applause and desk thumping by the Liberal faithful.

"The House now recognizes the Honorable Member from Calgary West."

"Mr. Speaker. The third question posed by Shannon Johansen is directed to the Honorable Prime Minister."

"Mr. Speaker. Why do the agents of the Canadian Security and Intelligence Service believe they are above the very laws they are paid to uphold?"

"The House now recognizes the Honorable Prime Minister."

"Mr. Speaker. I have no way of knowing what the C.S.I.S. agents believe."

More applause and desk thumping.

"The House now recognizes the Honorable Member from Calgary West."

"Mr. Speaker. This last question is my own."

"Mr. Speaker. Are these attempted murders of Joseph Ferguson, a worker in the Department of Immigration and Cecil Mann, the agent assigned to the case part of a botched cover-up of criminal activities by this Federal Government?"

Booing and heckling by the Liberal faithful.

"The House now recognizes the Honorable Prime Minister."

"Mr. Speaker. I have done nothing wrong. The Canadian Secrecy Act prevents me from commenting further on this matter but I can assure you we will be looking into it with all our resources." He begins to gather up papers. "I have important business elsewhere and cannot answer any more questions at this time."

More applause and desk thumping as the Prime Minister leaves the floor of the House of Commons.

Shannon Johansen has been watching Tom Jones, the leader of the Alliance Party. He is livid and can barely control himself. She returns to the Ottawa Citizen and writes about the demeanor of the Leader of the Opposition during question period and the imminent firing of the Alliance Justice critic. Before finishing the article, Shannon receives a phone call from McIntyre and amends the article to read of his firing.

At the close of question period, Alliance Party members converge on Terry McIntyre, congratulating him on the questions he asked during the question session.

Tom Jones walks past the entourage and growls "Be in my office in five minutes."

Puzzled by the tone of the retort from the opposition leader Amiel Gill asks, "What's his problem?"

"He's going to fire me as the Alliance Justice Critic."

"Why would he fire you? Your questions today made this Liberal Government look guilty in the actions of C.S.I.S"

"Yesterday he ordered me not to ask the questions I did. Afterwards he warned me not to continue along this vein of questioning and to clear any questions I plan to ask in the future with him."

A large gathering of Alliance members are listening intently to the exchange.

"What reason would he have to fire you Terry?" Inquires Amiel Gill.

"When I asked the last question about the botched cover-up in the Federal Government I hit a sore spot with both Tom Jones and the Prime Minister. I believe I got too close to the truth."

"Do you believe he is involved in something crooked?"

"There's something crooked going on at the Department of Immigration and I plan to find out who's involved. "

Terry McIntyre, Amiel Gill, and another five members of the Alliance Party walk to the office of the leader of the opposition. Terry McIntyre taps on the door, and walks in, leaving the door open. Waiting are Tom Jones and Tom Jones Jr. sporting a taped nose.

"Don't bother sitting down. You're fired from the Justice Critic Portfolio."

"What's your involvement in the Department of Immigration?" queries McIntyre.

Suddenly flustered Tom Jones begins to ask, "How did you...? What are you talking about? How could I be involved in anything in the Department of Immigration?"

Terry McIntyre turns and speaks to Tom Jones Jr.

"Your face doesn't look very good. The young lady inflicted a real ass kicking on you in my office. I presume you'll feel better after you beat your wife tonight."

Tom Jones Jr. storms out of his chair but stops short of swinging at McIntyre. McIntyre gives him a contemptuous look, then leaves the room.

Money, Money Everywhere

Early on the morning of June 28, Marcel Roy is carefully removing all electronic traces from the C.S.I.S. bank account computers of the $2.213 million transaction between the C.S.I.S. account and the illegal Joe Ferguson account in the Carling Avenue Royal Bank. He is surprised to learn the C.S.I.S. account again contains close to $2.5 million. The Ferguson account has the $1.764 million transferred from that account to the terrorist accounts of the Maple Hill Mob in Montreal. He removes the electronic transfer records of the $2.213 million deposit into the Carling Ave. bank. The next move is to remove the electronic trail showing the money transferred out of the Ferguson account to the fifty-six Montreal accounts and the seven Hamed Ahmidam accounts. Leaving the Wi-Fi-equipped computer in the Hamed Ahmidam residence, Marcel visits each of the seven banks where he has established accounts under the Hamed Ahmidam alias, withdrawing the $68,000 from each account and notifying the financial institutions he will be withdrawing a further $64,000 on Friday. Driving home, he locks the money in his safe. Marcel removes his disguise, cleans up and changes. From there it's back to the "Trojan Horse Program." Over the next few days he will repeat the process in the financial institutions and empty the Hamed Ahmidam accounts a second time.

A New Client

Rae drives Cecil back to his apartment, and then proceeds to his office at Carlingwood Plaza. Cecil's first concern is to retrieve his 9mm. American Eagle Luger and a box of 9mm. ammunition. Removing the weapon from the gun case he puts on the shoulder harness, then loading the Luger he places it in the holster. The American Eagle is an excellent automatic, which he prefers to the 45-calibre Glock, standard issue of C.S.I.S. Folding clothing into suitcases and boxes he places them in his car to take with him. After contacting a moving and storage company to store the remainder of his belongings, he has a cleaning company come in. Explaining the problems of the previous evening to the management of the apartment, they agree to terminate the lease immediately. They have no desire to hold him to his lease with the eminent possibility of another shooting occurring on the premises nor will they provide security to the building.

The law firm of Jones, Watson and Smythe hold a meeting and agree to represent Cecil Mann at his criminal trial. Rae then speaks to Joe Ferguson and Tom Jackson.

"Last night we were informed C.S.I.S. planted two assassins in the police holding cells to kill Cecil Mann. Marcel, Shannon and I read Mann's confession, which you have in front of you. We agreed to pay his bail. At this time, Mann is more dangerous to their plans than Joe ever could be. He never dreamed the leaders of C.S.I.S. were lying to him and were planning to execute him."

"Cecil was informed the proper warrants to arrest Joe were in an attaché case they had with them when they came to your home to kill you."

"I saw Rene open the case and shove it under the noses of the two C.S.I.S. agents just prior to arresting them," Joe acknowledges. "They were arguing pretty heatedly when Tom and I stepped in."

"Marc Leblanc previously informed Cecil, court orders were granted to C.S.I.S. to install the surveillance devices in Joe's home, in our office, and in Joe's office. Last night he acknowledged cutting the wires to the video camera and removing audio surveillance equipment from Joe's phone in the office. Cecil observed the audio/video surveillance recorders in Pierre Montague's office when he removed the wiring running to the equipment."

"This morning, Montague lost his temper when Rene and Marcel entered his office with a search warrant. His attitude deteriorated when they confiscated the illegal recording devices. Then they charged him."

"Montague never expected that development," Joe acknowledges. "I would have loved to see it. He doesn't get taken down very often."

"Cecil was presented with false evidence to prove Joe granted Landed Immigration Status to various terrorists, allowing them to enter Canada illegally. He was told Joe would be arrested to stop the illegal operation that's bringing terrorists into Canada. Joe was to be incarcerated while they completed their investigation and were able to bring more charges against him."

"Cecil realizes he could be going to jail for his part in the illegal operation against Joe even though he believed at the time the investigation was legal. He knew he had been lied to about the whole operation when he saw the knife in the hand of the terrorist entering the bedroom at the top of the stairs. Cecil hollered in a vain attempt to warn you. He was relieved to see you outside and alive and to learn from me the rest of the family was away during the ordeal."

"After Cecil was released on bail last night the police set up a sting operation in his suite and re-arrested the two C.S.I.S. agents. Rene Dubois had enough evidence to also re-arrest Marc Leblanc. This time the Judge refused to grant bail for the three men.

"Do you believe the C.S.I.S. agent?" Tom questions Rae.

"Yes I do. He knows he needs our help because both C.S.I.S. and the R.C.M.P. will be trying to kill him. That bullet in the back by his supposed partner was no accident."

Joe is thinking back to the early morning hours when the terrorists charged into the bedrooms.

"I heard a man holler just as the door slammed open. I assumed it was one of the terrorists venting a war cry."

Tom interrupts the conversation.

"Even with the taped conversation between Montague and Perrault it's still hard to trust a man who was sneaking around trying to gain evidence on you yesterday Fergie. I guess he was only doing his job and he did honestly believe that you were a criminal. We can't really blame him for the criminal actions of his superiors."

"That's true enough. Right now, I'm in a quandary worrying about the boys and I think Cecil Mann is the answer. He would certainly protect them far better than could my parents. C.S.I.S. and the R.C.M.P. wouldn't be looking for Cecil in Belle River, but Cecil would be looking for anybody who would hurt the boys for his own protection."

"Your right." Rae continues, "the last place C.S.I.S. would look for Cecil is with your sons. Another advantage, Cecil's training includes surveillance work. He is much more likely to respond to any unusual actions by other individuals than are the boys or your parents. Could you arrange for Cecil to stay with your parents Joe?"

"It's on a farm near Windsor. I'll give you the phone number and directions after I confirm everything with my parents. I will also package the satellite phones for the boys. He can deliver them."

Rae Jones invites Marlene Moore into his office. "We have decided to represent Cecil Mann in the court action against him on the charges of illegal entry into the Joe Ferguson residence."

"What about the attempted murder charges?"

Rae eases Marlene's worries. "He knew nothing about the attempted murder and believed the operation was for the arrest of Joe Ferguson to stop the illegal immigration of terrorists into Canada."

"Mr. Ferguson has to be stopped."

"Joe isn't the person involved in the criminal activity. His crime was learning about the criminal actions of his superiors in the Immigration Department. We believe that Pierre Montague, head of the Department of Immigration and Jean Perrault, head of the Canadian Security and Intelligence Service are two of the parties involved but it has to be a much larger operation than just those two. When they decided to kill Joe Ferguson they also had to kill Cecil Mann because he knew too much and could hurt their operation."

Marlene is suddenly relieved. "You are saying, Mr. Jones, Cecil knew nothing about the attempt to kill Mr. Ferguson when he went to the house."

"We would not have put up his bail if we didn't believe him. He was used by C.S.I.S. but would not commit murder and his superiors knew that. He no longer has any illusions about the integrity of C.S.I.S. or the Federal Government. He will be here shortly to give us a statement, then he will have to hide from C.S.I.S. and the R.C.M.P."

"He could hide at my apartment."

"The Justice Department knows about your place. C.S.I.S. will know every phone call you make and every phone call you receive. The same will hold true of Cecil's phone. It's imperative they kill Cecil. One call between you will seal his fate."

Bob Watson opens the door to Rae's office, "Cecil Mann has arrived, we're meeting in the conference room."

"We require your cell phone." Cecil hands William his cell phone, which William turns off. "Because the phone was turned on there is the possibility of C.S.I.S. agents waiting for you in the parking lot."

"I never thought of that."

"They did," William interjects. "You will be carrying two phones with you to Joe Ferguson's sons. The only numbers you will need are **01, and **03 which will reach Rae and myself. The numbers between the two phones are **19 and **20. No calls will ever, under any circumstance be made between those phones and land phones or cell phones for your own safety."

There is a tap at the door, and then Mary Watson opens the door.

Bob speaks to his wife.

"Good, you're here. Cecil, do you have anything you need in your car?"

"My clothes."

"Let's change them over to the station wagon."

"I'm keeping the Lexus."

Rae admonishes Cecil, "How many days do you plan to stay alive if you continue driving the Lexus?"

"I see what you mean. I'm going to have to change my way of thinking completely. I'll have to constantly remind myself to remain inconspicuous, because maintaining constant vigilance is my only protection."

"There might be hope for you yet," Bob interjects.

Cecil places his clothes in the blue station wagon. Mary Watson drives the Lexus home and parks it in the garage. Bob parks the station wagon with the lawyers' cars behind their offices.

In the office, William addresses Cecil, "Before you leave change into something more casual. That suit will be a bit too obvious in the station wagon. How is your money situation?"

"I withdrew $6,300 from my account. I'd better destroy my credit cards and bank card because C.S.I.S. will use them to find me."

"Leave your bank card and code with us." Rae continues with his explanation, "The odd small purchase around town will keep them thinking your still in Ottawa and they won't think to widen the search. We'll require all the information you can give us to properly represent you."

Cecil relates everything he knows in his statement to the lawyers. After changing, he talks to Marlene for a short time. Cecil feels guilty while stopping at the Ferguson residence before heading for the Peter Ferguson farm west of Windsor, Ontario. Resisting the urge to speed, Cecil sets the cruise control. Stopping for the night at the Tilbury Rest Station, he sleeps fitfully – events of the last few days have invaded his dreams. He arrives at the farm outside the town of Belle River early the following morning.

Wheels Within Wheels

Marcel enters the U.S. Embassy compound and asks to speak to Ambassador Henry Kilmer. A marine escorts him to the Ambassador's secretary, who presents him to the Ambassador.

"Please sit down Mr. Marcel Roy, Canadian Student at Large."

Marcel smiles at the quip from the Ambassador. "We've discovered a false bank account, established by the Canadian Security and Intelligence Service, made out in the name of Joseph Ferguson. They will use that account to continue to persecute Joe. I removed the money and all trace of the funds ever being in the account. Tomorrow Joe is planning to open a new account in the same bank with a legitimate check for $526,000 Canadian. We were hoping we could give you $526,000 in cash and have your government issue a cheque for $526,000 Canadian, made out in the name of Joseph Ferguson, showing it as payment for the death of the terrorist, Abu Zubaydah. We expect them to arrest Joe Ferguson but he will have proof that the account is legitimate and the courts will exonerate him. We plan to show this is another government blunder in a long list of government fiascos."

"It should work," the American Ambassador agrees. "I'm going to keep my eyes on the Canadian Press and see if it does. C.S.I.S.

has surely looked like an ass in their efforts to persecute Joe Ferguson and their efforts have made your federal government appear culpable. Before you give me any funds let me make a phone call."

The Ambassador places the call, and then addresses Marcel. "I won't require your money. The dead terrorist is Abu Zubaydah. I'll issue the check for you right now. What about the rest of the funds?"

"If the Fergusons have to flee to the U.S. they'll have funds waiting for them. I have more terrorist information on my I-Pod to download onto your computer."

Ambassador Kilmer rises from his chair, We'll see if my secretary is still here."

The secretary has left. Marcel sits down at the computer and begins to work the mouse and keyboard. The Ambassador smiles and steps behind Marcel, knowing that it is impossible to access the computer without proper codes. The smile disappears. Marcel brings up the program and begins downloading. He again operates the computer and stops with the mouse curser sitting on the send button.

"Do you wish to press the send button?"

"Where is it going?" asks the Ambassador.

Marcel is grinning. "The anti-terrorist files in the F.B.I. offices in Washington."

"You accessed the F.B.I. files!"

Marcel depresses the send button, and then files the terrorist information in the embassy computer.

Take Care

On the evening of June 28, 2001, eighteen members of the Maple Hill Mob meet in their hideaway. Andre Prichard is applying the disguises to the people in attendance. He has fourteen disguises, creating duplicate terrorists, to apply tonight and his wife's disguise tomorrow morning.

Using this opportunity, Marcel addresses them.

"You have all been given satellite phones for your personal safety. Use them to contact each other, and keep the calls strictly business. I cannot stress strongly enough the danger of using these phones to dial cell phones or land line phones. These phones are our only means of communicating with each other without putting all our lives at risk. We must never at any time put any person at risk because C.S.I.S. and the R.C.M.P. will be looking for the smallest mistake on our part and they have the resources to capitalize on any miscues."

"I think you're being paranoid," Marie Prichard proclaims, "and you're being far too dramatic."

Marcel takes a folder from his briefcase. From the folder he places a picture of the comatose Matt Spence in front of Marie Prichard. The second picture is Abu Zubaydah, lying face down on the bed his back covered in blood. The third picture is 19-year-old Omar Zubaydah with his back covered in blood. Fourth is 16-year-old Shaukat Zubaydah, his throat ripped out by the shotgun blast, his face and torso covered in blood. He then lays out close up pictures of the four fatal wounds. Marie grabs her mouth and scrambles for the bathroom. After cleaning up, Marie returns slowly to her seat and sits down, pushing the pictures away from her sight. Her features are still pallid and her motions unsteady, but she is ready to continue. Her natural color is beginning to return.

"These four men's deaths are the direct result of one intercepted telephone call.... One call.... Had we been complacent Joe and Eileen Ferguson would be dead instead of those three professional assassins and the C.S.I.S. agent."

Everybody is silent as Marcel Roy places the photographs back in his briefcase.

Planning to make withdrawals when the banks open Friday morning, fourteen Arabic "terrorists" are driving on Ontario Highway 417 towards Montreal.

The female Arabic terrorists all wear the traditional Muslim abaya, hijab, and niqab. They wear brown contact lenses and the mid eastern hue to their faces, hands, arms and legs hides their true skin color.

Rae Jones and Alex Johansen are wearing the classic Muslim hairstyle and beard, and wearing the disha dasha and the juba. On their heads, they wear the shora held in place with the egal. Tom Jackson and Maurice Solinger are resplendent in their heavy black, curly beards and wigs. They wear traditional western clothing but also wear the Muslim juba and the kufi. Henri Roy and Joseph Ferguson have heavy black beards and wigs. They wear the disha dasha and the mens' abaya and on their heads is the traditional turban cloth. All the men in this terrorist organization have the dark skin and brown eyes of their female counterparts.

By eight o'clock Marcel, accessing the Montreal terrorist accounts through the Hamed Ahmidam 'Wi-Fi-equipped' computer, learns which accounts already have funds deposited in them from the illegal Joe Ferguson account. He notifies the members of the Maple Hill Mob the financial institutions to visit first to begin their withdrawals. Marcel once again works the 'Trojan Horse Program'. When the banks in Ottawa open for business, he begins making withdrawals from the Hamed Ahmidam accounts.

By late afternoon funds from the last Montreal bank accounts have been withdrawn, and are on their way to Ottawa. The 'terrorists" have squirreled $2,400 from each account and informed the banks they will be withdrawing $29,000 on the following banking day. Tuesday, July 2nd, promises to be an excellent payday for the Maple Hill Mob.

William Smythe has a meeting with Rene Dubois, the city police detective in charge of the investigation into the attempted murder of Joe Ferguson, and the Crown Prosecutor on the case, Joshua Campbell. After two hours of intense scrutiny of the evidence in the investigation, the Crown drops the charges against Cecil Mann.

Friday afternoon the Prime Minister closes parliament. It will reconvene in the fall.

Marcel continues compiling the list of terrorists living in the Ottawa area. The more terrorist Wi-Fi-equipped computers he can access, the less chance of being discovered accessing his 'Trojan Horse Program'.

Early July 2nd, Marcel is again outside the Hamed Ahmidam residence transferring $2.012 million from the Ottawa C.S.I.S. account into the Montreal accounts and the Ottawa accounts of the aliases of the Maple Hill Mob. As the funds in the account drop below

$500,000, he is surprised to witness $2,000,000, suddenly jump into the account. He realizes the process is automatic. Transferring the last $32,000 to a Hamed Ahmidam account he carefully leaves the C.S.I.S. bank account.

Tuesday, the Maple Hill Mob withdraws the money from their Montreal bank accounts and informs the banks they will be making a withdrawal of $31,800 on July 4th. Leaving the last facility, they stop at an automatic teller to remove the last $100 from each account and turn the funds over to Henri Roy to put in his safe. Later this afternoon Marcel will remove all electronic traces of any funds ever being in the accounts.

Wednesday, July 3rd, carpet layers replace the carpet and underlay in the two bedrooms and the hallway in the Ferguson residence. Tom and Joe have already finished drywall patching and painting and the police have removed the bloody blankets, mattresses and pieces of carpet as evidence.

Visiting the Carling Avenue Royal Bank, Joe opens a new account by depositing the check he received from the U.S. Government for $526,000 in Canadian funds.

From the lists provided to the American government by Marcel Roy, the F.B.I. begin picking up terrorists and spiriting them across the border. Using the code name 'I spy', Marcel has been placing disinformation on the Internet, stating that Muslims were being arrested by the Canadian Department of Justice and held incognito then shipped to the US for remuneration from the US government. On Wednesday he states the next people disappearing would be Hamed Ahmidam, Mahboob al-Yawer, Basit Khawaja, Fazul Ghailani, Maha al-Hashimi, Salama Berwari and the identities of the rest of the male and female terrorist used as aliases by his partners in the money grab. They and their families go into hiding. The search for those particular terrorists by C.S.I.S. and the R.C.M.P. will intensify once they discover the Montreal and Ottawa bank records.

Thursday – the last day of the money grab. Marcel is attempting to make a left turn from the parking lot of the mini-mall where his sixth bank is located – he has one more withdrawal. A red sports car with the horn blaring, screeches to a halt behind him, the driver waving and hollering for him to get out of the way. Seeing Marcel looking at him through the mirror, the driver gives the one finger salute. Marcel slams the car into park and reaches for the door handle, forgetting for a moment he is dressed as an Arab. Still looking in the mirror he spies the bank teller who just helped him racing into the parking lot, looking wildly about, then racing back into the bank. Marcel puts the car in gear, switches the signal and carefully makes a right turn, slipping easily into the traffic. The sports car squeals out behind him, swings into the left lane and passes him, the horn blowing and the driver still waving a single digit. Marcel is too busy to worry, he is already on his satellite phone punching **14.

"Hello."

"Mom! C.S.I.S. is onto us! Get everybody out of the banks!"

"We're all finished. The Solingers are in one bathroom changing and the Joneses are in another.... Did I just hear a sigh?"

"Yes. A very loud one. I'm driving. We'll talk later tonight."

Marcel reflects momentarily on the operation, and is satisfied. The disguises worked in Ottawa and Montreal. They will work in Europe.

In the evenings, Marcel accesses chat rooms on the Internet, concentrating on groups using foreign tongues. His message, *who wishes to speak to I spy* is in both English and French. He has a hit in French.

I need information from I Spy.

What information?

Who are you?

Forget it!

Where do you get your information?

Too dangerous in a chat room, cautions I Spy.

Can you help us?

Again, too dangerous in a chat room.

What shall I do?

Leave the chat room and I will contact you.

Marcel types in the E-mail code s.al.y@aol.com. Then types, what do you want?

How did you find out C.S.I.S. was planning to arrest Mahboob al-Yawer?

None of your business! Get to the important questions.

Why are they after our people?

Greed! They're being paid for your family and friends.

They were paid once.

Greed! They want more. If you can't pay them the next time, the U.S. Government will. They'll take your money as long as you'll pay.

Will it ever stop?

Only when you are incarcerated in the U.S. unless you are willing to stop them yourself, warns I Spy. I'll contact you tomorrow with specific information. If you're not willing to act on the information, to guarantee your own safety, that will be our last contact.

The following evening, Marcel, accessing a terrorist's 'Wi-Fi-equipped computer, types this message for Salama al-Yawer. *You have two people whose demise will greatly slow down the actions of the Federal Government selling your confederates to the US Government. The first name is Guy Trembley, head of the R.C.M.P.* Marcel lists the home and *office addresses of Guy Trembley. He is instrumental in the collection of those individuals to be turned over to U.S. authorities and receives a large portion of the funds collected. When I hear of his liquidation I will give you the name of the individual choosing your people. If I hear nothing I will know you do not wish to secure your families personal safety, and I will not bother contacting you again.*

Get your brother out of Kingston – The R.C.M.P. has his address.
Print this information and delete it from your hard drive.
Marcel types in the E-mail code s.al.y@aol.com.
Salama al-Yawer types, *do you have information for us?*
Marcel hits send.

Members of the F.B.I. posing as R.C.M.P raid a safe house in Kingston. Two terrorists, failing to heed the warning, are whisked over the river and disappear.

The rest of the week is spent with Andre Prichard taking passport photographs of the 18 members of the Maple Hill Mob and then photographing them in their disguises for their alias passport photos. Keith and Jerry Ferguson send their passport photos from a library in Windsor via the Internet to the Prichards' home computer. Andre works on those photographs to perfect their disguises. The photographs, photocopies of operators' licences, birth certificates, social insurance cards, health care cards, passports and other pertinent information concerning each individual is placed in separate envelopes and delivered to the American Embassy.

The Arrest

On Sunday, Eileen Ferguson returns from visiting her mother, Angie Marks, in Toronto. Not willing to inform his wife about the two satellite phones in his possession, Joe leaves them with Tom Jackson.

In the afternoon of Monday, July 9th, two members of the R.C.M.P. enter the Carling Avenue Royal Bank with a court order to freeze the account established by C.S.I.S.

"We'll send the court order to our head office. The account will be frozen tomorrow," the Manager of Customer Service informs the R.C.M.P. Officer.

"That should be fine," replies the Mountie, "Ferguson isn't likely to remove the funds before then."

The manager peruses the account bank record on the monitor.

"He will definitely not take any money out. There's never been any money in the account."

"What do you mean there's no money in the account? There has to be $526,000 in the account."

"Not in that account."

"You said not in that account. Does he have an account containing $526,000?"

"Yes, but it's not that account."

"Change the numbers on the court order and send it in."

"You can forget that. I have no intention of breaking the law for you. Regardless, Head Office would only reject it," the manager explains.

"Print off a copy of the account and we'll come back tomorrow."

"I can't without a court order."

"I can leave my partner here with you while I get a court order to obtain the account numbers. I will then come back here and you will give me the information I require. I will return with the court order for you to send away and you will get home at midnight or you can give me the account numbers and we will return tomorrow afternoon with the proper court order."

"I'll tell you the numbers. You record them."

The following morning the same two R.C.M.P. Officers arrest Joe Ferguson at the Department of Immigration. Placing handcuffs on Joe and leading him through the building, they make a big show of the whole event. Reporters, waiting in front of the Immigration Building to photograph the event, are given a fictitious story about Joe's complicity in bringing terrorists into Canada. While placing Joe in a holding cell, the R.C.M.P. refuse his request to contact his lawyer.

Tom Jackson, observing the same two members of the R.C.M.P. arresting Eileen Ferguson, phones William Smythe. He continues to watch the proceedings and sees the Mounties leave the Ferguson home carrying a shotgun. Slipping out the back door of his home, Tom drives to the end of the alley to await the appearance of the R.C.M.P. vehicle. Following at a distance, he observes them pull into the R.C.M.P. Detachment at 1200 Vanier Parkway. Tom is talking on the phone to William when the lawyer's car, driven by Rae Jones, slips in behind him.

"Fergie was arrested earlier today. I don't know why we haven't heard from him but I presume the R.C.M.P. wouldn't allow him to contact us. I've contacted Shannon Johansen to meet us here."

Tom is observing the action at the R.C.M.P. detachment through his binoculars. "There's a police car pulling out now. Two passengers. Eileen on this side."

William replies, "We'll follow first and you follow us. When your phone rings pass us. We'll keep alternating places. They're likely heading for the courthouse."

Shannon answers her satellite phone.

"It looks like they're heading for the Court of Queens Bench. We'll meet you there."

Shannon is the first to arrive at the courthouse. She waits inside the building and observes William entering by the front door. William strides over to a courtroom directory, looks at it and steps into the elevator while placing a call.

"Rae Jones here."

"Courtroom 207. Tell Tom."

William and Shannon enter the courtroom and take seats close to the front. William, recognizing the Crown Prosecutor, mumbles, "Good." Rae Jones enters and sits beside William, while Tom Jackson takes a seat towards the back of the courtroom. Ten minutes later, the arresting R.C.M.P officers escort Joseph and Eileen Ferguson into the courtroom for their arraignment.

Crown Prosecutor Joshua Campbell addresses the presiding Judge, "Your Honor. Joseph Peter Ferguson is charged with illegally granting landed immigration status to Ayman al-Zawahri, a known al Qaeda terrorist. He has a secret bank account, which the R.C.M.P. discovered, containing five hundred and twenty six thousand dollars. He has given the R.C.M.P. a signed confession of his guilt."

William Smythe is standing, "Your Honor. May I approach the bench?"

Judge Steven Harris asks, "Do you have information on the case at hand?"

"Your Honor. I am William Smythe, legal counsel for the prisoner. Why was I not contacted when Joseph Ferguson was arrested?"

R.C.M.P. Officer Maurice Ducette addresses the court, "Your Honor. He never expressed any interest in having a lawyer present at any time during the interrogation."

"That's a lie," Joe interjects. "I asked to phone my lawyer when I was being booked and was refused, and there never was an interrogation, and I never signed any confession."

"Your Honor. The prisoner is lying," states R.C.M.P. Officer Robert Head. "He never asked for a lawyer before, or during the one hour interrogation Officer Ducette and I had with the prisoner, during which time he gave that confession and signed it."

William Smythe speaks out again, "Your Honor. My client is charged with granting landed immigrant status to a terrorist. That is impossible for him to do. His position at the Immigration Department is researching the number and types of jobs that Canadians cannot fill in this country and informing the Immigration Department the qualifications and numbers of immigrants needed to fill those positions. Mr. Ferguson's position is strictly research. He has never been responsible for accepting or rejecting immigrants."

"My second concern is the illegal bank account. Could I see the documentation on the account?"

The Crown Prosecutor hands the paper to William. William examines the paper then removes documents from his briefcase, placing them with the first document.

"I have here the check statement from the US Government showing they presented Joseph Ferguson with a check for $526,000 Canadian for killing Abu Zubaydah in the home invasion at the Ferguson residence. I also have here the deposit slip for the cheque, and photocopies of the back and front of the cheque, when he deposited the cheque for $526,000 from the U.S. Government, into that very account."

Crown Prosecutor Joshua Campbell now remembers where he heard the name Joseph Ferguson before. He examines the documents very thoroughly. He then compares the back of the cheque to the signed confession and the landed immigrant document on Ayman al-Zawahri.

Joshua Campbell angrily turns to the arresting officers.

"What time did you arrest Joseph Ferguson?"

"Shortly after nine o'clock this morning," Officer Maurice Ducette informs the court.

"It was ten after ten," interjects Joe Ferguson. "Coffee break runs from nine thirty to nine forty-five. I had a short meeting with two of the staff after the break to clarify a problem."

Joshua Campbell continues his interrogation of the R.C.M.P. officers, "What time did you place Joseph Ferguson in the cell?"

"About ten-fifteen," says Maurice Ducette.

Joe Ferguson continues to discredit the arresting officers' testimony.

"It was ten forty-four when I took off my watch and asked to phone my lawyer."

Joshua Campbell continues his interrogation of the arresting officers.

"What time did you arrest Eileen Ferguson?"

Maurice Ducette does some quick calculations, "It's a ten minute drive and we arrived just after twelve o'clock."

"May I speak your honor? My name is Thomas Jackson. I live next door to the Fergusons. The R.C.M.P. arrived at the Ferguson residence at eleven thirty. They left at eleven fifty-five. Because of the problems the Fergusons experienced with C.S.I.S. agents, I followed them. They arrived at the R.C.M.P. detachment at ten minutes past twelve and left for the courthouse ten minutes later."

Joshua Campbell sums up the information he has deciphered during the hearing.

"According to my calculations the members of the R.C.M.P. spent two ten minute time periods at the detachment during which they booked Joseph and Eileen Ferguson, locked up their possessions, put them in cells, removed them from cells and held a one hour interrogation to gain a confession. Checking the documents I find the signatures of Joseph Ferguson on the immigration documents and on the confession are exact duplicates while the signature on the back of the cheque and the deposit slip are somewhat different. Since no person signs his name exactly the same every time he signs any document, the signatures on the immigration documents and the confession must be either forgeries or fraudulently obtained signatures."

Judge Harris scrutinizes the documents. Before he finishes his examination, he is visibly angry, "I must concur with your findings. Officer of the Court I am charging you to arrest these two members of the R.C.M.P. charging them with forgery, laying charges using forged documents and perjury."

The Crown Prosecutor addresses the court, "Your Honor, I recommend that the charges against Joe and Eileen Ferguson be dropped and they be allowed to go free. The evidence is clear. They have been falsely charged with these crimes."

Judge Harris examines all the court documents.

"I concur with your recommendation and the prisoners are free to go. I wish to extend the apologies of the court for the illegal activities of certain members of the Canadian Justice System."

William accompanies Joe and Eileen into the Vanier Parkway R.C.M.P. Detachment to recover their belongings. Shannon tags along.

"We've come for the Fergusons' personal effects," William informs the clerk.

"Just one moment, I'll have to check with Commissioner Guy Trembley."

"Can I assist you?" the Senior Official of the R.C.M.P. asks William.

"Yes I represent Joe and Eileen Ferguson. We're here to collect their personal effects."

"Certainly. Will you give them their belongings Ken? I see they made bail. When is their trial date set?"

"The Judge dropped the false charges against Joseph Ferguson. You should get your facts straight before you trump up charges in an attempt to railroad an innocent citizen. Your two dupes were arrested and charged with forgery, laying charges using forged documents and perjury."

"The evidence presented to the courts is true," snarls Trembley.

"Yes the evidence against the R.C.M.P. officers is true," William Smythe snaps back. "The evidence against Joe Ferguson is a complete fabrication and you know it."

The clerk places the personal belongings of Joe and Eileen Ferguson on the desk.

"Where is the shotgun that was removed from the Ferguson residence?"

"We're holding it as evidence in an ongoing investigation."

"What investigation?"

"The murder investigation into the deaths at the Ferguson residence."

"The deaths of three terrorists trying to murder innocent citizens."

"Five Canadian citizens," growls Trembley. "Now get the hell out. You're not getting the gun." He sees a young lady standing off to one side. "What do you want?"

"Nothing really," Shannon replies. "I'm just a reporter looking for a story."

Shannon Johansen drives back to the courthouse in time for the arraignment and bail hearing for the two R.C.M.P. officers. At her desk, she prepares her article for the morning edition of the Ottawa Citizen.

The saga of the Canadian Government persecution of a Canadian citizen continues. Joe Ferguson was arrested today and charged with bringing a known terrorist, Ayman al-Zawahri, into Canada and receiving money from the terrorist to be granted landed immigrant status in Canada. The R.C.M.P. officers produced as proof a bank account in the name of Joseph Ferguson, containing $526,000.00, documentation granting landed immigrant status to Ayman al-Zawahri, documentation granted to Ayman al-Zawahri under the alias Adbed Moez, and a confession purportedly signed by Joe Ferguson.

By the time the judicial hearing was finished, we learned that the R.C.M.P. denied Joseph Ferguson his civil rights by refusing his request for legal counsel. The bank account is legal, and had nothing to do with any criminal action by the accused. The confession and the signatures on the landed immigrant documents produced by the R.C.M.P. were fraudulent.

R.C.M.P. Officer Maurice Ducette and R.C.M.P. Officer Robert Head, were arrested in the courtroom, and charged with forgery, laying charges using forged documents and perjury.

The Federal Government again paid the bail for the members of the Federal Justice Department charged with criminal wrongdoing.

Although Judge Steven Harris and Crown Prosecutor Joshua Campbell dropped all charges against Joseph and Eileen Ferguson, R.C.M.P. Commissioner Guy Trembley refused to return the shotgun confiscated by the R.C.M.P. during the arrest. The reason given by Commissioner Guy Trembley, "The gun is part of an ongoing investigation into the murder of five Canadians at the Ferguson residence." The five Canadians murdered are Abu Zubaydah, known al-Qaeda terrorist wanted by the US Government for his part in the bombing of the US Embassy in Somalia, living illegally in Canada using false immigration papers under the alias Muqtada Musharrof. He illegally entered the Ferguson residence, directed by C.S.I.S., and attempted to kill the family as they slept. Omar and Shaukat Zubaydah, sons of Abu Zubaydah, al-Qaeda trained terrorists, killed while trying to murder the Ferguson family as they slept. Matt Spence, C.S.I.S. agent, shot trying to kill a neighbor of Joe Ferguson when ordered by the neighbor to raise his hands. He shot twice at the neighbor before the neighbor shot him. This C.S.I.S. agent was also in on the attempted murder of the Ferguson family and the attempted murder of a fellow C.S.I.S. agent. The fifth Canadian killed was John Winston, C.S.I.S. agent, who killed a sixteen-year-old boy in the basement of the Ferguson residence and was shooting at Joe Ferguson's son and two other boys when he was shot and killed.

The defendant never fired the shotgun confiscated by the R.C.M.P. during either home invasion by members of the Canadian Justice System, nor is this shotgun considered evidence by the City Police detachment still conducting the investigation into C.S.I.S. involvement in the Ferguson home invasions. The Federal Department of Justice has consistently blocked this investigation by the Ottawa police.

How long will the Federal Government and members of our Justice system continue their illegal conduct against the person of Joe Ferguson?

Included in the news article were the landed Immigrant documents of Ayman al-Zawahri and his alias Adbed Moez.

William Smythe, Joe Ferguson and Tom Jackson meet with Chief Henri Montford of the Ottawa Police Force. Chief Montford returns the Fergusons' two shotguns and the 30-06 and shotgun belonging to Tom Jackson. On the way home, Joe buys a box of steel shot 3½", 12 gauge shotgun shells for his Mossberg Ultra-mag 835 shotguns.

Joe retrieves his satellite phone from the Jackson residence and Tom goes to bed, setting his alarm for 11:00 p.m.

Joe removes the $526,000 from the Royal Bank, leaving it with his lawyer.

Belle River

Peter Ferguson is driving into Windsor, Ontario to pick up repairs needed for his corn harvester. Jerry sits in the front seat of the car beside his grandfather and Keith who lost the race to the car climbs into the back seat. Cecil Mann brings a grocery list from the house and sits behind Peter. Driving down the country road, they encounter a motorcyclist on a Harley Davidson bike. Cecil notices the cyclist paying undue attention to the car and passengers as he passes, and then turning the bike around he follows them. Cecil removes his seatbelt and rolls down the window.

"Roll up the window. There's too much dust."

"In a minute." Cecil's voice is suddenly cold.

"The motorcycle turned around and is following us," Keith informs his grandfather

"He can pass if he wants."

Peter is watching the cyclist very carefully, alerted by the tone of Cecil's voice.

Cecil unzips his jacket and removes the automatic from its shoulder holster, holding it under his jacket. The motorcycle pulls out to pass and Cecil slides to the middle of the seat turning to face the open car window as he does so. The motorcycle slowly begins to pass, then Cecil watches as the biker reaches under his Hells Angels jacket, and pulls out a handgun.

"**Grandpa he has a gun!**" shrieks Jerry.

Cecil raises his weapon and fires three times in quick succession and three-9mm. shells drive into the cyclist. The bike leaves the road with the driver still balanced on it and rolls into the cornfield before toppling. Peter ducks, slams on the brakes, then grabs his ears. Cecil is out running after the bike before the car stops. Keith jumps out of the car and runs back to retrieve the weapon dropped by the motorcyclist. Cecil suddenly appears, riding the motorcycle out of the cornfield and up onto the road. After shutting off the bike, he and Keith straighten up the damaged corn. Minutes later Cecil is driving the motorcycle back to the farm followed by the car. In the machine shed, he shuts off the bike. While the boys remain in the vehicle, Peter Ferguson hurries to confer with Cecil.

"Is he dead?"

"Yes he is. We'll need somewhere to dispose of the body, preferably some distance from here. The R.C.M.P. or C.S.I.S. will be looking for him shortly and we can't have him found close to your farm."

"How much time will we have Cecil?"

"They won't start looking for him for a few days – probably not until Monday."

"That's enough time. Those hogs are the greatest garbage disposal units in the country. If we throw him in the feeder pen, we'll be able to dump the bones in Lake St. Claire on Saturday."

The following night Cecil is on the motorcycle headed for Montreal. Stopping at the Fifth Wheel truck stop in Milton, Ontario, he disposes of the personal effects of the biker in a garbage disposal unit, then he is heading west again on Highway 401. Nobody will give any notice to the bag of clothing when it exits the dumpster. Cecil keeps only the $20,000 he found in an envelope in the saddlebags of the bike, the cash from the biker's wallet and a beautiful diamond ring he will have resized. In Montreal, Cecil Mann rides the bike to a house occupied by the Rock Machine motorcycle gang. Shutting off the motorcycle, he leaves the key in the ignition and places the helmet on the seat. He takes off, the overly large, 'Hells Angels Jacket' with the bullet holes and a smattering of dried blood on it, drops the coat over the handlebars and leaves, removing his gloves as he walks away. Two hours later, he is sleeping soundly on the Greyhound bus heading for Windsor. Cecil will soon be safely back on the Ferguson farm in Belle River.

Keith Ferguson phones his father and leaves a message on the satellite phone answering service.

Joe Ferguson, recognizing the same panic in Keith's voice as he heard previously when Art was killed, returns the call from Belle River, while sitting on the back step of the Jackson residence. Keith fills his father in on the attempt to murder his grandfather and the disposal of the biker. After talking to his mother and Jerry, Joe disconnects the call. Sitting at the Jackson dining room table Joe explains the latest developments to his neighbour. He phones Maurice Solinger to apprise him of the situation.

Leaving the Department of Immigration early, Pierre Montague meets Guy Trembley for a round of golf at the Royal Ottawa Golf Club. Enjoying dinner and conversation the two conspirators pay no attention to the man of Arabic descent who sits behind Montague and orders a cup of tea. When the stranger rises and heads for the bathroom Montague turns around, picks up two suitcases sitting on a chair, and slides them under the table where he and Trembley are seated. The Arab returns, finishes his tea and leaves the clubhouse. Another Arab, drinking tea at another table, has witnessed the exchange between the two parties.

Montague and Trembley finish their dinner. The sun has set when the pair leave the clubhouse. Arriving at Champaigne Apartments, Pierre Montague drives slowly past the building. Spotting a vehicle's headlights illuminate on the opposite side of the street, he pulls a U-turn and enters the just vacated parking stall. Stepping from the vehicle, Montague never sees his antagonists until too late. Grabbing and pinning him to the pavement, they whip a garrote over his head and jerk it tight, cutting off the air to his lungs. Within seconds, the assassins forcibly remove keys, wallet, rings, wristwatch, cell phone and shoes from the dying man's possession. Removing the golf equipment, suitcases and briefcase from the trunk of his car, they ignobly force Montague into the enclosure. The door to the trunk is closed and the car doors locked. Three Arabs step to the sidewalk and wait patiently as the thrashing subsides inside the trunk. Nobody has noticed the skirmish. The Arabs, their dark grey robes flowing as they walk, quickly leave the scene. Turning the corner, they find a van waiting for them. The golf equipment and suitcase are set behind the seats and the four Arabs sit and wait for ten minutes – no one speaks. One Arab, leaving the van, quickly returns to the Montague vehicle. Opening the trunk, he removes the garrote from the corpse and checks the trunk for any other evidence pointing to the assassins then closes the lid. Checking the site, he can find nothing dropped by his accomplices. Inside the vehicle, he searches the glove compartment and under the seats but can find nothing of interest. Locking the doors the Arab continues in the same direction as he was previously walking. Turning the corner, he slips into the waiting van. Forty minutes later the van parks at Maple Hill.

While Marcel is busy recording the numbers in the call display on Montague's cell phone, Joe is perusing the documents found in Pierre Montague's briefcase. After thoroughly examining the papers, Joe speaks to Marcel.

"Can you get these papers to the U.S. Embassy tomorrow morning?"

"Yes. What's the problem?"

"I don't really know but it looks like some people want to get to Canada from Saudi Arabia in very short order. They are willing to pay very well to be here by August 4th with no problems and no questions asked."

"I'll try to learn as much as I can through my 'Trojan Horse Program' and my Internet contacts. If I do learn anything I'll pass that information right through to the U.S. Consulate also."

Marcel removes from the suitcases two large, wrapped packages containing $753,000 in cash. After a cursory examination of the packages, they go back into the suitcases and Marcel places them on the floor. Remaining on the table are Montague's wallet, the contents of the wallet, rings, Rolex, keys, cell phone and shoes. Marcel slides the cell phone and credit cards to the side and addresses the group.

"Does anyone want these items?"

"I already have what I want. That animal tried to kill my sons. He would never stop, so I had to stop him."

"If it's all right with the rest of you," Tom Jackson interjects, "I'd like to claim first dibs on the golf equipment."

Marcel reaches into a pile of cards and slides three across to Tom, "You might as well take these cards also. There are no names on them and they'll give you membership in three country clubs. The rings, wallet, watch, Guccis and money I'll lock in the safe until we require them."

Marcel slides the keys and bankcards over to Maurice Solinger. "Adrian Montague will likely need the information these items will provide. The credit cards and cell phone I'll dispose of tonight."

"Maurice, I want to thank you for tailing Montague and informing us when to leave the parking stall," Joe interjects, "and I have to thank the rest of you for helping me tonight."

The Arabs have been removing their disguises and cleaning up. They are now dressed, ready to head home. Marcel detours to a park frequented by drug addicts, and walks across the park, dropping the credit cards and the cell phone at various intervals. This should keep C.S.I.S. and the R.C.M.P. busy for a week.

Arriving home at one o'clock in the morning, Caroline Tremblay drives into the underground parking and takes the elevator to her floor. Entering the suite she finds Pierre Montague has not yet arrived. She's not worried, Pierre has missed a couple of nights, and Caroline has learned there is a big difference between being lovers and living together and she now prefers the former where Montague is concerned. Marriage to Montague is no longer an equation in her life. 'I wonder when I will see Eric the Red again'. Caroline's body quivers in anticipation.

Tom Jackson arrives home and drives down the alley and into his garage. In the Jackson residence, Joe collects his satellite phone, two shotguns and some shells, and walks to his own home. Eileen is asleep when he enters the house. Joe sleeps in Keith's bed not wishing to disturb his wife.

Strangers in the Night

At two forty-five, the buzzing of his satellite phone awakens Joe.

"Hello," is Joe's sleepy response.

"It looks like company, I'll call you back if they walk past."

Joe is instantly awake. He quickly removes the clothes and hangers from Keith's closet. Joe has previously cut a large hole in the drywall in the hallway end of the closet, and a peephole from there into the hallway. Looking through the hole, he can see the stairwell. The night light in the ceiling casts a pale glow in the hall. Joe waits patiently with the shotgun cocked sighting through the peephole. He hears a stair squeak. It squeaks a second time. Joe waits. He watches one shadowy intruder sneaking up the stairs, then spies the second stalker close behind him. The prowlers become more visible as they slowly and carefully advance into the light. The first intruder is four feet from Joe when he pulls the trigger. Moving the gun quickly to the side, he pulls the second trigger, shooting from memory, unable to see the second target for drywall dust. Leaping from the closet, he grabs the second shotgun. The Uzi cuts loose as the dead assassin involuntarily pulls the trigger – blasting into the wall, the door, and the floor – spraying hot lead into the master bedroom. Shells from a handgun blast into the closet. Their message of death whistling harmlessly through the area he just vacated, smashing into the opposite closet wall. Joe hears the boom of a shotgun firing outside, followed immediately by the roar of a second shotgun. Footsteps pound down the stairs, a clatter resonates up the stairwell, then the front door opens. Joe, racing down the stairs, looks out the door but can see nothing. Eileen, in the bedroom, screams and screams and screams. Joe, scrambling back up the stairs to the bedroom, tries to calm her fears.

Tom Jackson sets the satellite phone on the bed and picks up the shotgun, cocking both hammers. Watching three people walking down the street, he sees one lie down partially behind the lilacs, and point a weapon towards his front door. The other two continue to the front door of the Ferguson home and enter the house. Tom hears the blasts of the shotgun, and then the rattling of an automatic and small arms fire. The man behind the lilacs lifts himself, looking towards the Ferguson residence. 'Why were there shotgun blasts emanating from the home'. Tom fires. The would-be assassin, when hit by the shotgun shells, jerks involuntarily, firing his shotgun and knocking stucco off the house. Tom, hearing footsteps pounding past under his bedroom window, shouts "Fergie" out the window. Receiving no answer, he dials Joe's number, knowing that stepping outside could get him shot.

"Joe Ferguson."

"Are you okay?"

"We're alive. Eileen is hysterical right now."

"I'll make the phone calls."

Tom calls Rene Dubois, 911, and William Smythe. He quickly apprises each party of the situation. Picking up the satellite phone, he contacts Shannon Johansen.

The phone in the Ferguson residence rings.

"Joe Ferguson."

"Joe this is Bonnie Neumann. We saw one man run and jump into a car in front of our house. He's just sitting there in the driver's seat. Clark has him covered from a bedroom window."

"Thank you Bonnie. The police are on their way and should be here within a few minutes. We'll inform them about the man."

Tom Jackson spends a few minutes calming Ralph down. He has never been wakened before by a shotgun blast in the house. When the dog has quieted down Tom lets him out to run in the backyard. Entering the Ferguson residence, he spots the 9mm. automatic the second assassin dropped while opening the door. Tom calls out, "Joe? Eileen?"

"Upstairs. Come on up."

Joe and Eileen finish dressing as Tom climbs the stairs and steps around the dead assassin. Lying on the floor is an Israeli manufactured Uzi. Joe spots his satellite phone lying on Keith's bed. Not wanting the police or his wife to discover that phone, he puts it in his pocket to take to the office later.

Tom, Joe and Rene are standing talking beside the body in Tom's yard when an R.C.M.P. vehicle slowly cruises past. Rene turns and watches them leave.

"If they weren't involved they would have stopped. It's natural to stop and see if you need help, if only out of curiosity."

The police forensic unit is finishing in the Ferguson residence and moving to Tom Jackson's home when Detective Rene Dubois begins his interrogation of Joe and Eileen Ferguson and Tom Jackson.

"I see the R.C.M.P. as well as C.S.I.S. are now trying to kill you. Have you found out yet why they want you dead?"

"They weren't here to kill us. They were going to arrest us," Eileen Ferguson staunchly informs Rene Dubois, unwilling to believe anything evil of the government or any of its agencies.

"You don't honestly believe that do you Eileen."

"Yes I do."

"Not again," William intones.

Rene tears a sheet of paper from his notebook and writes 'Legal Arrest' at the top. He then itemized the procedure necessary to follow for a legal arrest.

Came in police car
Stopped in front of house
Wigwags flashing
Uniforms
Knocked on door
Produced badge
Produced warrant
Guns in holster
Handcuffs
Police issue weapons
Ring doorbell. Announce presence
Safety on gun
On duty-legal to carry weapons
On duty, legal with proper documentation to enter home to make arrest.

On a second page he writes 'Criminal Action'.

Came in stolen car
Stopped down the street from the house
Dark civilian clothing, running shoes to suppress noise
Home invasion
Not carrying badges

No warrants
Guns drawn
No handcuffs
Home invasion
Street guns, not registered, Uzi-illegal weapon
Guns cocked ready to fire
Removed from active duty-illegal to carry weapons
Removed from active duty-illegal to enter home to make arrest.

"A policeman can't do anything illegal when arresting a person," Rene informs Eileen. "The first list is normal procedure for any officer of the law. The list on the right is the pattern they followed. Can you show me one item on the right hand list that is comparable to one item on the left hand list when those same officers did arrest you?"

Eileen sits at the table looking at the list, unwilling to answer the question posed by the detective.

"I'm still waiting for an answer Eileen."

Eileen speaks very softly, "No."

"No what!"

Eileen speaks softly again, "There is nothing in the right hand list the same as when I was arrested."

"I can't hear you!" Rene is annoyed at her attitude. **"Say it again!"**

Eileen speaks slightly louder, "There is nothing in the right hand list the same as when I was arrested."

"Comparing both lists, did they come to arrest you?"

"No, I don't think so."

Rene asks Eileen, "What was their purpose, sneaking into the house way they did?"

"I don't know. I guess they may have come to kill us like you think."

"Can't you ever give an honest answer?"

Eileen is stunned, "Are you saying I'm lying to you?"

"Worse than that, I'm saying your lying to yourself."

"They came to kill us."

"Finally! Joe if Eileen goes back on what she just admitted grab your two sons and get as far from her as you can, otherwise she'll get you killed."

Shannon Johansen has her story.

July 12th, 2001

Once again, The Ferguson family owes their lives to the watchfulness and concern of their neighbors and their own diligence. When R.C.M.P. Commissioner Guy Trembley refused to return the shotgun confiscated by the R.C.M.P., Joe Ferguson secured the release of his familys' other shotguns from the Ottawa City Police Force. Believing the City Police were still holding the shotguns, three members of the R.C.M.P. staged another home invasion in an attempt to murder Joe Ferguson and his family.

Observing a car driving past at 2:45 a.m. with no lights and then stopping perked the curiosity of a neighbor of the Ferguson family. The neighbor observed three adults exit the car but no light came on when she saw the car doors swing open. The neighbor phoned Joe Ferguson and Tom Jackson to warn them in case this was another attempt on the lives of the Ferguson family.

The neighbor and Tom Jackson both watched one individual lie down partially concealed behind some lilac bushes and point a weapon at the Jackson residence. The other two individuals walked up to the front door of the Ferguson residence and the neighbor observed them unlock the front door and enter the house. Tom Jackson ran downstairs, grabbed his shotgun from the gun cabinet, and raced back to the bedroom.

Joe Ferguson had already taken his guns upstairs and was loading them when the front door opened. Hearing the floorboard squeak in the upstairs hallway, Joe Ferguson fired blindly through the end wall of the closet killing one member of the R.C.M.P. and wounding the second. The wounded officer fired three times into the closet then fled the scene, blood flowing profusely from an arm wound. That officer was later found dead from shock and loss of blood, in a car illegally removed from an R.C.M.P. impound yard.

Tom Jackson ordered the sniper lying behind the lilacs to drop his gun. The sniper fired his gun then Tom Jackson fired, killing the sniper.

Dead are:

R.C.M.P. Officer Maurice Ducette was arrested and charged with forgery, laying charges using forged documents and perjury on Tuesday July 10 in the arrest fiasco of Joseph and Eileen Ferguson.

R.C.M.P. Officer Robert Head was arrested and charged with forgery, laying charges using forged documents and perjury on Tuesday July 10 in the arrest fiasco of Joe and Eileen Ferguson.

R.C.M.P. Officer Margaret Thornsbury.

When R.C.M.P. Officer Maurice Ducette was killed in the hallway, outside the master bedroom he was carrying a cocked Israeli Uzi. A weapon banned in Canada. The other two officers were also carrying unlicenced firearms

All three of these officers work directly under Guy Trembley, Senior Official in the R.C.M.P.

How much longer will the Federal Government allow this scandal to continue in the Federal Justice Department?

Is the Federal Government involved in criminal behavior inside the Department of Immigration and are these attempted assassinations of Joseph Ferguson a cover up of their illegal activities?

When questioned the Prime Minister of Canada has only two answers. "I have done nothing wrong and I cannot answer any more questions because I have urgent business elsewhere."

Does anybody in the government have an honest answer?

Shannon Johansen

The morning of July 11th, finds William Smythe back at 1200 Vanier Parkway. With the court order in-hand, he will have no problem collecting the shotgun confiscated by the R.C.M.P. Commissioner.

"I've come for the Ferguson shotgun and shells you refused to give us yesterday."

"You're not getting them," Trembley informs the lawyer." They're part of an ongoing investigation."

"This court order says I'm taking them with me."

Trembley can barely control his temper. His face turns red and he balls his fists. After glaring at the smiling William Smythe, he turns to an office clerk.

"Get the shotgun and shells from the evidence lock-up."

"If you haven't already heard, the charges against your two goons have been dropped."

The Senior Official of the R.C.M.P. turns and stalks angrily from the room. He will bide his time, but he will exact his revenge from this insolent lawyer.

Guy Trembley tries to contact Pierre Montague. His calls to the Department of Immigration elicit the reply, "Mr. Montague is not in his office right now, would you like to try later or leave a message." His calls to Caroline Tremblay give him no more clues as to the whereabouts of Pierre Montague and any call by Guy Trembley to Montague's cell phone are either taken by the answering service or the phone rings busy. An R.C.M.P. constable entering the Montague residence finds nothing. This is an enigma. If Guy hears nothing from Montague by morning, he will begin a search to determine his whereabouts.

Finishing breakfast, Trembley again tries to reach Montague – to no avail. He activates the remote start on his vehicle before leaving the house. Five minutes later, he leaves the house to drive to his office. The R.C.M.P. have investigated many instances of bombs rigged to explode by activating the car starter. Trembley used the same method to dispose of an unwanted enemy. This is the reason Guy Trembley always starts the vehicle with the remote start. He has never heard of a bomb rigged to the brake lights….

Marcel types in the E-mail code s.al.y@aol.com and hits send. The terrorists now have a list of names and addresses of a portion of the Liberal Cabinet Ministers involved in the illegal immigration operation, thirty-two top members of the Immigration Department, C.S.I.S. and the R.C.M.P. Also included is a list of sixty-three foreign diplomats and support staff involved in the immigration swindle. He includes a note saying these foreign diplomats and staff are attempting to route certain immigrants into Canada through US terminals where the F.B.I. will have the authority to arrest them.

Andrea Jones, Heather Smythe, Mary Watson, Kathleen Solinger, Gloria Johansen, and Marie Prichard begin a campaign of unrest by sending letters to certain Arab leaders in their communities in Ottawa, Montreal and Toronto saying, "Your life and your family's safety is at risk from the Canadian and US governments. E-mail s.al.y@aol.com for full particulars."

Sowing Dissention

Marcel has been busy in the Swiss bank accounts of the government officials involved in the immigration ring. He opens numbered bank accounts under the projected aliases of the members in the Maple Hill Mob in the DC Bank, Deposito-Cassa der Stadt in Bern, Switzerland – the bank used by the government in the immigration swindle, and other banks in Bern, Switzerland. The next step is to open numbered accounts in Zurich, Geneva, Lausanne, Fribourg, Neuchatel, Luzern, Sankt Gallen, Basel, and Brig Switzerland. He will also establish accounts in the Channel Islands, and the Bahamas.

Friday afternoon, police find the car issued to Pierre Montague. The city police investigation into his death reveals Montague carried two suitcases from the Royal Ottawa Golf Club, delivered surreptitiously to him by an unknown Arab. Staff at the country club reveal he has been given suitcases on a regular basis for the past ten years. Widening the investigation reveals Montague has picked up suitcases, packages and envelopes at other country clubs in the Ottawa area.

It's time to seed discontent in the ranks of the crooked politicians and civil servants. Marcel Roy enters the DC Bank, Deposito-Cassa der Stadt in Bern, Switzerland. He transfers the Swiss bank accounts of C.S.I.S. agent John Winston, C.S.I.S. agent Matt Spence, R.C.M.P. Officers Robert Head, Maurice Ducette, and Margaret Thornsbury, Director of C.S.I.S., Jean Perrault, R.C.M.P. Commissioner Guy Trembley and the Senior Official in the Department of Immigration, Pierre Montague, from those accounts into the bank accounts of the Cabinet Ministers involved in the immigration ring. He program's the accounts to automatically transfer any new funds entering those accounts. The next stage is to freeze the numbered bank accounts of the civil servants. This bank account freeze does not apply to the top two levels of the civil service. These moves are to split the three factions, and destroy any trust they have enjoyed until this time.

Dragen Yankovich is patiently waiting in the parking lot for the staff to exit the offices of the Treasury Department. In his hand is a small box containing a letter and two sets of computer disks. The one set of disks contains photographs, names, addresses, phone numbers and positions in the civil service of all the people involved in the immigration ring whose bank account has been frozen and the information the frozen accounts are to be transferred to the Members of Parliament in the event of a change of government. The second set of disks contains the identical information on the top eulachon of the civil service, the mandarins and the cabinet ministers also involved in the immigration ring. The second file also contains a dossier of the funds from the dead member accounts transferring to the Cabinet Ministers.

Keeping in his mind the pictures of numerous workers involved in the immigration ring, Marcel spots Mildred Wentworth. Intercepting the path Mrs. Wentworth is taking to her vehicle, Dragen Yankovich addresses the lady.

"Pardon me are you Mildred Wentworth?"

The lady stops and looks at the man addressing her, "Yes I am."

Dragen Yankovich hands her the box containing two sets of disks and a letter.

"What is this?" asks Mildred.

"I have disconcerting evidence that our Swiss bank accounts are to be pilfered by our superiors," replies Dragen Yankovich. "Distribute the information in these files to our fellow workers on the large file. I have removed the name of Jack Campbell from the list. I gave him this same information three days ago. He tried to cut a deal with his superiors to get his own account back and disappeared yesterday. I will scrutinize your activities and warn you if you if your superiors begin to get suspicious. Do not under any circumstance look at the information contained on those disks using any government computers."

Mildred Wentworth gives Dragen Yankovich a look of skepticism.

Spotting John Francis, a co-worker of Mildred Wentworth, he calls the man over and instructs them to work together on the information. Mildred must now tell John about the information on the disks in her possession. The seeds of distrust will soon take root and grow.

Marcel visits a library computer where he types the message,

The mandarins and cabinet ministers have compromised your numbered Swiss bank accounts. Mildred Wentworth and John Francis of the Department of Finance have access to the information you require. The following names, addresses and home phone numbers belong to members of the civil service I have contacted on this matter.

Ten envelopes containing this information bear the name of the recipient and the caption 'urgent and confidential'. Rae Jones and Andre Prichard now join Marcel Roy wearing disguises. These "postmen" will hand deliver the envelopes to their respective destinations.

Dragen Yankovich has computer disks to deliver to the new Senior Official in charge of the Immigration Department, and the new Senior Officials in charge of the RCMP and CSIS in the Justice Department. Handing the disk to each mandarin he says, "You will find this information on these numbered Swiss bank accounts very disturbing." Enclosed with the disks is the following missive,

Within these disks is a record taken from the secret bank accounts in Bern, Switzerland. You will find the funds transferred from the accounts of the dead civil servants to the accounts of the Cabinet Ministers. You will need to contact other Senior Officials and act to put an end to the pilfering of your bank accounts by the members of the Liberal Party. I have entrusted this information to the Senior Official in charge of the Department of Immigration, the Senior Official in charge of the Department of Finance, and the two Senior Officials in the Justice Department. You will be required to contact other Senior Officials in the government and inform them about this development.

From this day forward, distrust of their superiors by the members of the civil service involved in the illegal immigration of terrorists into Canada will intensify. These workers will hinder all attempts by the government to bring new terrorist immigrants into the country.

Civil Rights

Ayman al-Zawahri, living in Canada under the alias Adbed Moez, disappears from his home in Toronto, Ontario. Kidnapped by the F.B.I., he is spirited across the Niagara River to Grant Island, and then transported to New York City, where he is detained in isolation. Five days later, a New York newspaper reporter, Gregory Brown, from a very tipsy guard, learns of the abduction and imprisonment of Ayman al-Zawahri.

"Yeah the F.B.I. kidnapped the guy over the border in Canada and brought him to New York. I seen the Arab locked up by hisself in a cell in the jail. He sez his name is Adbed Moez, but the F.B.I. claims his name is Ayman al-Zawahri or somethin like that."

Gregory Brown orders two more beers for the guard.

"When did they capture the man?"

"They caught him in Toronto, Ontario last Friday the thirteenth," replies the guard. "I guess it was a bad day fer him, huh. They broke into his suite when he was sleepin and dragged him out of bed. They sez they threw him in a van an took him to the Niagara River an den took him across in a boat so the Canadian and American border guards couldn raise a fuss. Pretty smart eh. Then they brought him to New York and hid him in that jail. They been questioning him but don't know nuttin yet. He's a real cool customer an jest sits there and don't say a word."

The Wednesday, July 18, 2001 edition of the New York Times comes out with a scoop.

This reporter has just learned of the civil rights violation of a Canadian citizen by the F.B.I. In the early morning hours of July 13, 2001, five F.B.I. agents entered the home of Adbed Moez, kidnapped him and forced him into a van at gunpoint. This Canadian citizen was smuggled into the US across the Niagara River in a boat, so neither U.S. nor Canadian border guards would be able to stop this travesty of justice by the F.B.I. and to hide this flagrant injustice from the Canadian and American public. The man is now in solitary confinement in New York City.

The F.B.I. claim the man they have kidnapped is a member of al-Qaeda by the name of Ayman al-Zawahri and not Adbed Moez as he claims to be. Whatever his name US authorities have no right to enter his home in Canada and kidnap the man.

The U.S. Government, by its criminal actions, has violated the civil rights of a Canadian citizen. These kinds of actions can only result in worsening relationships with our northern neighbors and condemnation of our actions by the international communities of this world. How can we champion the democratic rights of others and commit the same atrocities we abhor in dictatorial nations?

If this travesty continues without our intervention, who will be the next person to lose his civil rights? The citizens of our great nation must rectify this illegal action by our government, and this citizen of Canada must be safely returned to his own country. If the F.B.I. believes they need to arrest this Canadian there are democratic processes at their disposal, which will bring Adbed Moez back here for questioning.

We must never allow our government to be involved in any criminal actions that can destroy the rights we have enshrined in our constitution and hold so dear to our hearts.

Gregory Brown

Friday sees civil rights demonstrations in New York and Washington with larger demonstrations organized in most of the major cities over the weekend. Toronto, Ottawa, and Montreal in Canada hold anti-US rallies to protest the actions of the F.B.I.

Patrick Champlain, Prime Minister of Canada, appears on camera, publicly denouncing the actions of the F.B.I. and Chantelle Pilon, a Liberal cabinet minister calls the U.S president an 'idiot' for believing he can get away with these actions.

The F.B.I. have proof that Adbed Moez is Ayman al-Zawahri, a high-ranking member of the al-Qaeda terrorist organization, but civil libertarians have their own agenda and are enjoying their popularity on this issue. The F.B.I. attempts to learn why Ayman al-Zawahri was in Canada proves futile under the present circumstances. Knowing the civil rights demonstrations will only intensify, U.S. authorities finally decide to return Ayman al-Zawahri to Canadian authorities.

Adbed Moez flanked by two F.B.I. agents and followed by a large contingent of civil rights activists steps onto the Rainbow Bridge at Niagara Falls to begin his walk to freedom. The Prime Minister of Canada, a large group of Canadian dignitaries, and a contingent of Canadian civil libertarians greet him at the center of the bridge and invite him to enter Canada as a free man again.

Speeches given by Prime Minister Patrick Champlain and the civil liberty groups, praise the actions of civil rights activists to secure the freedom of Adbed Moez and preserve the rights of all free people. Adbed Moez steps off the bridge and disappears. Six weeks later Ayman al-Zawahri returns to Afghanistan, having completed his mission in Canada.

Dissention

The civil servants receive confirmation from a financial agent their Swiss bank accounts are frozen and the money from the dead members Swiss bank accounts has been transferred to other accounts. The agent secured by the mandarins confirms the money from the accounts of the dead agents was transferred out of those accounts to the other numbered accounts on their list, this list being the cabinet ministers. The intrigue continues to split the various groups with the Members of Parliament completely unaware of any problem except a radical slowdown in the processing of terrorist immigrants.

Adrian Montague returns to Ottawa to deal with the funeral of her husband. Meeting with her, Maurice Solinger informs Adrian, Eric will transfer $200,000 into her accounts before the end of September with another $43,000 to follow by the end of October.

Maurice, wearing rubber gloves, removes the jewel case containing the 22 incriminating computer disks and the documents from the safe. The only individual with any knowledge of the disks is a senior official in the Department of Finance. He gave the disks to Montague without informing his superiors and will be very quiet about this information.

After informing Adrian of the whereabouts of three bank accounts containing $578, 900, Maurice warns her not to give anyone access to the safe until all the funds are in the U.S. accounts. Armed with a power of attorney, Adrian and Maurice visit the banks to search the safety deposit boxes. They discover $4.5 million in foreign securities and title to Champaigne Apartments. With the account numbers Adrian has provided, Marcel will be able to transfer funds from Europe to her accounts in the US.

Marcel Roy and Rae Jones again visit Ambassador Henry Kilmer at the US Consulate. They pick up four satellite phones that do not have the speed dial keyed in and return the phone originally designated for Eileen Ferguson. Marlene and Cecil, to enable them to speak to each other with no opportunity for the R.C.M.P. or C.S.I.S. to overhear their conversations, will use two of the satellite phones. The third phone will be given to Joe Ferguson's parents in Belle River and the fourth to Angie Marks. Two other phones are specifically keyed to reach and receive calls only from and to Andrea Jones and/or Marie Prichard. With those phones, their babysitters can contact the parents if the need arises, and both sets of parents will be using those phones to contact their children.

Marcel explains to the American Ambassador the plans they have to break up the illegal immigration operation, "We have penetrated nineteen branches of different terrorist organizations in Canada and informed them that members of the Canadian Government have been selling different members of their organizations to the US Government. These terrorist organizations have links to the remaining terrorist groups in Canada and the U.S. At this time, the terrorists have a list of the top 35% of the members in the government involved in their disappearance. As these individuals are eliminated, I will keep giving them more names."

"We are splitting the civil service into different camps by freezing the Swiss bank accounts of the workers, leaving the accounts of the mandarins and their closest allies alone and transferring the accounts of any of the group that dies to the accounts of the Members of Parliament involved in the conspiracy. We have transferred this information to the two levels of the civil service to sow distrust in their ranks. The final stage of our operation will be to remove all the money from the numbered accounts and make it disappear. We believe these acts will severely limit or destroy the governments illegal immigration organization."

The American Ambassador to Canada ponders the information for a minute then asks, "Couldn't you achieve the same results by going to the citizens of Canada with the information?"

Rae Jones breaks into the conversation.

"The Prime Minister of Canada has far more power than the American President. While in office, the Prime Minister has powers comparable to King Charles 1st of England and is answerable to no one. He chooses the members of the Senate, his cabinet ministers, and all the Senior Officials in each department of government. He chooses all the judges, beginning in the Supreme Court down to, and including, the judges sitting on the Courts of the Queens bench in each province and territory in Canada. He selects the directors controlling all the Canadian Crown Corporations. He selects and fully controls 40% of the government. In no other democracy does the leader have the dictatorial power possessed by the Canadian Prime Minister."

"If we went to the people with this information there would be a hue and cry for three weeks and on the fourth week the people of Canada would look for any excuse they can find to support these traitors. Their main excuse is 'the other parties are just as crooked.' The other parties are not involved in the criminal actions this government is and will continue to be if they are not stopped."

"Doesn't the murders of the civil servants and parliamentarians bother you?"

"Yes," Marcel replies, "but their greed has fueled a total disregard for the lives of all the citizens in both our countries. They have demonstrated a willingness to eliminate any innocent person they consider a threat to their criminal activities. These criminals have shown only one priority to me – pure, unadulterated greed at the risk of everybody else's life. We are following the same course of action they have demonstrated in their callous attitude for the lives of others."

Rae and Marcel drive to the office of Jones, Smythe and Watson. Marcel picks up his vehicle in the Carlingwood Plaza parking lot and heads for the nearest terrorist Wi-Fi-equipped computer to continue his research through the Trojan Horse Program. He has accessed over twenty five thousand names of terrorists and their families, but realizes by the time he accesses these current Immigration Department files and the archived immigration files he could find another ten thousand names.

Rae calls Marlene Moore into his office, gives her the satellite phone and warns her, "This phone is safe for contacting Cecil up until you contact somebody with a land phone or cell phone. Once you do that C.S.I.S. and the R.C.M.P. will be able to trace Cecil's phone and kill him. Don't use the satellite phone in your suite or car because there is a very great possibility they are both bugged and your car will have a tracer installed. When you are in the apartment or your car, shut off the phone – you can't answer it. Never leave the phone in the car or apartment. C.S.I.S. will continue to search them looking for leads to find Cecil. The safest place to use the phone is walking in a crowd."

Bob Watson calls a short staff meeting, "We are planning to take an extended holiday in a few days. Your wages will continue to be paid by direct deposit. We will require some staff in the office while we are absent to take care of day-to-day contingencies. Enjoy your holidays and we'll see you when we get back."

The Beginning of the Plan

Joe and Eileen Ferguson drive to Toronto to visit with Eileen's Mother. Joe leaves a satellite phone with Angie and cautions her, "Don't let Eileen know that I left this phone with you because she is likely to go to the authorities and get me and the boys killed. I'll be leaving her with you for our safety."

Joe's next stop will be Belle River where he delivers satellite phones to his parents and Cecil Mann and picks up his sons. Leaving Belle River the following morning the trio soon enter Windsor, then a drive through the Detroit-Windsor tunnel puts them in the good old U.S. of A. Two hours later, they are on Interstate 80/90 headed for New York City and a rendezvous with their cohorts.

In New York, the members of the Maple Hill Mob turn their Canadian passports, operators' licences, health care cards and social insurance cards over to the F.B.I. in exchange for duplicate information showing their 'American terrorist citizenship'. The Maple Hill Mobs American passports, drivers licenses and other proof of U.S. citizenship and the clothing they will wear as European origin Americans is waiting for their arrival in the U.S. Embassy in Switzerland.

The money the Maple Hill Mob acquired from the C.S.I.S. account, the funds in the suitcases, and the money received from the US Government for Abu Zubaydah was sent previously, via diplomatic pouch to the United States, and deposited by the F.B.I. After signing the proper documentation at the bank, they receive bankcards and cheques under their names and under their aliases.

The Maple Hill Mob all travel in their disguises to Switzerland. Using their fake "terrorist" passports, operator's licence, and social security numbers, they confirm their numbered accounts under their aliases in the banks in the major cities of Bern, Zurich, Geneva, Lausanne, Freibourg, Neuchatel, Luzern, Sankt Gallen, Basel, and Winterthur Switzerland. Using their true U.S information each member opens four numbered bank accounts in the major centres with Marcel Roy opening eight accounts. With each account, the members of the Maple Hill Mob also lease a large safety deposit box. A deposit of two hundred and fifty Euros will secure each box and make the monthly safety deposit box rental payments.

Their next move is a flight to London, England. A short domestic flight sees them in Portsmouth, England, on the English Channel. A trip by ferry and they are visiting the Channel Islands. On Guernsey, the Maple Hill Mob confirms one hundred and twenty numbered accounts using their aliases and on Jersey, they open another one hundred and twenty numbered accounts. The members of the Maple Hill mob return by ferry to Portsmouth then to London, England where they take the flight from Heathrow airport to Nassau in the Bahamas. The Maple Hill Mob confirms eighty bank accounts in Nassau and another eighty accounts in Freeport on the Island of Grand Bahama. They open another 42 accounts with safety deposit boxes on different islands in the island chain. Their last stops are the Islands of Turks and Caicos, with sixty accounts confirmed on each Island. Two days later they turn their alias passports and personal information in to the F.B.I. in New York City and receive their U.S. passports. All the terrorist information will be waiting for them at the American Embassy when they arrive in Bern, Switzerland. The new Ferguson passports, like all their personal information reads Peter Joseph Ferguson, born April 11, 1951. Henry Keith Ferguson, born March 23, 1983 and John Gerald Ferguson, born January 15, 1981. A similar change in documentation appears in the personal identification of all the members of the Maple Hill Mob with corresponding information on the passports. All addresses on the 20 passports and personal information list them as residing in the states of New York, New Jersey or Pennsylvania, U.S.A.

In the New York offices of the F.B.I., Marcel Roy reads about some interesting developments that have taken place in Canada.

A government jet carrying George Branch, the Canadian Minister of Justice and his secretary, the newly installed R.C.M.P. Commissioner Jeffrey Molokai and three of his staff, the newly appointed Director of C.S.I.S., and five of his top officers, exploded over Northern Ontario killing everybody on board. These dignitaries, from the Department of Justice, were scheduled to conduct a symposium on combating terrorism in Winnipeg, Manitoba. Police are searching for Abu Bakar Ba'asyir, a baggage handler at the airport who disappeared after the plane exploded.

The Prime Minister has moved Josef Malekano from the Minister of National Defence portfolio to the Justice portfolio. The new minister in charge of the Armed Forces portfolio is Doreen Juricic.

Pakistan: Last night rocket fire killed the Canadian High Commissioner to Pakistan when it destroyed the Embassy limousine carrying him and two secretaries to a social gathering of dignitaries at the U.S. Embassy. The Pakistan military is conducting an extensive search in Lahore to find the terrorists responsible for the attack.

Egypt: Early this morning, terrorists invaded the Canadian Embassy in Cairo, Egypt, killing the ambassador and his staff. This is the second attack on Canadian Foreign Officials in the last twenty-four hours. Why are terrorists singling out Canadian Embassies? Is there a connection to the airplane explosion that killed the Canadian Justice Minister and a number of his immediate staff?

Saturday, August 25, Marcel Roy is busy on a computer in the F.B.I. offices in New York City. Entering the E – mail code s.al.y@aol.com Marcel enters the computer of Salama al-Yawer leaving her with the names, home addresses, office addresses and pictures of the remaining members of the government involved in the illegal immigration program.

Marcel, again using the F.B.I. computer, enters the bank accounts in the DC Bank, Deposito-Cassa der Stadt in Bern, Switzerland, containing the numbered accounts of the government conspirators. He first accesses the frozen accounts, releasing them and then transferring the funds, through the accounts held by the members of Parliament, into 400 terrorist accounts located in 400 banks in the cities of Bern, Zurich, Luzern, Sankt Gallen, and Winterthur, Switzerland, routing all the accounts through the accounts of the elected Members of Parliament. He continues throughout the night until he has finished setting up the transfer of every account. By four o'clock, Marcel Roy is sound asleep in the infirmary at the F.B.I. headquarters in New York City.

While Marcel Roy is busy on the computer. Maurice and Kathleen Solinger and Andre and Marie Prichard leave on flights from LaGuardia airport and Kennedy Airport in New York City, bound for Zurich and Geneva, Switzerland. Rae and Andrea Jones, Tom Jackson, and Alex, Gloria and Shannon Johansen embark on flights from both airports to Frankfurt, Germany. William and Heather Smythe, Bob and Mary Watson, and Joe, Keith and Jerry Ferguson board flights to Paris, France using both airports.

A diplomatic box containing the terrorist information and disguises of members of the Maple Hill Mob and extra personal clothing is awaiting their arrival in the American Embassy in Bern, Switzerland.

At nine fifteen, Marcel Roy and his parents are boarding a flight at Kennedy airport bound for Bern, Switzerland. Marcel sleeps during the flight.

The members of the Maple Hill Mob in Frankfurt, Germany meet with a lady driving a small school bus. She drives them close to the Swiss border. Darkness has fallen long before the bus arrives at its destination. The driver sees a light flash and pulls to the side of the road. Six shadows leave the bus carrying knapsacks. A guide escorts them quietly along obscure paths. Branches grab their clothing, then snap away into the gloom, slashing at the next shadow flowing in the line. They are about to step from a corpse of trees close to the river when the smell of smoke alerts them to danger. The shadows glide silently forward. Three teenage boys are sitting around a small campfire talking and drinking beer. The guide motions for Tom Jackson, Alex Johansen, and Rae Jones to follow him and starts retracing the path they had previously used to access the river. At the top of the hill they find another path, wider and with a more gentle slope. They begin marching, thump, thump, thump, thump, thump, steadily down the hill.

The snap of a dead branch awakens the boys to people coming down the path. Listening carefully, the boys hear feet marching, thump, thump, thump, thump, thump, thump, moving progressively closer to their refuge. Not willing to leave any evidence at the scene, the boys pick up the remaining full cans of beer and flee along the river, then up a path and away from the site. Even as they race away, the boys consume small gulps from their partial cans of beer to maintain their energy levels.

A powerboat delivers the Maple Hill Mob and their guide across the lake, and then again, the shadows follow winding paths through the bushes. Entering a farmyard, the guide escorts them into a shed containing a waiting U.S. Embassy van and chauffer. Their chauffer drives the Maple Hill Mob into Basel, Switzerland, and soon the van is on the highway, moving towards the capital of Switzerland. The use of the U.S. Embassy vans almost totally negates any possibility of routine check-stops by the Swiss authorities

The members of the Maple Hill Mob landing in Paris take a domestic flight to Besancon. A tour van chauffer drives them to a site near the France/Switzerland border. A short boat trip and they are in Switzerland. As the Guide leads them along various footpaths through the bushes, they approach a van sitting in a small clearing. A few minutes later, the Maple Hill Mob is driven to their rendezvous in Basel Switzerland. From Basel, they will proceed in a U.S. Embassy van to Bern Switzerland, where hotel accommodations await them.

Upon landing in Bern, Marcel Roy heads directly to the U.S. Embassy. Previous arrangements were made for his use of a computer. Marcel is soon accessing the numbered bank accounts of the Canadian Government Officials involved in the illegal immigration ring, removing all the electronic information of the transfers of the funds to the terrorists' accounts in Bern, Zurich, Luzern, Sankt Gallen, and Winterthur, Switzerland. Going back, he leaves a faint trail from the account of Patrick Flaherty to the account of the Maurice Solinger alias, via the account of the Canadian Prime Minister, in the DC Bank, Deposito-Cassa der Stadt in Bern, Switzerland. Searching the Maple Hill accounts he discovers the funds already in the seven DC Banks, Deposito-Cassa der Stadt in Bern, Switzerland. Marcel removes all electronic traces of the money entering the Maple Hill accounts except for the slightest trail to Maurice Solingers account in the DC Bank, Deposito-Cassa der Stadt. On Monday 20 men and women of Eastern European, North African, and Arabic descent will begin the process of pilfering $1.94 billion Euro from the Swiss Banks.

Pilfering

Monday, September 3rd, 2001. The members of The Maple Hill Mob, in their disguises wait as the banks in Bern, Switzerland open. At the tills they will withdraw $2,000 to $5,000 Euro and inform the banks they will be withdrawing $1million to $3 million September 4. At the banks in Luzern and Zurich, the withdrawals will take place September 5. On the evening of the third, Marcel is again at the computers cleaning up the accounts in Zurich, Sankt Gallen, and Winterthur. There is now no electronic trace of the funds transferring into the terrorists' accounts.

September 4th, Marcel, disguised as Hamed Ahmidam, withdraws $3 million dollars from his account in the DC Bank, Deposito-Cassa der Stadt in Bern. Standing three tills from him is Maurice Solinger making a similar withdrawal. Marcel walks over to Maurice and lifting his briefcase onto the counter, places it beside Maurice's briefcase, then exits the bank. Maurice fastens both briefcases to his wrists. Marcel is waiting outside the bank when Maurice, carrying two briefcases locked on his wrists, exits the building. Maurice Solinger in his disguise is a perfect replica of Gabriel Champlain, the brother of the Prime Minister, who is the current Canadian Ambassador to Switzerland. Although Maurice Solinger is slightly shorter than the Canadian Ambassador, this discrepancy will not be noticeable on security cameras.

Maurice and Marcel change their disguises and with the rest of the Maple Hill Mob continue withdrawing funds from the remaining Bern accounts. That evening Marcel transfers the remaining funds from the terrorists' Bern accounts to the terrorists' accounts in Geneva, Switzerland. Tomorrow night he will be closing all the accounts in Bern except for the "Gabriel Champlain" account in the DC Bank, Deposito-Cassa der Stadt. The removal of all electronic transfers sending and receiving funds between the bank accounts will drastically reduce any speedy discovery of the transfers of the money between the various financial institutions. The remaining paper trail will be slow and tedious to follow and it will dead-end once the last account is empty.

Marie Prichard enters the Schweizer Verband der Raiffeisenbanken in Sankt Gallen. She and Andrea Jones have a friendly wager on who will withdraw the most funds each day. Andrea has won the last two days, but not today. Marie addresses the teller in English – the language he used with his previous customer.

"My name is Aquila al Hashimi. Yesterday I informed the bank I would be making a withdrawal of $3million.

The teller, a Taliban, speaks to her contemptuously in an Afghanistan dialect. Marie reading the manner and speech of the man begins to seethe. She poses the question again, this time in French. Again, the teller speaks in the Afghanistan tongue, his mannerism contemptuous and his speech derisive.

Marie, her nerves already drawn taut from the pressure of making the withdrawals, explodes in her French tongue.

"You insolent pig. Find me a teller for me who is knowledgeable enough to understand either English or French."

The room is suddenly quiet. No Muslim woman dares speaks to a man like that. Everybody is watching and listening – not believing what they've heard.

The teller can't believe this woman would speak to him in this manner. He'll show her. Does she not know he's a man? He fails to see the security guard moving up behind him as another guard moves toward Marie. A lady has left her office and is rushing towards the scene of the confrontation. The teller again confronts the Muslim lady. This time in French.

"You dare you speak to me like that you old cow! May the wrath of Allah destroy you where you stand."

"Get out of my sight you insolent bastard!"

The teller feels a tap on his shoulder. Spinning around he finds himself looking into the unpleasant face of the security guard. The lady addresses the guard.

"Take him to my office and keep him there until I can take care of this customer – then I will speak to him."

"My name is Corinne. I must apologize for the behavior of that teller. It should never have happened, and it won't happen again. How may I assist you?"

"I want my money and I want it now!"

"Please don't condemn me for the boorish behavior of that teller. Will you give me your account number and I'll see how I can assist you?"

"My name is Aquila al Hashimi," Marie hands Corinne the bankcard with the account number on it.

Corinne accesses the number on the computer. The account leaps out at her – $19 million dollars!

"There is a notice in the account showing you wish to withdraw three million dollars today. The funds are waiting in a box in the safe. I'll take you to the safety deposit box cubicle to give you the funds."

"I've changed my mind. I require six million."

Corinne realizes the behavior of the teller has precipitated this problem but she must attempt to salvage the account.

"Would you give me a moment and I'll see if I can release the rest of the funds?"

Corinne quickly accesses the bank records.

"We do not have sufficient funds in this bank to release six million dollars. Would you accept five million, two hundred thousand dollars today and the remaining eight hundred thousand dollars tomorrow morning? I must apologize to you for the inconvenience we're causing you."

"I'll take five million at the present time," Marie answers in a slightly mollified tone. "I won't bother with the other million at this time."

"Thank you for your understanding. Meet me at that door," Corinne turns and points "and we'll complete the transaction within the safety of the vault."

Marie's actions will precipitate a much more aggressive stance in the rest of the Maple Hill Mob and the withdrawals will quickly increase in dollar volume.

That evening Marie collects her $10.00 wager from Andrea.

On the morning of Thursday, September 6th, the funds have been withdrawn from the banks in Luzern, Zurich, Sankt Gallen, and Winterthur, with the accounts transferred to the waiting accounts in Lausanne, Freibourg, Neuchatel, and Basel. The Maple Hill Mob now have $448 million Euro hiding in 42 safety deposit boxes in

Switzerland and $100 million Euro in a U.S. diplomatic pouch on a flight to Washington, D.C. In the afternoon, they begin duplicating the process in Geneva and Lausanne. Friday they make the withdrawals from the banks in Geneva and Lausanne then move on to the accounts in Freibourg and are working the accounts in Neuchatel when the banks close for the weekend.

Cecil Mann has talked to Detective Rene Dubois a couple of times but the information today is very disturbing. The courts have granted the R.C.M.P. jurisdiction to investigate the deaths of terrorists, C.S.I.S. agents, and the members of the R.C.M.P. in and at the Ferguson residence. The Crown dropped the charges against C.S.I.S. agents Marc Leblanc, Donald Prince and Roger Dugan and those men have returned to active duty. New arrest warrants were issued for Joe Ferguson, and Tom Jackson, charging them with murder. The R.C.M.P. are looking for Eileen, Keith and Gerald Ferguson for questioning in the shootings and they have issued a new warrant for the arrest of Cecil Mann for his complicity in the case. The investigation into the deaths in the Ferguson residence has now turned into a vendetta by the Canadian Justice Department.

Cecil places a call to William Smythe and apprises him of the situation in Ottawa.

"Will you be able to remain with Fergie's parents until we return and have a chance to find a safer place to disappear?"

"I don't think I can find a safer place to stay. Since the biker incident I've become their favorite son."

"I bet you have. You'll have to watch. The Mounties will begin observations on the farm in an attempt to find out when the Fergusons will be returning from Disneyland. They'll intensify their scrutiny of the farm when Joe doesn't return to work."

"Rene informed me customs is alerted for their return. Peter has become a lot more observant of his surroundings and I usually patrol the farm at night so the Mounties chance of surprising us is minimal. The fact they won't be expecting me to be on the farm is to my advantage and I've grown a beard and my hair is longer since you last saw me."

"Take care Cecil. Apprise me of any new developments."

During dinner, William sits with Tom and the Fergusons.

"I've been talking to Cecil Mann. He informed me the Justice Minister intervened to change the jurisdiction of the criminal investigation into the deaths at your residences. The R.C.M.P. are now conducting the investigation. Warrants have been issued for the arrest of Joe and Tom, charging them with murder. Keith, Jerry and Eileen also have warrants sworn out for their arrest. They are wanted for questioning. Cecil is charged with conspiracy."

"I was wondering when the Federal authorities would get involved. I presume they'll have the same reception planned for us as failed with Cecil."

"What was that dad?" asks Keith.

William explains, "When Cecil was incarcerated, C.S.I.S. placed a couple of assassins into the cell with him. We posted his bond before they had an opportunity to murder him. Later that night two C.S.I.S. agents broke into his suite in a further attempt to silence Cecil."

"Why did they try to kill Cecil?" asks Jerry.

"He was a witness against C.S.I.S. in the attempted assassination of your father."

"You don't believe they would try to kill us do you?" Jerry asks.

"It would be the simplest solution to the governments problem. With your family, Tom, and Cecil dead their problem would be quietly solved."

"I want to see my friends again."

"If you do go back to Ottawa you're not likely to see your friends although they will probably see you," William advises Jerry.

"Why won't I see them when they see me?"

"You don't see anything lying in a coffin."

"LLLLike AAAArt."

"Exactly like your friend Art. Remember – they've already tried to kill you twice."

"When?"

William explodes.

"**When… You ask me when… When the terrorists broke into your home and butchered the beds…. When the biker tried to shoot your grandfather…. That's when…. Quit acting like your mother.**"

"We'll have to stay in the States when we finish our little escapade Tom. The Canadian climate isn't healthy anymore."

"I've been thinking the same thing myself. I'm sure going to miss my Government Pension Cheque though. It's not like I'm made of money."

Saturday morning Marcel eats a quick breakfast, and then walks to the U.S. Embassy. He leaves a second $100 million in a diplomatic pouch destined for Washington DC, then begins working the computer transferring the terrorists' bank accounts in Geneva and Lausanne to the terrorists' accounts in the Channel Islands. Going back, he finishes cleaning up the terrorists' bank accounts that have the funds removed.

At noon on Wednesday, September 12th, Marcel is in the Office of the Pierre Richeau Shipping Company in Basel, Switzerland consigning boxes of freight for overnight delivery to Paris, France. The freight consists of all the disguises of the Maple Hill Mob, and the extra clothing of the members sneaking back into France and Germany. They are to be picked up by the Montreal based, Cirque du Soleil on Thursday for a performance Thursday evening. A gentleman sporting flaming red hair and beard named Eric Jensen, better known to his friends as Eric the Red, signs the bill of lading.

Marcel, sitting in the airport in Basel, relaxes a bit. Everything has gone as planned. Over one billion Euro dollars is sitting in 84 safety deposit boxes in 84 different banks in Switzerland, and another two hundred million Euro dollars is waiting for them in Washington DC. Each member of the group is carrying $20,000 Euro on their person. These funds will take care of any unforeseen contingency.

The Ferguson, Smythe and Watson families are back in France and flying to Paris where the Watson and Smythe families will board a flight to land in Heathrow airport in England. The Jones and Johansen families and Tom Jackson are in Germany, headed for Stuttgart where they will board flights for London, England. Maurice and Kathleen Solinger will board a flight tonight from Bern, Switzerland to Paris and Andre and Marie Prichard will be on a flight to the same destination from Zurich. The boarding call comes and Marcel Roy and his parents are on their way to Paris.

Terrorist Attack

The Roys are clearing customs at Charles Degaulle Airport when a marine steps up to him and speaks.

"Pardon me, are you Marcel Roy?"

"Yes I am."

"Ambassador John Patterson is inviting you to dinner at the U.S. Embassy tonight. I am to escort you."

"I will require some time to shower and change. What time is the dinner?"

"You are to come as you are. The dinner is informal but the Ambassador requires your presence as soon as possible."

Marcel asks his parents to pick up the van waiting at the rental agency, and then book into their hotel room. The marine escorts him to the waiting Embassy limousine. Forty-five minutes later, the car enters the Embassy grounds. There are six marines on high alert located behind barricades in the compound. Marcel looks over the situation for a moment then asks the marine seated beside him, "What's the reason for the extra security in the Embassy?"

The marine looks hard at Marcel, and then answers with a question of his own.

"Haven't you heard about the terrorist attacks on the World Trade Center in New York City and the Pentagon in Washington DC?" They hijacked four commercial airliners and crashed two of them into the Twin Towers and another into the White House."

Marcel is shocked. This is unbelievable. He finally responds, "I'm truly sorry. Will you excuse my ignorance of the events? I just didn't know."

Suddenly Marcel remembers – 'the letter Montague was carrying – men from Saudi Arabia. The Internet information he found – wtc – World Trade Centre – wh –White House – a al-z? a al-z? a al-z? Zawahri! **Ayman al-Zawahri!** That's why he was in Canada. I should have searched further.'

In the Embassy, Marcel introduces himself to Ambassador John Patterson. The Ambassador, in turn introduces the two gentlemen who will be dining with them, David Kaiser and Andrew Dahl, two key members of the U.S. State Department.

"Marcel in light of the terrorist attacks inside our borders we need people of your expertise to help us to track down and destroy the al-Qaeda terrorist organization responsible for the attack on our country and also to provide us with the knowledge of other planned activities of this, and other terrorist groups. Henry Kilmer, the U.S. Ambassador to Canada, gave us a full account of your expertise with a computer. He informed us he was watching as you bypass the security on the Embassy Computer and within minutes, you were able to access the FBI computer in Washington. We are willing to pay you $200,000 per year and cover all your expenses. If, after six months you require further funding, we will be willing to re-negotiate with you on the money you will require to do the job."

Marcel thinks carefully on the offer before answering.

"I'm willing to assist you in the tracking of these terrorists because it's in my interest as well as yours, but I would never accept any remuneration for my help. The American government will have to cover all my expenses, but I must remain, at all times, a visitor to your country. Under the present circumstances, I could never accept American citizenship. Even if I sit at desk in Washington every day for 30 years, I must remain a visitor."

Andrew Dahl becomes upset with Marcel's statement and blurts out, "What do you have against American citizenship?"

The Ambassador to France replies quietly to the outburst, "I don't believe he has anything against American citizenship. His problem is American taxation."

"I have a bigger problem with Canadian taxation. Within the next two years, I will be obtaining citizenship in either Ireland or Costa Rica. At the present time I am favoring Costa Rica, but both countries have their benefits."

Ambassador Patterson is laughing, "The main benefit of both those countries is their tax laws. Neither country taxes the income received from offshore accounts – right Marcel?"

The four men discuss the situation for another hour. Marcel borrows the use of a computer and transfers the last accounts from Basel Switzerland to the terrorists' accounts in the Channel Islands, then cleans up the remaining electronic information on the bank accounts in Switzerland. The three men standing behind him are amazed at his proficiency in entering and exiting the accounts without leaving any trace of his presence.

"Andrew, why don't you get Marcel to do your banking for you?" David Kaiser jokes with his friend.

"I was thinking of having him do your banking for me," is Andrew Dahl's repartee.

Marcel joins in the frivolity, "Why don't you leave me your account numbers and we'll see what happens?" Then Marcel gets serious, "I'll come back here tomorrow morning and catch a commercial flight to Cherbourg. I could be back here Saturday afternoon to look for information – we'll be sitting around Sunday."

"There's an airport on the Isle of Jersey," the U.S. Ambassador interjects. "What time Saturday afternoon should we pick you up?"

After a short discussion, a marine chauffeurs Marcel to the hotel.

Night Shift

Cecil Mann, still believing there could be danger from C.S.I.S. or the R.C.M.P. continues to patrol the farm each evening from 11:00 p.m. until 5:30 a.m. Leaning against a tree, Cecil enjoys the chorus of the frogs emanating from the pond beside the road. The song ends.... Why?... He slips beneath a bush and lies on the ground, gripping his 9 mm automatic. The cloudy night is thick – you can almost cut it with a knife. The frogs begin their song again. First one – then two – then in full chorus. Listen… listen… listen…. Nothing…. The crickets stop chirping. The frogs continue their melody. Still…. No crickets singing…. Muscles tightening…. Shhh – shhh – shhh – shhh…. Something in the grass… A coon…? Cigarette smoke…. Cecil freezes.

A ghostly whisper emanates out of the dark, "The lights are out – they'll be sleeping."

Another voice whispers back, "I'll set the timer for half an hour and put the bomb on the front step. There's enough plastic explosive to blow the house down and the incendiaries should finish the job. By the time the fire department arrives there won't be anything left."

The first voice whispers eerily through the black of the night air, "Sounds good. We'll wait in the car and leave after the explosion."

Quietly placing the bomb, two shadows slip past Cecil. Soon the clop, clop, clopping of running feet is heard, moving down the lane and onto the road. Cecil, having retrieved the bomb, is gliding silently behind them, a wraith in the darkness, floating eerily above the road.

Again, the frogs stop their chorus. As the two men enter their car, Cecil slips into the cornfield, and moving quickly, is soon behind the car backed into the edge of the cornfield. The two officers, conversing in the car, are oblivious of the danger Cecil poses as he advances on hands and knees and slides the bomb under the car. Crawling backwards, he is soon moving quickly through the corn and then gliding down the road – A ghost returning to his lair.

One Mountie steps out of the car and moves towards the back of the vehicle. He stands looking – waiting for the bomb to explode….

B-O-O-O-M. The night sky lights up behind Cecil as the sound blasts through him – tearing at him as it passes – ripping at the essence of life within his body…. Silence – the song of the frogs is no more – no crickets to relieve the monotony with their pleasant chirps – nothing but the sound of running feet, swish, swish, swishing down the road towards a light in a window.

Peter and June Ferguson, awakened by the explosion, dress quickly. Explaining the visitors, Cecil packs his belongings and leaves knowing the R.C.M.P. will be conducting an investigation into the bombing. Cecil is soon driving west on the 401 and stops to sleep at a rest station. He awakens to the light patter of raindrops on the roof of the station wagon. Lying quietly in the car, he soon drifts off to sleep again. The rain will continue for the next three days, removing all evidence of his participation in the explosion that killed two members of the R.C.M.P.

Peter Ferguson phones his neighbors to discuss the explosion and three neighbors decide to join the Ferguson's to survey the site of the explosion. When the neighbors drive up to the flaming wreck, Peter and his wife join them. The four families are walking around in the cornfield when the Ontario Provincial Police arrive. Peter and June have guaranteed there will be no footprints linking Cecil to the blast. After giving statements, the four families drive home.

As Cecil Mann drives west on the 401, he receives a phone call from Marlene Moore. The lovebirds arrange to meet at three o'clock the following morning. Two days later, they are entering the town of Orangeville, Ontario. Cecil spots a private airport. The sun is shining brightly in a clear blue sky after the rain of the previous days. Soon he and Marlene are enjoying a tour of the area with Cecil at the controls of the plane he has rented. The trees and grass are magnificent in the beautiful green hues that only a rain can deliver. A crop of golden barley stands proudly waiting for the swather to make an endless yellow brick road in the field. Their flight carries them over a herd of Holstein cows grazing peacefully in a well-trimmed pasture, unseen tails flicking at the flies and mosquitoes that are their constant companions. Lakes and ponds, sparkling in the golden sun, are turquoise jewels scattered everywhere. The beautiful rainbow that flows along beside the plane and leaves as suddenly as it appeared captivates Marlene.

Late in the afternoon of the day following the explosion, two members of the R.C.M.P. drive into the Ferguson farmyard.
June and Peter Ferguson step onto their front step to speak with the Mounties. A light drizzle is falling.

"I'm Officer Josh Brown and this is Officer Mary O'Neill. We're here to follow up the investigation of the car that exploded down the road from your house. We were wondering if you might have found any new evidence or remembered anything new."

"A loud explosion wakened my wife and me," Peter Ferguson explains. "When we looked out the window we saw a fire burning which we thought was on the road. We phoned the Provincial Police, and then phoned our neighbors. When we saw a neighbor drive up to the fire we went to investigate ourselves. We were there when the police arrived.

"After it started to get light, my neighbor found the licence plate fastened to the bumper of the car in my cornfield. The police checked the licence and found it belonged to the R.C.M.P. detachment stationed at 1200 Vanier Parkway in Ottawa. The Provincial Police had no idea why Mounties from Ottawa would be parked on my land with a bomb. Maybe you could tell us?"

"We hadn't heard they were members of the R.C.M.P." Officer Brown lies. "Do you and your wife live here alone?"

"Yes we do." Peter replies.

"Could we step inside and talk it's quite miserable out here?" Officer O'Neill asks the Fergusons.

June Ferguson is thinking about the question posed by Officer Josh Brown. 'That's why they were here. They thought Joe and Eileen were here and the bomb was to kill them'. "You came out here to find out if Joe and Eileen were here or to find out where they are. Get off our farm and stay off. **Go! Go!**"

Officer Brown denies the allegation, "No. We're here to investigate the explosion."

"My wife told you to leave. Now go!"

Peter Ferguson whirls on his heel and starts to enter the house. The two Mounties jump and grab Peter, throwing him to the ground, then handcuffing him. June races into the house, slamming the door behind her. While they are controlling Peter, she dials 911, "This is June Ferguson! Mounties are beating my husband! We farm a half-mile north of highway 42 on Rourke road just east of Belle River! Please, please, hurry!"

Josh Brown hurls through the closed door, peeling it from the wall. He grabs the handset from June Ferguson, ripping it from the phone. The Mountie jumps for June as she grabs the pot of boiling soup from the stove and hurls it in his face. He pulls his gun from the holster and fires but misses – he is unable see her. June steps in and swings the heavy aluminum pot, catching the officer full in the face and knocking him down. He drops his gun and is on his knees trying to find the weapon when June hits him on the temple with the pot. Bung! – He's out cold. June picks up the gun from the floor as Officer O'Neill hollers.

"Do you have her under control Josh?"

June screams at the officer on the porch.

"If you try to come in here I'll shoot him in the head."

"June she's going to shoot through the window," Peter hollers, warning his wife.

"Now she's standing four feet from the window and pointing her gun at me."

CRACK! June shoots through the wall missing Officer O'Neill.

"She's running to the car," Peter hollers to his wife. She has a rifle pointing at me. Don't come out."

June rolls up a string mop and slides it partially into view in a window. **Crack!** The missile, blasting from the rifle, smashes the window and sends the mop spinning from her hands.

"She's running towards the house."

June steps into the doorway. The Mountie whirls and races back to the cover provided by the car. She looks back to see June dragging her husband into the house. **Crack!** The missile plows through Peter's still extended leg, then he's out of sight. June slides the mop into the window opening again then jerks it back. Another projectile blasts into the house.

June quickly bandages Peter's leg.

Officer Brown begins to stir. Bung! – He's not stirring any more.

Officer O'Neill is behind the car pointing her rifle at the house when the Ontario Provincial Police (O.P.P.) arrive on the scene. Two more Provincial Police vehicles arrive in short order. An intense argument ensues. Officer O'Neill's weapons are confiscated and the O.P.P. order her into the back seat of their vehicle. The police remove the cuffs from Peter's wrists. An ambulance is contacted.

June and Peter Ferguson give their accounts of the developments that led to the altercation and then the fight itself. The ambulance staff examines Peter who has a split on his forehead, broken nose, split lip and contusions on his face, all consistent with having his face driven into the deck of the front porch. On his back is a bruise and cracked rib caused by a fist while the Mounties were controlling him on the ground. In the doorway is blood from the leg wound. Peter stated in his evidence he was opening the door of the house to get him and his wife away from the argument. The Mounties could look at the closed door as long as they pleased. June Ferguson has a bruise on her arm and a strained shoulder consistent with the Mountie grabbing and jerking her. The police find the smashed door, the smashed window, evidence of three rifle shells entering the home, the broken phone in the corner of the kitchen and they have the 911 dispatcher's evidence, including the crash of the breaking door.

The O.P.P lay charges of assault and assault with a deadly weapon against R.C.M.P. Officers Josh Brown and Mary O'Neill. Officer Brown will give his statement from his hospital bed in Windsor, Ontario where the first ambulance is transporting him. A second ambulance will deliver Peter to the same hospital in Windsor. The story of the shooting is on the evening news telecast and the persecution of the Ferguson family continues to receive extensive coverage on all the major Canadian news stations.

In identifying both officers, the press lists them as members of the same Ottawa R.C.M.P. detachment as the two members of the R.C.M.P. killed by a bomb, in their car, at the Ferguson farm the previous night.

The Search

"Eric the Red" is waiting when the Pierre Richeau Shipping Company opens its doors. At the hotel the Ferguson, Prichard, Solinger, and Roy families take two vans and the disguises and leave on their drive to Cherbourg, on the English Channel.

Marcel returns to the U.S. Embassy. Seated at a computer he removes the evidence of the transfer of funds from the terrorist accounts in Basel. Completing that task he begins the search for the al-Qaeda terrorist, Ayman al-Zawahri, whom US authorities believe masterminded the terrorist attacks of September 11th. Slowly he traces the terrorist's movements. Late in the afternoon of September 13, he completes his research.

<u>Ayman al-Zawahri</u>

Confederates in Canada are Abdulaziz Issa Abdul-Mohsin al-Mogrin, located in a safe house at 173 Forest Hill Road in Toronto, and Hamed Ahmidam, in a safe house at 96 Powell Avenue, Ottawa.

Left Canada from Pearson International Airport August 22nd, 2001, using the alias Adbed Moez and landed in Paris, France.

From Paris he flew to Cairo, Egypt.

Using the alias Amin Othman, from Cairo he flew to Khartoum in the Sudan. Met with Abdullah Ahmed Abdullah for three days.

Flew from Khartoum, Sudan to Riyadh, Saudi Arabia using the alias *Mahmoud el-Hafnawi*.

Met with Riduan Isamuddin for two days

Flew from Riyadh, Saudi Arabia to Lahore, Pakistan then on to Kabul Afghanistan. He met with Osama bin-Ladin in a camp north of Kabul. He is now in the Hindu Kish Mountains in northeastern Afghanistan.

Ambassador John Patterson reads the report and speaks to Marcel

"Our experts in Washington lost the trail in Cairo and don't have the names of his fellow operatives in Canada. I'll send this missive in to the F.B.I. and the C.I.A. The C.I.A. will be following up the leads in Khartoum, Sudan and Riyadh, Saudi Arabia. The people we will want most are his confederates in Toronto and Ottawa in Canada."

The Ambassador leaves Marcel Roy to his work then returns a few minutes later and hands him a note.

Donald Prince and Roger Dugan of C.S.I.S. arrived in Bern, Switzerland this afternoon. They proceeded to question the bank manager of the DC Bank, Deposito-Cassa der Stadt about the state of certain accounts. They have rooms at the Freienhofgasse # 3, 3600 Thun in Bern.

Marcel contacts Salama al-Yawer by entering the E – mail code s.al.y@aol.com.

Donald Prince and Roger Dugan of C.S.I.S. arrived in Bern, Switzerland this afternoon. They have rooms at the Freienhofgasse # 3, 3600 Thun in Bern.

These two members of the Canadian Justice Department represent a real danger to me and thus the danger automatically extends to you and your compatriots. These officials of the Canadian Justice System will not remain in Bern past the 18th day of September because they will have all the information they require by that date to destroy us. I spy.

Marcel enters the bank accounts of the government civil servants and the Members of Parliament in La Premiere Banque de Commerce de la Bern, Suisse. Working cautiously, he makes all the accounts drain directly or indirectly into the bank account of the Prime Minister. Three hours later, he exits the bank accounts with $1.17 million in the account of the Prime Minister.

Marcel, working the Internet, discovers pertinent information. Two Saudi Arabian terrorists, Abu Rusdan and Nasir Abbas are currently on a flight to Toronto, Ontario using Canadian passports obtained from the Canadian Consulate in Paris. They will be arriving at Kennedy Airport in three hours for a short layover then continuing on to Pearson airport in Toronto. Marcel's dossier includes photographs, flight number, seat numbers, arrival, and departure times at Kennedy airport. Ambassador John Patterson passes the information to his head office in Washington, D.C. The F.B.I. will be waiting for Abu Rusdan and Nasir Abbas when their plane lands.

Marcel again contacts Salama al-Yawer.

Canadian authorities have received $834,000 from the F.B.I. for the information Abu Rusdan and Nasir Abbas will be arriving in Kennedy airport. The F.B.I. will be arresting the two men upon arriving in the U.S. at 4:09 a.m. Arrangements were made through the Canadian Embassies in Washington and Paris. I spy.

Salama al-Yawer will find this piece of information on her E-mail two hours after the terrorists are in custody.

Channel Islands

Marcel flies to the airport in Cherbourg, France. From there, his parents drive him to the waiting yacht. Members of the Maple Hill Mob will enjoy a cruise along the coastline of France in United States Embassy yachts leaving from Portsmouth, England and Cherbourg, France. Part of the tour includes visits to the Isle of Guernsey on September 14th and again on the 18th, and visits to the Isle of Jersey on the 15th and 19th. The second phase of operation money grab is about to begin.

In the afternoon of September 15th, an Embassy jet picks up Marcel on the Isle of Jersey and whisks him off to the American Embassy in Paris. He returns on the evening of September 17^{th,} to Jersey. A cab drives Marcel to the waiting yacht, which sails to join the other yacht, docking at the Isle of Guernsey.

Also on September 17th, the offices of C.S.I.S. and the R.C.M.P. in Ottawa receive faxes showing the Canadian Ambassador to Switzerland, Gabriel Champlain withdrawing three million Euro dollars from La Premiere Banque de Commerce de la Suisse in Bern, Switzerland, then receiving another briefcase containing another three million Euro dollars and carrying both briefcases out the door of the financial institution. Patrick Flaherty, the new R.C.M.P. Commissioner is not impressed watching his ill-gotten funds disappear. Somebody is going to pay for this. Included in his information is evidence of all the accounts of the people involved in the illegal immigration operation still draining into the account of the Prime Minister of Canada.

All work ceases in the illegal immigration ring as the civil servants and mandarins learn of the loss of their funds. Accusations fly in Ottawa and in the Canadian Foreign Embassies.

Tuesday, September 18th, the Maple Hill Mob remove their funds from the banks on the Isle of Guernsey, then visit the Isle of Jersey and repeat the process September 19th. With their successes in Switzerland and the knowledge the Canadian and Swiss authorities are attempting to trace the funds, they are far more aggressive in their withdrawals from the financial institutions in the Channel Islands – with excellent results.

At the airport on the Island of Jersey the Roy family, the Solinger family and Andre Prichard wait for the plane belonging to the American Embassy in Paris. The plane lands, and Marcel greets Bill Johnston, personal secretary to the U.S. Ambassador to France, and escorts him to the waiting van. Inside the van the secretary stamps the boxes containing the disguises to be sent to Washington DC and 250 million pounds sterling is transferred into diplomatic pouches, which Marcel will carry with him. They place the terrorist information and passports into anther diplomatic pouch for delivery to the F.B.I. Office in Orlando, Florida. The Roy and Solinger families leave on the U.S. Embassy plane with Bill Johnston. Andre Prichard returns the van to the rental company then walks to the waiting yacht. The embassy yacht destined for Portsmouth, England is already on its way and the embassy yacht stationed in Cherbourg, France will soon return to its homeport.

On the flight back to Paris, Bill Johnston fills Marcel in on the murders, in their hotel beds, of two members of the Canadian Security and Intelligence Service in Bern, Switzerland. The Maple Hill Mob have a brief respite from their fears of being caught removing the funds from their terrorist accounts.

In the American Embassy, Marcel transfers the funds remaining in the Channel Island accounts to one hundred and sixty terrorist accounts in the Bahamas. The accounts break down to eighty accounts in Nassau on the Island of New Providence, eighty accounts in Freeport, Grand Bahama Island. After removing the funds from those accounts the remaining funds will make their last transfer to sixty terrorist bank accounts on the Island of Turks and sixty terrorist bank accounts on the island of Caicos, in the Bahamas.

Ambassador John Patterson enters the room, "Well Marcel. It looks like you've pulled off the coup you planned. Interpol knows Canada is shielding terrorists. Knowing the loss of the money received by the Canadian Government will destroy the ring they plan to dead-end any police action on the disappearance of the money from the Swiss banks."

"Your saying there won't be any investigation in the Channel Islands."

"That's right. With the discovery of the Canadian Ambassador to Switzerland on the bank security films, relations have really soured between the governments of Switzerland and Canada. Continued belligerence by the Canadian government, and they're really battling to recover their money, will force the Swiss

Government to expel the Canadian Embassy. When the Swiss government expels the Canadian Embassy, they will deal Canada a major blow in international relations.

The discovery of the Canadian Ambassador illegally removing funds from the DC Bank, Deposito-Cassa der Stadt has allowed that financial institution to refuse repayment of the funds. The bank dares not conduct too intensive of a search because word of your achievements would destroy their credibility. They also realize that an extensive investigation might prove the Canadian government correct and the bank would then have to reimburse the bank accounts. That's a scenario neither the DC Bank, Deposito-Cassa der Stadt, nor the Swiss government has any intention of allowing to happen.

Interpol has their own reason for dropping the case," adds John Patterson. The dossiers you provided on the terrorists in Canada is bringing their files on those terrorists up to date. Most of them had disappeared off Interpol's radar and they want to continue working, through you, with us, to obtain the information on the rest of the terrorists."

"This is a relief to me," states Marcel, "and will be a relief to everybody involved with me. This is a major step to end this government's illegal activities."

"When the Canadian Embassy is removed from Switzerland the Swiss government and the DC Bank, Deposito-Cassa der Stadt de la Suisse will stop all Canadian investigation of their records. The Canadian government cannot allow anybody to discover why the funds were in the bank and they certainly can't do anything that will get the reporters snooping. You have achieved your goal and the results must be greater than even you believed possible."

Marcel smiles, "The news keeps getting better and better. My hope is to remove this corrupt government from power but I certainly can't complain about the results. I hope to work with your agencies and eliminate more of the security risks posed by these terrorists. Members of the Canadian government have, through their greed, exposed both our countries to terrorist actions. I know we will never rid Canada of all the terrorists the Liberal Government has admitted inside our borders but by working together we may yet hope to negate their actions and expose them to the public.

We all need to thank you for all your government's assistance in our efforts to destroy the government immigration ring. Without the full co-operation of the American Government we could never have achieved the results we have in such short order."

"The disclosure of the terrorists within the borders of Canada and the destruction of the government organization bringing them in is invaluable to the U.S. Government," states the Ambassador. "For diplomatic reasons you don't exist but my orders to help you came right from the top."

The Embassy chauffeurs Marcel to the airport, where his parents are holding his boarding pass. He joins his parents and the Solingers for the flight to Washington via New York. Chained to Marcel's wrists are the diplomatic pouches containing 250 million pounds destined for a vault in the F.B.I. offices in Washington D.C.

The Airplane

The plane lands in Washington in the early hours of September 20th. An F.B.I. helicopter chauffeurs Marcel to the F.B.I. offices to place the diplomatic pouches in a vault, and then a government limousine chauffeurs him to the hotel for some much-needed sleep.

Marcel arrives at the headquarters of the F.B.I. to begin working. He removes all traces of the transfer of funds from the financial institutions in the Channel Islands to the waiting accounts in the Bahamas.

Marcel Roy is searching for a terrorist in Spain when Robert Green, a top ranking F.B.I. agent enters the room and speaks to him.

"Muslim terrorists broke into the Canadian Embassy in France early this morning, killing all the Canadian staff. Two of the terrorists were killed trying to escape and one member of the group was captured after being wounded."

"The Canadian Government never expected these kinds of repercussions from their policies," Marcel acknowledges. "In some ways it's gratifying to see them bearing the fruits of their labors."

Yes it is," agrees Robert Green. "The Swiss Government has learned that the Canadian ambassadors to France, Denmark and Germany along with five Liberal Cabinet Ministers were in Switzerland while you were so busy in their country. One of those Cabinet Ministers just happened to be the Prime Minister. When he returned to Canada he just happened to be carrying two large suitcases that bore diplomatic seals. I gather your Prime Minister is no longer a happy camper. Swiss intelligence has also discovered Canadian Members of Parliament and civil servants visited Italy, Austria, France and Germany during the last two weeks. With the preponderance of evidence and the belligerence of the Canadian Government, I expect the Canadian Foreign Embassy to be expelled from Switzerland within the next few days."

Joe and Tom are poring over government newsletters when Tom finds an airplane the F.B.I. has confiscated as part of a drug bust listed for sale. The two men discuss the benefits the plane would accord them then Joe phones Marcel.

"Marcel here."

"It's Joe. Tom found a Cessna 414 we could use for flying to both the Bahamas and Cayman Islands. I'm interested in buying it if the U.S. Government will sell it to a Canadian. The F.B.I. confiscated the plane when they caught drug runners using it."

"What other information do you have on the plane?"

"It's eight passenger, pressurized cabin, retractable running gear, cruises at 200 miles per hour and with the locker tanks has a range of 1,000 to 1,100 miles. This plane has a satellite guidance system for long-range navigation. The US government is asking \$280,000 for the plane, which is probably worth closer to \$350,000 because it has less than 200 flying hours."

"I don't believe any of the Maple Hill Mob has a pilot licence but I'll contact Robert Green and see what we can do. I'll give you a call when I have information for you, but you need to ask around to see if we have a pilot in the group.

Marcel phones Robert Green at his residence.

A child answers, "This is the Green Residence."

"Could I speak to Robert Green please?"

"Poppa, It's for you."

"Hello. This is Robert Green."

Marcel relates the reason for the call and gives Robert the phone number and lot number for the sale of the Cessna.

A few minutes later Robert returns the call. "Yes they'll deal. Their asking price is $280,000. He won't tell me the highest bid but he did say anything over $196,000 would take it.

Marcel laughs. "He won't tell you the highest bid eh. How does $220,000 U.S. sound to you?"

"Sounds like you might have just bought a plane. Stay on the line while I confirm the transaction."

Robert comes back on the phone. "You've bought a plane. He's faxing the bill of sale to my office. Who's name do you want on the bill of sale?"

"Peter Joseph Ferguson. I'll give you the money in the morning."

Marcel contacts Joe.

"You've bought a plane – $220,000 U.S."

"Good. I still have $210,000 in the New York account. I'll borrow the rest from the boys."

"Just withdraw $125,000. It's worth $5,000 apiece from the rest of us for the convenience and security the plane will provide. Instead just take out $120,000 and I'll kick in $10,000 for my share."

Marcel hangs up the phone and speaks to Shannon Johansen, seated across the table.

"This dinner hasn't turned out to be very romantic for our first date."

Shannon laughs. "Maybe we'll have to make our second date our first date?"

Joe and Tom speak to the other members of the Maple Hill Mob but no one has a pilot licence. Bob Watson had flown planes before but that was twenty years ago. In desperation, Joe calls his father in Belle River.

"No Sammy had to quit flying but we have a character sitting in the house who just might be able to fly the plane. I would say, by the looks of him, he could really use the work. Scruffy looking character though. I don't know if you'd want to be seen with him. If you do see him make sure you stand upwind. I can handle it – I'm a pig farmer. Still he's on the front step and we're talking through the screen door."

Joe can hear laughter in the background.

"What experience does he have?"

"What experience do you have?"

Peter is back on the phone to Joe again. "His parents own a Cessna 180. He had his pilot licence before his driver licence. While attending Simon Fraser University, he held summer jobs flying water bombers for the B.C. Department of Forestry. Yes, I would say he has the ability to fly your plane."

Marcel Roy and Joe Ferguson are waiting in the F.B.I. building when Robert Green arrives. Two hours later Joe Ferguson and his sons, Keith and Jerry leave for Orlando, Florida. Three cars are making the trip to Orlando, the Fergusons', Tom Jackson's and the Pritchards'. Passengers in the cars are the Joneses, Solingers and the disguises.

In the afternoon, Cecil Mann and Marlene Moore are on a flight from Detroit, Michigan to Orlando, Florida. When Cecil arrives the airplane registration for the Cessna and his green card and gun permit will be waiting for him. Looking at the young lady sitting beside him, Cecil decides that's where he would like her to be for the rest of his life.

On Monday, September the 24th, The Maple Hill Mob begin removing funds from the terrorists' bank accounts in the Bahamas and on Tuesday October 2nd, the last pound sterling is safely stored in the last safety deposit box and the members are back in Orlando, Florida. The Cessna has performed beautifully hopping between the islands picking up and dropping off the members of the Maple Hill Mob as required. The Arabic clothing has disappeared into a dozen dumpsters located throughout the city and the terrorist passports and personal information is back with the F.B.I. They exchange the U.S. passports and information for their Canadian passports and documentation. Once again they are citizens of Canada.

Time to Relax

The Maple Hill Mob gathers for a final luncheon together at the Imperial Hotel in Orlando, Florida when Tom Jackson stands up to speak.

We all drew straws to see who would have the opportunity to speak. I lost. I guess I better get on with what I was told to say. We all decided that divvying up the money with Marcel getting two shares and the rest of us getting one share just isn't fair. No sir, it just isn't fair to Marcel. We all noticed Marcel enjoys flying as we hopped back and forth between the islands. Marcel even took over the controls for a short time on a few of those hops. I was so scared I almost wet my pants and Fergie had a look of pure terror on his mug. Anyways, back to what I was saying. Marcel enjoyed the flying so much we decided to do something for him so show them what we bought him Fergie. (Joe is holding up a World War 2 flying helmet). The members of the Maple Hill Mob pass the helmet down the table to Marcel. Now the outfit isn't complete without this (Joe holds up a fleece lined flight jacket) and this (a long white scarf) and this (a pair of goggles). Now I thought we'd already spent enough money but some smart guy comes up with the bright idea of finding a plane for you. I went along with the idea until I found out they expected me to help pay for it. I lost again. It's funny how some people want to tell me how to spend my own money. Anyway, we started looking around. I found a plane that had hit a tree and came with a hundred and fifty pounds of glue. Then we found a Harvard that has the seats one behind the other. As we all know, Shannon vetoed that plane. I'm not as dumb as I look. I know why she vetoed that plane. Then we looked at a Cessna 180 but Shannon didn't want that one either because she didn't want Alex and Gloria or Henri and Irena tagging along when you went flying. Anyways Cecil assured me you weren't worth a Cessna 180. We looked at a lot of two-seater planes and finally came up with one we figured you both might be satisfied with. When you get back to Washington, your going to find the plane these other snooks voted to spend my money on, a brand, spanking new two-seater, Cessna 414 with spare back seats. Then some smart guy comes up with the idea of flying lessons – using my money again. My money! I'm not going to tell you his name but his initials are Bob Watson. Anyways, we spoke to Cecil about teaching Marcel to fly and he assured us that if he instructed you for two hours a day he would guarantee you would have your pilot's licence in fifteen years, give or take a month."

Joe picks up his glass of wine, "To Marcel Roy, Don of the Maple Hill Mob – the man who made wanted criminals of us all."

Cayman Islands

Tomorrow the Prichard and Jones families will visit Disney World for two days then leave on their long drive back to Ottawa.

Andre Prichard has neatly packaged all the wigs and beards in their traveling cases. Marcel will be taking them to Washington with him. From there, the U.S. government will transport them, under a diplomatic seal, to the American Embassy in Ottawa.

Marcel and Joe have retrieved three diplomatic pouches from the hotel vault and the Maple Hill Mob move 142.8 million pounds sterling from two diplomatic pouches into eleven briefcases. They remove the 100 million Euro dollars from the other diplomatic pouch and place those funds into seven different briefcases.

Joe returns the briefcase containing the remainder of the Pounds Sterling to the safe of the Imperial Hotel. Stopping at a convenience store in the hotel, Joe picks up a newspaper to search for an apartment on Wednesday. Sitting down in his room, he reads the news on the front page.

Canadian Ambassador to Switzerland killed. Swiss authorities arrest four Canadian Embassy workers and charge them with the crime.

Cecil Mann has been sleeping since 3:00 p.m. At 1:00 a.m., he will be piloting the Cessna on a flight to the Cayman Islands. His passengers for the trip are the Johansen and Solinger families, Marcel Roy and William Smythe. These members of the Maple Hill Mob are asleep by 7:00 p.m.

At midnight, Tom Jackson and Joe Ferguson leave the hotel, driving to a private airport with the seven members of the Maple Hill Mob destined for the Cayman Islands. Cecil Mann checks the airplane and then fires up the motor. After checking the gauges, he clicks on the satellite guidance system. Cecil had earlier entered the flight coordinates into the system but he checks it once more before taking off. Snapping on the landing lights, Cecil starts down the runway. An hour later, he is dropping down to land at Key West to top up his fuel tanks. Taking off again Cecil flies the Cessna west, circling around Cuba, then on to Georgetown on the Island of Grand Cayman. The members of the Maple Hill Mob have dozed for most of the trip. Marcel takes control of the plane for the last hour, turning it back to Cecil to land.

Cecil finds the private airport he is looking for. Taxiing up to the hanger, he stops the plane next to a waiting van and steps out of the plane. Signing the necessary documents, Cecil receives the key and starts the van. After transferring the briefcases to the van, Cecil pilots the Cessna to a designated site and secures it to the ground. The van, driven by Gloria Johansen, is on its way to the first bank in Georgetown.

The bank opens for business. Cecil exits the sliding door and steps towards the rear of the van – his eyes miss nothing. Marcel exits the van and steps to the front, scrutinizing both ways on the sidewalk. The bulges under their jackets are deliberately obvious. Shannon Johansen steps from the van carrying two briefcases secured to her wrists. Marcel follows her into the area between the double doors and stops while Shannon proceeds past the security bars and into the bank. Cecil keeps guard on the sidewalk in front of the bank. Alex Johansen steps from the van and closes the door, moving to the back of the van. He surveys all the activity on the streets. In a private office, Shannon signs the necessary documents and deposits 11.9 million pounds sterling into her account. When she moves to the vault with the safety deposit boxes, Maurice Solinger exits the van followed by his wife, Kathleen, carrying two briefcases fastened to her wrists. They enter a different financial institution following the identical procedure.

The process continues until 142.8 million pounds sterling are deposited into ten accounts of 11.9 million pounds sterling each and Marcel Roy's account containing 23.8 million pounds sterling. The 100 million Euro dollars is safe – locked in the seven safety deposit boxes of these members of Maple Hill Mob. They drive back to the Cessna, unfasten it from its anchors, fuel up and begin the flight back to Florida. On Friday morning, Cecil Mann will be making the trip to the Island of Little Cayman. Tom Jackson, Joe Ferguson, Henri and Irena Roy, Bob and Mary Watson and Heather Smythe will be depositing 107.1 million pounds sterling into nine Maple Hill accounts and hiding the remaining $100 million Euro funds from the second diplomatic pouch in seven safety deposit boxes.

Taking off from Grand Cayman Island Cecil climbs to the cruising height then turns control of the plane over to Marcel. Cecil dozes for an hour then helps guide Marcel around the loop of Cuba. He sleeps soundly for two hours more before taking back control of the plane.

Joe Ferguson, Tom Jackson, and Marlene Moore find an apartment with three suitable accommodations. Joe rents a three-bedroom suite on the 18th floor of Choctaw Apartments. The trio visits a rent-to-own store and select furniture for delivery the following morning. Joe enrolls his sons in the local high school.

On Thursday morning, Joe and Tom drive members of the Maple Hill Mob to the Orlando airport. William Smythe, Marcel Roy and Shannon Johansen will fly to Washington D.C. Shannon plans to fly to Ottawa the following week. William Smythe will drive west from Washington D.C. to meet his wife and the Watsons in Detroit, Michigan. The Solinger and the Johansen families will fly to New York and pick up their vehicles. The Solingers will drive north from New York and enter Canada through Quebec. The Johansens plan to enter Canada over the Rainbow Bridge at Niagara Falls.

Friday morning Bob Watson sits beside Cecil Mann as they fly to the island of Little Cayman.

"I enjoy flying. Twenty years ago I had my pilot's licence but then business and family took over so I let it drop."

"After we top up the tanks in Key West would you like to take over the controls for a while Bob?"

"I'd love to, but are you really willing to let me handle this beautiful machine?"

"Only for three minutes and that includes the time it takes you to move your pudgy little butt into this seat and back into your own seat," Cecil jokes.

"Your generosity underwhelms me," Bob quips back.

Once back on course Cecil turns control of the plane over to Bob, instructing him on the satellite guidance system and showing him how to operate all the bells and whistles on the plane. Bob enjoys handling the plane for over an hour before turning the controls back to Cecil.

On the return flight, Bob and Cecil do the preflight inspection together. Inside Bob starts the plane and checks the gauges, and then Cecil and Bob enter the co-ordinates for the return flight into the global positional system. That finished, Bob taxis onto the runway and begins the return flight. Twenty minutes later Cecil is sound asleep. He awakens to a light touch on his arm.

"Will you take over now? I'm beginning to feel sleepy."

Looking at his watch, Cecil realizes they will be landing within two hours. As Cecil checks the gauges, he hears Bob begin to snore in the seat beside him.

Six a.m. Sunday morning, Cecil Mann is taxiing the Cessna onto the runway for a flight to Detroit, Michigan. Henri and Irena Roy will board a flight in Detroit for Ottawa. William Smythe will pick up his wife and the Watsons at the Detroit airport, and then cross over the Detroit River into Ontario. They will rendezvous with Peter and June at Belle River to pick up the station wagon before continuing the drive home.

Joe will be meeting his parents, Peter and June Ferguson, and mother-in-law Angie Marks at the Detroit airport. Eileen will be flying back to Orlando, Florida with him. Marlene tags along to make sure Cecil stays out of trouble.

Two hours out of Orlando Bob Watson takes over the controls on the plane and Mary Watson sits beside him to watch the skies for air traffic. It's a beautiful day with very little wind and only a smattering of fluffy white clouds interspersed along their flight path. Two hours later Cecil replaces Bob piloting the Cessna. At 11:00 a.m. Detroit time, Marcel is taxiing the plane to a parking site to allow everybody to exit.

Joe is eating lunch with the Watsons and Smythes when Eileen, Angie, June and Peter arrive. Peter is still moving awkwardly on crutches because of the broken leg bone.

"Where are the boys?" Eileen asks her husband.

"I believe they are with Tom Jackson in Disney World right now."

"Why didn't you bring them with you, then we could go home?"

"I'm not returning to Canada to give those butchers another chance to kill me or the boys."

"Why would they try to kill you?"

"Because I learned that a group of elected parliamentarians and mandarins in the civil service have received millions of dollars to grant Canadian citizenship to terrorists, including the al-Qaeda terrorist who planned the attack on the World Trade Centre in New York."

Eileen then asks, "Why don't you tell the Prime Minister and he can have the R.C.M.P. investigate and charge those responsible?"

"The Prime Minister and the Justice Department are two of the chief protagonists involved in the criminal activities bringing the terrorists into Canada."

"The Prime Minister would never do anything like that to hurt Canadians."

Angie Marks interrupts the argument.

"This isn't going to work Joe. If Eileen goes with you, she could compromise the lives of you and the boys. I can take her back to Toronto with me and she can go back to Ottawa from there. I'd hate to see anything happen to you and the boys because of her stupid actions."

Marlene and Cecil rise from the table when they finish eating their lunch and start walking towards the table where Joe is sitting. Joe observed them entering the cafeteria previously and realized the plane is refueled. It's now time to head back to Florida.

Joe speaks to his wife, "The decision is yours Eileen, but if you ever do anything – anything at all that could result in the deaths of me or the boys you will never see any of us again."

"I want to live with you and the boys. I'll go with you."

Peter spies Cecil and Marlene walking up to their table and speaks to them.

"Hey turkey, is that angel still condescending to hang around with you?"

"Listen you old pig farmer you better be careful who you call a turkey."

Peter rises from his chair and the two men grab each other and hug as Marlene and June begin to talk to each other.

Eileen is upset to find Cecil at the airport. "What's he doing here?"

"I'll tell you one thing," Peter replies, "June and I will sleep a lot better knowing Cecil is close to Joe and the boys…. Yeah we'll sleep a whole lot better."

Angie, June and Peter, sitting in the observation lounge, watch as Cecil pilots the Cessna onto the runway, then increasing the throttle, races away from them and begins to climb into the sky.

Angie admires the airplane. "That's a beautiful plane the man has."

"Yeah it is." Peter responds.

What Angie doesn't know won't hurt Joe.

No Time for Complacency

Marcel learns terrorists destroyed the Canadian Embassy in Indonesia, killing all the staff. After the killing of the Canadian Ambassador to Switzerland, the embassy in Switzerland is closed and the staff expelled by the Swiss government. This is the first time the Swiss Government has ever expelled a Foreign Embassy.

Marcel Roy notices there has been no action by the terrorists in Canada for the last two weeks. He enters the E – mail code s.al.y@aol.com and types *Why no action against the government?*

Salama al-Yawer types, *Most of the R.C.M.P. and C.S.I.S. have been dealt with. The government has promised us new identities and new passports.*

Two nights later, members of the F.B.I. disguised as R.C.M.P., pursue Mahboob al-Yawer and he barely escapes. They show up at his house with a search warrant, tear the house apart and wake up the children. Salama al-Yawer receives a phone call at midnight from her distraught sister-in-law. A family friend, a wanted terrorist, disappears following an arrest by the fake R.C.M.P. Once again, Salama al-Yawer is sufficiently motivated. Terrorists lure two members of the R.C.M.P. into a house and kill them.

Marcel Roy contacts Salama al-Yawer once again. *Why those two Mounties?*

The Mounties are after our people.

They only follow orders. They are meaningless.

We must stop the Mounties from taking our people.

You can kill one thousand Mounties and they will continue to arrest you and your partners. They are not involved. They are only following orders. They are meaningless.

What must we do to protect ourselves? Salama al-Yawer asks Marcel Roy.

You know what you must do. You can quit playing games with me. I know you have deliberately shied away from the people who are the most dangerous to you. Don't ever believe you can deal with them. The department of Foreign Affairs collects the names. The Finance Department collects and distributes the money. The Immigration Department has the names and addresses. The mandarins control the departments. The Members of Cabinet control the mandarins. The Prime Minister and the members of the Liberal party control the Cabinet. We require the Finance Department and the MPs receive most of your attention at this time. You have the list – use it or accept the consequences.

A short time later Marcel is into the computer, gleaning information on her partners. Two weeks later, the F.B.I. has spirited one of them across the border. The two factions are battling once again.

The Evidence Search Continues

Sunday the Maple Hill Mob gathers at the apartment of Marlene Moore and packs her belongings. Within hours, everything is in storage with Cecil's gear. Before moving the belongings, Alex removes the surveillance equipment from the car and telephone.

Monday morning, Bob Watson registers the sale of the Tom Jackson residence to himself and the Joe and Eileen Ferguson residence to Henri and Irena Roy. These transfers will stop the Federal Government from confiscating the properties, because there is no family link between the buyers and sellers. Visiting the two residences, Tom discovers the Jackson home has an occupant and Ralph is in the yard. Returning that evening, he learns the culprit is Harold Jackson, Tom's son.

Bob questions Harold. "What are you doing here? You seem to have moved in."

"My wife kicked me out of the house claiming I hit her. She showed the police a bruise and they arrested me. The next day she filed a restraining order against me. I can't see the kids or get my clothes from the house. Two days before she kicked me out, she emptied our bank account. She has filed for spousal and child support and is trying to take most of my paycheck. On Saturday Tommie came over here and told me a man that Sheila works with is sleeping with her every night."

"How are you doing financially?"

"Dad had my name on his bank account so I was able to get some immediate cash. I plan on putting it back as soon as I get some money."

"How much money is in Tom's account?"

"About $52,000."

"Take it out early tomorrow morning," Bob advises Harold. "The government will be watching the account for any activity to try to find Tom. Take the money before they freeze the account. If you can't get all the money, open an account, transfer the remainder of the funds, and then take it out the following day. I'll open an account that you'll have signing authority on. Nobody, including your wife's lawyer will be able to find that account."

"Your father transferred the house to me so the government couldn't grab those assets. Once we clean up your mess, we'll transfer it to you. You'll have to rent the house for now. I'm not worrying about the money and Tom won't worry about the money but you'll require the expenses for your divorce action. I'll deposit the money back into the account of Tom's money we're setting up and if you need any funds you'll have immediate access to it. Tom turned his stocks and bonds over to me to transfer to you but that will also wait until after the divorce. We'll have to sit down tomorrow and discuss all the facets of your divorce so you will get everything you deserve. Your priority right now has to be visitation with your children. Come in to my office tomorrow morning to discuss this problem further."

Bob makes a phone call to Tom Jackson and informs him of the problems his son is undergoing then turns the phone over to Harold.

When the phone conversation is finished, Harold again speaks to Bob. "Dad says for me to take the money and the house because he doesn't need them."

"If you take the money and house now you have to list them in your assets for the divorce settlement and your wife will be entitled to half of your assets. After the divorce your wife can't touch them."

"That makes sense. He also mentioned you knew a couple of men."

"Yes I'll be talking to Maurice and Alex later. I'll need the keys to your house, garage and shed."

While Harold Jackson is in the office of Bob Watson, Maurice Solinger and Alex Johansen are installing audio surveillance equipment in the Harold and Sheila Jackson residence. Finishing in the house, they hide the reception equipment in the garage. After locking the cabinet, the two men clean up the evidence and leave.

R.C.M.P. constables enter the offices of Jones, Smythe and Watson with a search warrant for the dossiers on Joe Ferguson, Cecil Mann and Tom Jackson.

"Where is the rest of the material?"

"That's all I have," William replies.

The R.C.M.P. constables tear the place apart looking for more evidence. They find the safe under the wastebasket.

"Open that safe."

"There is nothing in the safe pertaining to Tom Jackson, Cecil Mann or Joe Ferguson."

"Open that safe."

"No I won't."

One constable leaves to procure a court order. The second constable remains in the office, guaranteeing the contents remain safely stored in the safe.

At eleven o'clock William, Bob and Rae leave the office. They visit travel agencies looking for information on Ireland and Costa Rica. Returning to their offices at three they find two very unpleasant R.C.M.P. constables waiting for them.

"Where have you been? We've been waiting for over three hours"

"That's none of your business where I've been." William quips at them while placing the travel brochures on top his desk.

The lead R.C.M.P. constable is having problems controlling his temper. "I should charge you with hindering a police investigation."

"You can't so don't even bother trying."

Rae and Bob are watching and enjoying the exchange. The constable is ready to explode.

"Here's the court order. Open the damn safe."

William diligently reads the court order. Then he thoroughly reads it again.

Placing the Court Order on the desk, he kneels on the floor and opens the safe. Removing a file folder, he carefully places it on the desk.

The R.C.M.P. constable grabs and opens the file folder. It contains a $20 bill.

Rae stumbles into the hallway, unable to control his laughter any longer.

William picks up the money and puts it in his pocket. "I couldn't remember where I left that twenty."

The R.C.M.P. constables are storming out of the office when William speaks to them again. "Would you constables sign for all the evidence on Joseph Ferguson, Tom Jackson and Cecil Mann you are removing from our offices?"

The evidence the Justice Department was hoping to find is stored in a cardboard box in the Maple Hill Building, having been removed from the office safe when the security camera and the audio surveillance equipment was removed prior to their trip to Europe.

In the following weeks, Henri and Irena Roy move into the Ferguson residence and their daughter and son-in-law rent their home.

Learning the Truth

When parliament resumes Terry McIntyre attacks the Prime Minister and his party about the lack of action on the murders of Members of Parliament and government staff.

Tom Jones, Leader of the Opposition, removes Terry from membership in the Alliance Party. He now sits in the House of Parliament as an Independent.

"Speaker of the House."

"The House of Commons begins question period."

Terry McIntyre stands.

"The house now recognizes the Honorable Member from Calgary West."

"Mr. Speaker. I still have received no answer from my question to the Prime Minister last week. Why has our Embassy in Switzerland been expelled from that country?"

"The house now recognizes the Honorable Prime Minister."

"Mr. Speaker. The matter is being resolved with the Swiss Government as we speak."

The Prime Minister sits down amid backbencher cheering and desk thumping.

"The house now recognizes the Honorable Member from Calgary West."

"Mr. Prime Minister. I didn't ask if it was being resolved I asked why has the Swiss government dishonored our country by having the Canadian Embassy so ignominiously expelled from Switzerland. What has this Liberal government done to humiliate our country like this? What could our country have possibly… the banks – it has to be something with the Swiss banks."

Terry McIntyre sits down.

"The house now recognizes the honorable Prime Minister."

"I cannot speak further about this matter until the problem is resolved."

The Prime Minister sits down amid backbencher cheering and desk thumping. He sits in his chair brooding. If McIntyre goes to Switzerland, he could learn the truth about the money he and his cohorts had deposited in the Swiss bank accounts.

Terry McIntyre arranges to leave for Switzerland the following day. Shannon Johansen of the Ottawa Citizen meets with Terry McIntyre later that evening.

"You have to go to Washington DC first and talk to a man I know," Shannon informs Terry. "He will tell you everything that is going on. Then go on to Switzerland."

"I have my flight booked and hotel accommodations confirmed. I'm leaving for Switzerland tomorrow afternoon."

"How do you hope to learn anything?"

"I'll check in the banks and find out what is going on."

"Which banks?"

Terry McIntyre begins to explain to Shannon, "I'll start in Geneva. Switzerland isn't that large of a country."

"Geneva has over 800 banks, and that's only one city. With the stunt pulled by the Federal Government don't expect any co-operation from the banks or the Swiss government."

"What stunt?"

"You'll have to ask Marcel that question in Washington."

"How else will your friend be able to help me?"

"It's easy to ask the right questions when you already know the answers and who to ask," Shannon explains. "Do you want me to make the arrangements?"

Later that evening Shannon phones Terry McIntyre, giving him the information he requires to meet with Marcel Roy.

The following morning Terry McIntyre changes his flight plan and with his wife, Jerry, flies to Reagan Airport in Washington, DC. In the F.B.I., Washington Bureau he meets with Marcel Roy.

"Hello Terry. I'm Marcel."

"You have information for me?"

"In a minute. Tell me about yourself first."

"I'm in a hurry."

"Tough," Marcel responds. "I'll give you the information after I decide you're worth the information."

After twenty minutes of deliberations Marcel tells Terry, "You're ideals and feelings for Canada correspond to our own. You'll definitely help us in our endeavors to remove this corrupt government from the position of power which it now enjoys."

"The present program of granting citizenship to terrorists first began under the Progressive Conservative banner in 1992. The Liberal Government has since endorsed it and they have profited handsomely under the program."

"Your saying the Liberal Government is granting Canadian Citizenship to known terrorists."

"Yes."

"Is the leader of the Alliance Party involved?"

"Yes he is, as is the Leader of the Progressive Conservative party. This policy began under the Progressive Conservative Party and because the Liberals could pocket millions of dollars continued under their banner."

"You're telling me this is a very large operation. I knew there was something criminal going on but I was never able to find out what it was. That immigration worker – what's his name – Ferguson? – Yes Ferguson. He found out."

"The members of the government involved in this immigrant ring have received between $300,000 and $900,000 per terrorist or terrorist family, which they deposited in the DC Bank, Deposito-Cassa der Stadt in Bern, Switzerland. The elected MPs transferred all the funds to other accounts and withdrew the money in September. They were planning to blackmail the bank into replacing the money in all the accounts before the civil servants found out. Bank security cameras filmed Ambassador Gabriel Champlain and a terrorist accomplice removing $6 million Euros using an alias."

"You're telling me they actually have the Prime Minister's brother on film carrying money from the bank – whew-whee."

"Armed with that evidence the bank in Switzerland refused to replace the funds. The Swiss Government expelled the Canadian Embassy breaking off diplomatic ties with the Canadian Government because they continued in their attempts to blackmail the bank."

"Now everything is beginning to make sense. I knew the government was corrupt. It's hard to believe they would sell out the country for their own greed – but they have."

"The civil servants in the Canadian Embassy in Switzerland learned about the Canadian Ambassador to Switzerland removing the money from their Swiss bank accounts and killed him in retaliation."

"So that's why he was killed. Up until now, I felt sorry for the Prime Minister because his brother was murdered. Now I feel he...."

"The government now has the terrorists killing the civil servants who could incriminate them in their immigration swindle. They are also selling the names and addresses of the terrorists to the US government. We know the government has granted citizenship to over 33,000 terrorists. In these computer disks, you will learn who is involved and how much they received. Prominent in the list are both the Prime Minister and the Leader of the Alliance Party. A majority of the cabinet ministers are also involved as are members of the executive of the Liberal Party."

"If I can find proof of what you've just told me the Canadian electorate will kick them out of power in the next election."

"You have more faith in Canadians than I do. The Canadian citizens are the reason this government can steal with impunity. With all the facts of the Liberal Government's corruption, they will still find some excuse to endorse them. When the electorate endorses the Liberal Party, they also endorse the Liberal policy of corruption."

Marcel gives Terry a list containing the people to see and the questions to ask.

In Switzerland, Terry McIntyre learns the flight on which he was originally booked disappeared over the Atlantic Ocean. Search parties find no sign of debris or passengers.

'Did this corrupt government kill 117 innocent people in an attempt to stop my investigation into their crimes?' wonders McIntyre.

From the banks, the Swiss Government, and Interpol, Terry will learn how corrupt this government is.

R.C.M.P. Commissioner Patrick Flaherty makes a phone call to his counterpart in the National Defence Headquarters, Chief of Defence Staff, Yves Plante. They arrange a meeting for the following week.

Election Call

Landing at Ottawa International Airport, Terry McIntyre is met by Shannon Johansen. On the drive to his place of residence in Ottawa, he learns the Liberal Party has dissolved parliament and called an election for November 19th, 2001. Terry will be defending his seat in Calgary West against the Alliance appointee, Thomas Jones Jr., son of the leader of the Alliance party. At the Ottawa residence of Terry and Jerry McIntyre, Terry and Shannon prepare a series of news articles to be printed in the Ottawa Citizen. The following morning, Terry McIntyre leaves for Calgary to begin his campaign for re-election to the Canadian parliament.

Realizing there will be danger to her person once she publishes her first article on the story obtained from Terry McIntyre, Shannon moves the bed and dresser from the Solinger residence into the hideout of the Maple Hill Mob. Since Ottawa operates with a city police department, the R.C.M.P. and C.S.I.S. will have limited resources to trace her whereabouts.

On October 27th, Bob and Mary Watson leave Kennedy Airport in New York bound for Geneva, Switzerland. They stop at the BFC Banque Financière de la Cité. Bob removes $1,100,000 from the safety deposit box, and deposits $50,000 dollars into the account. Mary establishes an account with a deposit of $50,000. The remaining funds will make $100,000 deposits into ten Maple Hill accounts in Geneva. The following day, Bob removes a further $1,100,000 from the BFC Banque Financière de la Cité for deposit into ten Maple Hill accounts in Lausanne and to establish two new accounts. Over the next few days the Watsons will each establish four more bank accounts with deposits of $50,000, deposit $50,000 into each of their three remaining accounts and deposit $100,000 into each of the remaining seventy-six accounts of the Maple Hill Mob. The final step will require the aid of the U.S. Embassy in Switzerland. In four trips of the chauffeured Embassy van the remaining funds from the eight safety deposit boxes is removed and $87.64 million is placed into a diplomatic pouch in the U.S. Embassy, for delivery to Marcel Roy in Washington D.C. After a bit of holidaying the Watsons will make the return flight from Geneva, Switzerland to New York City arriving on Wednesday, November 7th. From New York City, they will take a connecting flight to Ogdensburg, N.Y., to pick up their car for the drive home.

Over the next year the other members of the Maple Hill Mob will establish an additional seventy-six accounts in Switzerland and by the end of three years all the funds in the safety deposit boxes will be safely deposited into the 168 Swiss bank accounts of the Maple Hill Mob and the 42 bank accounts in the Bahamas.

On Sunday, October 28th, 2001, Shannon Johansen publishes her news story entitled:

The 9/11 Story

In the early morning hours of July 13th, 2001, five F.B.I. agents entered the home of Adbed Moez and kidnapped him. They were holding him in a cell in New York State when a reporter broke the story. Civil rights activists in the U.S. demanded he be freed. Canadian civil rights activists joined the cause. On July 22nd, the Canadian Prime Minister attacked the American government on television and ordered them to return the Canadian citizen Adbed Moez claiming he was not the al-Qaeda terrorist Ayman al-Zawahri. The Prime Minister knew this was a false statement.

On April 4th, 2001, Ayman al-Zawahri was granted landed immigration status in Canada after paying $400,000 to the Canadian Embassy in Turkey. When Iraqi refugees discovered him in West Van, British Columbia on May First, 2001, al Qaeda paid the Canadian Embassy in Switzerland a further $165,000 to give him false papers under the alias Mahmoud el-Hafnawi and he was moved to Montreal, Quebec. The Canadian government was given another $153,000. Ayman al-Zawahri was given the alias Adbed Moez and then was moved to Toronto, Ontario.

On July 10th, 2001, The Canadian Justice Department produced documents in an Ottawa court proving Adbed Moez was the al-Qaeda terrorist Ayman al-Zawahri.

On July 11th, 2001, the US Government paid the Canadian Embassy in Washington $250,000 for information as to the whereabouts of Ayman al-Zawahri.

At 11:35 a.m., on July 22nd, 2001, the Canadian Embassy in Switzerland received $750,000 Euro for the Canadian Government to pressure the US Federal Government and to achieve the release back into Canada of Ayman al-Zawahri alias Adbed Moez. By 9:00 a.m., the Canadian Prime Minister, Patrick Champlain, was on television condemning the US Government for their actions and threatening to take them to the World Court if they did not release Adbed Moez.

Under the shelter of the Canadian Government, Ayman al-Zawahri planned and orchestrated the terrorist attack on the World Trade Center in New York City and the attack on the Pentagon in Washington DC.

Two days after the attacks on the World Trade Center and the Pentagon, the Canadian Government finally offered their condolences to the US Government. They were one of the last countries to do so.

These copies of the documents proving Ayman al-Zawahri and Adbed Moez are the same person, were obtained from the Court of Queens Bench in Ottawa. This Evidence was presented to the courts by the R.C.M.P. detachment of the Senior Official of the R.C.M.P. and made headlines in every major newspaper in Canada on July 11th, 2001.

Shannon Johansen

Patrick Champlain, Leader of the Liberal Party, is on camera answering questions from a reporter:

"Mr. Prime Minister. Did the Department of Foreign Affairs receive money as outlined in the news article in this morning's paper?"

"I can state unequivocally the Department of Foreign Affairs has never accepted any money from any terrorist or terrorist organization to grant landed immigrant status to terrorists. I must also state no ambassador representing Canadian interests in a foreign country would ever accept money to allow a terrorist into this great country of ours. You all know I love my country and will always strive to protect it from any and all forces of evil."

"Why did you personally threaten the US government with court action when you had proof Adbed Moez was Ayman al-Zawahri?"

"At the time I had seen no evidence proving Adbed Moez was Ayman al-Zawahri and I still have seen no proof. The newspaper article is a lie concocted by the American Government to discredit the Liberal Party during this election campaign."

Sunday, November 4th, 2001.

Terrorists in Canada

The Prime Minister of Canada has claimed there are no terrorists in Canada. Today, with information provided to me, I will prove him wrong.

For the past nine years, members of the Federal Government have been bringing terrorists into Canada. The terrorists have been paying the Department of Foreign Affairs between $350,000 and $873,000 to immigrate to Canada and receive landed immigrant status. At the nearest count there are over 39,000 known terrorists in Canada for which the members of this illegal immigration scheme have received over $1.94 billion Euro dollars. There have been four hundred and seventy three Members of Parliament, Foreign Diplomats, government mandarins, and civil servants involved in this scheme in Canada and in Canadian Embassies abroad. The money these people received was in numbered accounts in The DC Bank, Deposito-Cassa der Stadt in Bern Switzerland. Shannon proceeds to list each individual responsible beginning with the Prime Minister Patrick Champlain, his position in the government, the amount of money in his account before its removal, and the number of his bank account. She continues through the list naming each person in the government involved in the immigration fraud.

Shannon Johansen

Patrick Champlain makes the evening news to explain his actions for a second Sunday in a row:

"Mr. Champlain. Your name has been put forth as the lead conspirator in an illegal operation to bring prohibited immigrants into Canada. The news article charges that you profited personally to the amount of $317million dollars. What do you have to say about these allegations?"

"They are lies by the American Government to discredit the Liberal Party during this election campaign and to destabilize the electoral process in Canada. I have instructed our government lawyers to take immediate action against the reporter and the newspaper and sue them. We have laws in Canada to protect people against malicious slander by any individual or organization. I refuse to allow anybody to slander me because I have done nothing wrong."

Beginning Monday, November 5th, Shannon Johansen will begin printing the names, aliases if applicable, addresses, phone numbers, terrorist organization affiliation and the amount of money each terrorist paid and where the money was paid to obtain landed immigration status in Canada. These lists, for 1000 terrorists per day, will appear directly onto the Canadian Press web site. At the beginning of each daily disclosure, she will again record every Member of Parliament involved in the scheme.

Two members of the R.C.M.P. arrive at the Ottawa Citizen bearing a search warrant. They confiscate the files belonging to Shannon Johansen and leave.

Mahboob al-Yawer, Basit Khawaja, Fazul Ghailani, Maha al-Hashimi, Salama Berwari and the rest of the terrorists used as aliases by the Maple Hill Mob to remove the money from The C.S.I.S. bank account are arrested in Montreal and charged.

Becky Hillman, a reporter, looks out the window at the Ottawa Citizen, and then rushes to Shannon.
"Mounties just drove into the parking lot. You'd better sneak out the back before they come in."

Shannon checks her watch, "The next bus will come in about twenty minutes. I hope they don't spot me."

"I'll get my car and meet you in the delivery bay."

"No I'll be...." Becky is gone.

While waiting for Becky, Shannon fills out the bill of sale on the back of her vehicle registration. Becky drives up to Shannon and steps out of the car – handing her the keys.

"Drive it carefully. The brakes are a bit weak."

Shannon quickly hands her the registration and keys, "I don't need it any more. I'll be leaving." She slips behind the wheel of Becky's car and is gone.

'What did Shannon mean – I don't need it any more'? Becky looks at the registration and keys.... It slowly dawns on her. Shannon gave her the car. 'I can't keep it'. She said, 'I'll be leaving – she's not coming back'.

The editor hands his assistant Shannon's news article. "I need two photocopies. Give one to the printer and hide one in the dead files where the Mounties won't find it. After you've done that download the article onto the Canadian Press web page then return the original to my IN file."

Ten minutes later, the Mounties enter the Ottawa Citizen building and speak to the Editor.

"Where's Shannon Johansen?"

"I don't know. She got a phone call and left with a photographer at nine-thirty."

"Her car's in the parking lot."

"Yes I know. They took a company car."

The assistant editor returns Shannon's news article to the IN file on the editor's desk.

"I'm busy and have to edit this news article for tomorrow's newspaper."

The Mountie looks at the papers.

"I'll take those papers."

"No you won't. They belong to the newspaper."

"You give me the papers or we'll be arresting you for hindering an investigation." After reading and pocketing Shannon's news article, the Mounties conduct a cursory search for Shannon and leave.

Becky phones for insurance. She leaves at noon to pick up new registration for the car. Rushing to the parking lot, she sees a Mountie standing beside a vehicle. As Becky gets closer, she recognizes Shannon's vehicle and presses the remote start.

The car lifts as the blast drives Becky backwards, spinning her to the pavement. The roar of the explosion tears at her eardrums, threatening to tear her head apart. Flames leap and dance consuming the car and the dead Mountie. Becky lays in shock…. She tries to stand up but crumbles to the ground. Again, she tries. Hands raise her up and support her, as friends help her move away from the roaring flames. Terror grips her and she holds tightly to her benefactors for protection. The pain from her skinned knees is excruciating, but she is still alive. Becky shakes violently from the shock…. The wail of sirens slowly awakens everybody, as from a bad dream. Only after the tow truck lifts the car will they discover the charred remains of the second body.

From a pay phone, Shannon phones the Hillman residence. The car is parked close to the law offices in Carlingwood Plaza on Carling Avenue. The keys are under the passenger seat. Her second call is to her mother.

"I can't pick you up now," Gloria explains. "There's a car parked down the street with two people watching the house and Alex phoned to say another vehicle pulled into his lot and he's being watched. I know Mary Watson is home again. Give her a call."

Time to Leave

Mary drives Shannon to Maple Hill and she packs her suitcases for the trip to Washington. At the Watson residence, Mary packs up an overnight case and by early afternoon, they are on highway 106 heading east to Belle River. The two ladies will take turns driving until they arrive at the Ferguson farm to spend the night.

The following afternoon Peter, June and Shannon are enjoying a boat ride on Lake St. Clair. The boat enters the Detroit River. A short time later Peter swings his craft to the east side of Belle Island Park. A U.S. Coast Guard Cutter pulls along side.

A loudspeaker blares – "Turn your boat into the current and hold your position."

Peter complies.

Netting, fastened to a rope, drops down into the boat as a winch begins lowering a cable with a stirrup. Shannon places her suitcases in the netting and as they are being hoisted places, her foot in the stirrup. As she begins to rise, Peter swings clear of the U.S. Coast Guard Cutter, and with a wave, the Fergusons begin the journey back to Belle River.

As Shannon steps onto the deck of the ship, the captain steps forward to extend a helping hand.

"Welcome to the United States Miss Jacobsen. My name is Captain William Scott. Would you please excuse me for a few seconds?"

Captain Scott steps to the rail and waves to three men in a large speedboat. The men wave back and take up a position following the Coast Guard Cutter. Shannon stares at the speedboat.

"Those are the men who helped Mr. Ferguson launch his boat this afternoon. Did they follow us from Belle River?"

"Yes ma'am. That's one of the boats."

'One of the boats….' "Who are those men?"

"Navy Seals ma'am."

'Navy Seals ….'

"Did they follow us for our safety?"

"You've been under constant United States security since your arrival at the Ferguson farm at 19:23 hours yesterday ma'am."

'19:23 hours….' "Thank you for your concerns. I really had no idea…."

The Coast Guard ship docks to rendezvous with Mary Watson. Soon the two ladies are at the airport waiting for Mary Watson's flight back to Ottawa.

Marcel, from the F.B.I. computers in Washington, is extracting information from the files of the Canadian Immigration Department. This is his first excursion into the archived terrorist files. He suddenly realizes something is happening – they've found a "Trojan Horse" – they're trying to trace him – let them trace. He jumps to another F.B.I. computer and accesses more files all the while calling for more computers. The same at a third, fourth, until he has all nine "Trojan Horses" in the basement of the Canadian Immigration Department operational. He jumps back to the first computer. The Security in Canadian Immigration is finished the trace and begins to remove the

"Trojan Horse Program". Marcel blocks them, and blocks them and blocks them. Immigration security is twenty minutes removing the "Trojan Horse".

"This computer Marcel."

The battle continues. Twelve minutes into the seventh computer everything stops…. No more information. Security has shut of the power to the computers. Life promises to be very interesting in the Canadian Department of Immigration when they begin to re-boot the computers. With all the files withdrawing forcibly at one time, information has jumped between files and other information has disappeared completely. In four days Marcel will learn he pulled over nineteen thousand terrorist files from the Canadian Government Immigration records in that single operation – by far his best day. The American Government now has documentation on over seventy-one thousand Canadian terrorists.

Cecil

November 5th, finds Rae and Andrea Jones and Andre and Marie Prichard on a flight from Ogdensburg, New York bound for Orlando, Florida. Rooms are waiting for them at the Imperial Hotel. Tom Jackson and Cecil Mann are returning from Washington with a briefcase containing $86.5 million Euro. Bob Watson, Rae Jones, and Maurice Solinger have all put in orders to Marcel for Cessna 414's or comparable planes. Marcel keeps sufficient funds to purchase the airplanes as they become available. Tom Jackson is at the controls. Joe Ferguson has booked a room at the Imperial Hotel for Keith and Jerry, sent a note saying the boys would be missing school on Tuesday, and told Eileen, Keith and Jerry would be spending Monday night with some school friends. It will be a long time before he mentions the Maple Hill Mob and the numbered bank accounts to his wife.

Tom Jackson carries the diplomatic pouch to his suite where he and Joe Ferguson place $100,000 Euro into one briefcase, $400,000 Euro into a second briefcase and split the rest of the $86.5 million Euro amongst six more briefcases.

At midnight Cecil Mann and Tom Jackson place eight briefcases into the trunk of Tom's car and they both drive a vehicle to the Imperial

Hotel to pick up six passengers for the flight to the Cayman Islands. A quick preflight check by Cecil and Tom and the Cessna is moving down the runway, beginning its flight. They land in Key West to top up the fuel tanks, then they are moving down the runway and beginning to climb, but this time Tom Jackson is at the controls. Cecil drops off to sleep comfortable in the knowledge Tom will wake him at the first sign of a problem. Two hours later Cecil is back at the controls of the plane and Tom is asleep.

Eight people are waiting in the van when the first bank in Georgetown, Grand Cayman, opens its doors. The side door of the van opens, Tom exits the door and steps to the rear of the van, Cecil follows Tom out the door but moves to the sidewalk in front of the van. When they are in position, Marie Prichard exits the van with a briefcase cuffed to her wrist, followed by Keith Ferguson. Once those two are inside the financial institution Andrea Jones, followed by Jerry Ferguson, enters a different bank. Inside the first bank Marie Prichard signs the documents verifying her account containing 11.9 million Pounds Sterling and places the Euro dollars from her briefcase into a safety deposit box.

Two hours later, the Cessna is climbing into the air, heading for the island of Little Cayman. Keith and Jerry Ferguson will verify their accounts and deposit the Euro dollars in their briefcases into safety deposit boxes.

The van moves to the last bank. Tom Jackson will carry in the last two briefcases. One bag of money for a deposit, and the second to place the funds in a safety deposit box.

Andre Prichard exits the van and steps to the back of the van. Rae Jones steps out of the vehicle and moves to the front.

Tom speaks to Cecil Mann, "Leave your weapon in the van and follow me inside."

The two men enter the bank and Cecil follows Tom to an office. Tom hands the teller a piece of paper.

"You will have to sign some papers to finish setting up the account. I presume you also wish to make a deposit."

"We will also require a medium sized safety deposit box," Tom informs the clerk.

The bank clerk fills out all the papers and hands them to Tom Jackson. Tom in turn hands the papers and pen to Cecil.

"You want me to sign," Cecil queries.

"I can't sign for your account."

Cecil, signing the bank papers, has a puzzled look on his face.

Tom speaks to the bank clerk, "Do you have a counter for Euro dollars?"

The clerk locks the door as he exits. He returns with the automatic counter, a box and a key to a safety deposit box. After placing the items on the desk, he re-locks the door to secure the office.

Tom unlocks the briefcase from his wrist. Placing it on the desk, he unlocks then opens the briefcase and removes a letter. As the bank clerk runs the Euro dollars through his machine Tom hands Cecil the envelope.

To Cecil Mann and Marlene Moore - A present for your upcoming wedding.

The card bears the twenty signatures of "The Maple Hill Mob".

Cecil has difficulty controlling his emotions. This is totally unexpected.

The Bank Clerk interrupts Cecil's thoughts. "I counted $100,000 Euro. Does that tally with your figures?"

"That's correct," Tom replies.

After making the deposit, the bank official escorts Cecil and Tom to the safety deposit stall.

Cecil stops outside the stall. "I'll wait here while you put the rest of the funds into the safety deposit box."

"You put your own money away."

Cecil carefully places the remaining funds into the safety deposit box. His mind is going in circles. His attempts to count the money end in failure. Sitting in the van Cecil blurts out, "I can never hope to repay all of you for your generosity."

Rae Jones asks, "What's the guy talking about Tom?"

"I have no idea, I think he must be hallucinating from all the flying he's being doing."

"When we get back to Orlando we'll have him committed," interjects Marie.

"That or feed him to a gator."

"That dainty morsel would only make a gator angry," Andre remonstrates. "We'll have to get Marlene to put some meat on those bones first."

Tom Jackson lifts the plane off the tarmac to begin an interesting flight home. Cecil Mann, watching the sky for air traffic, reminisces about everything that has transpired in the last few weeks. Eventually while relaxing and looking out at the sky, he falls asleep.

On Wednesday and Thursday, Cecil Mann, Tom Jackson, and the Prichard and Jones families visit the Bahamas where the Prichards and Joneses remove the funds from their safety deposit boxes and deposit the money into the forty-two bank accounts belonging to the Maple Hill Mob.

On Friday, the Prichards and Joneses will leave Orlando on their return flight to Ogdensburg, New York then a short drive to Ottawa, Ontario.

Scandal

Sunday, November 11th, 2001
Scandal in the Canadian Embassy in Switzerland

The Liberal Party and some of their cohorts devised a scheme to increase their illegal earnings. These elected officials diverted all the funds in their own numbered Swiss bank accounts, and the numbered Swiss bank accounts of the mandarins and civil servants, involved in their illegal immigration project into different accounts in the DC Bank, Deposito-Cassa der Stadt in Switzerland. After withdrawing the funds, they attempted to force The DC Bank, Deposito-Cassa der Stadt in Switzerland to restore the accounts to their original standings. The bank managed to trace one account and found on film the Canadian Ambassador to Switzerland, Gabriel Champlain, brother of the Canadian Prime Minister, withdrawing funds from an account under a false identity. With this evidence, the banks refused to restore the funds to the bank accounts of the members of the government. When the Canadian government threatened to expose The DC Bank, Deposito-Cassa der Stadt for losing the money the Government of Switzerland expelled the Members of the Canadian Embassy.

The Swiss Government believes the Canadian Government moved the money from Switzerland to Canada in diplomatic pouches. Two members of the R.C.M.P. assigned to the Canadian Diplomatic Corps have admitted to transporting diplomatic pouches to Canada during the period involved. Diplomatic Couriers, not members of the R.C.M.P., normally transport diplomatic pouches. Prime Minister Patrick Champlain returned from holidays in Switzerland with two large suitcases bearing diplomatic seals. What was in those suitcases?

These frames from the security camera clearly show Gabriel Champlain, the Canadian Ambassador to Switzerland, standing at the till signing a false name and then receiving $3 million Euro from the teller. The cameras then record another man, Hamed Ahmidam, a known al Qaeda terrorist, and a Canadian Citizen, also withdrawing $3 million Euro, placing his briefcase on the counter beside Gabriel Champlain, and the Canadian Ambassador to Switzerland locking both briefcases to his wrists. The last frames of the film show the Canadian Ambassador to Switzerland carrying the two briefcases containing $6 million from The DC Bank, Deposito-Cassa der Stadt.

The members of the R.C.M.P. stationed at the Canadian Embassy admitted killing the Ambassador because he was involved in the scheme to steal the illegal money they had acquired under their illegal immigration project.

The two R.C.M.P. officers, Malcolm Kennedy and Jean Fontaine, killed in the line of duty installing a bomb on a car I sold to Debbie Hillman can now be deleted from the still active list of conspirators published previously.

Shannon Johansen

A reporter catches the attention of the Leader of the Liberal Party. "Mr. Champlain, a Swiss Newspaper checked the accounts in The DC Bank, Deposito-Cassa der Stadt in Bern, Switzerland. The bank confirmed the account numbers and the amounts of money that were previously in each account. They refused to substantiate any names but did say that every account belonged to a Canadian working for the Federal Government. They confirmed the account containing $317million Euro, which was by far the largest sum, belongs to a man working for the government in Ottawa but with a residence in Montreal, Quebec. The reporter learned that account was empty for a short period, but now contains over $1 million. The other four hundred and seventy three accounts receive money, but those funds automatically drain into the major account. Could you cast some insight on why that particular account still contains funds and who, working for the government, but with a residence in Montreal, has that particular account in Switzerland?"

"Are you insinuating that the bank account belongs to me? I have no need for a Swiss bank account."

"I have no need for a pair of pants with a thirty-two inch waist but I have a pair," replies the reporter. "Do you have a numbered bank account in Switzerland?"

"I have already answered that question. Next question please."

"Those are great pictures of your brother in The DC Bank, Deposito-Cassa der Stadt in Bern, Switzerland," interjects a second reporter. "He makes a great bank robber. Do you know of any other reason he would be carrying two briefcases containing $6 million Euro from the bank and using a false identity to obtain the funds?"

"Are you insinuating Gabriel is a thief? My brother never stole any money from that bank. I refuse to answer any more questions."

"What about the two large diplomatic cases you brought back to Canada from Switzerland with you? Did they contain Swiss watches?"

The Prime Minister stalks angrily away from the cameras. 'Those reporters will never ride on the government plane with him again. They know better than to voice those allegations against him.'

Sunday, November 18th, 2001.

Over the last three Sundays, I have brought the criminal activities of the party in power in front of the public. Now it is up to the Canadian voters to do their part.

With information gained from a Member of Parliament, I have shown to the Canadian public how this government is willing to sacrifice this country for their personal gain. For them patriotism is nothing. Greed is everything.

The party in power, through its policies, has stigmatized the citizens of Canada by having our Foreign Embassy kicked out of Switzerland.

Four hundred and seventy three Members of Parliament and Civil Servants have conspired to bring over 61,000 terrorists into this country for the sum of $1.949 billion Euro dollars.

Tomorrow you will vote to reject the party in power with its corrupt practices or you will endorse the corrupt practices of the government and re-elect them to power. Their greed has placed the lives of Canadian families at risk and jeopardized the freedoms we enjoy. How much does Canada mean to you as a voter and as a citizen? We will find out tomorrow.

Shannon Johansen

In the election of November 19th, 2001, the Liberal Party retains power in Ottawa by winning twenty-one seats in the Maritimes and Newfoundland, one hundred and two seats in Ontario, twenty-four seats in Quebec, six seats in the Prairie Provinces, five seats in B.C. and two seats in the northern territories. A Conservative wins the seat in Parliament for the riding of Medicine Hat, Alberta, defeating the incumbent leader of the Alliance Party. The Independent Member of Parliament retains his seat in Calgary-West.

Terrorist Strike

Monday, November 26th, terrorists led by Abu Bakar Ba'asyir, occupy a school in Ville St. Laurent, on the Island of Montreal. Both male and female terrorists have plastic explosives strapped to their bodies. The weapons carried by the fifty-three terrorists includes, rocket launchers, Uzis, street sweepers, M-16's, grenades and flamethrowers, plus an assortment of automatic sidearms and knives. Included in their arsenal are night vision goggles, shooters-earmuffs, and gas masks.

The terrorists knock out the glass in the windows and doors in case the police, using some form of knockout gas, attack them.

Marcel Roy receives a phone call.

"Ray Jones here. Terrorists have taken students and staff hostage in a Montreal school. They are demanding the release of sixty-three terrorists held in jail without due process under new Canadian anti-terrorism legislation. Included in the group are fourteen men and women who channeled money from a C.S.I.S. bank account into banks in Montreal and removed the funds. Will you be able to get in touch with the terrorists you have been in contact with through the Internet?"

"Salama al-Yawer was extremely upset by the arrest of her brother and her friends, and is very likely involved in the terrorist action. I will attempt to reach her on her computer but I expect no answer. The simplest method for me to contact the terrorists will be to obtain the phone number and e-mail of the school computer. I will also require the phone number and e-mail address of the Montreal police station in charge of the operation. Call me once you have that information."

Half an hour later Marcel Roy has the required information and phones the school. "This is I Spy. Inform Salama al-Yawer I am on the office computer." Marcel hangs up his phone.

"What are your demands?" is the message on the computer.

We require the release and safe passage to a country of our choice, for our friends, unjustly incarcerated in Montreal, Ottawa, and Toronto. We also require safe passage of ourselves to the same destination. We require immediate action on these demands. Any attempts to storm the school will result in the deaths of our captives.

Salama al-Yawer

Lebanon, Syria and Libya are willing to grant safe passage for your group. Would you be willing to exchange your hostages for the Prime Minister and the members of the Privy Council? Would you be amenable to members of your community, branded as terrorists in the press, also leaving Canada under your protection if they so desire?

I Spy

Tuesday, November 28.

News releases appear on television and the Canadian Press web site:

Under an agreement reached between the Canadian Government and the terrorists holding the school in Ville St. Laurent on the Island of Montreal, terrorists listed in press releases over the last six weeks are to receive free flights from Canada to Lebanon, Syria and Libya.

Negotiations to release sixty-three terrorists currently incarcerated in Ontario and Quebec are now in progress.

The Liberal Government is attempting to suppress the information the terrorists are willing to exchange the six hundred plus students and staff currently being held hostage in the school for the Prime Minister and the members of the Privy Council. The Members of Parliament, who received hundreds of millions of dollars from the terrorists and granted the terrorists landed immigrant status in Canada, are unwilling to correct a travesty caused by their greed. The Prime Minister and his caucus refused to even speak about this decision by the terrorists. Over two hundred members of the opposition and Liberal backbenchers offered themselves as hostages in place of the children but the terrorists declined knowing this government would be willing to sacrifice those parliamentarians to serve their own agenda.

Using the cover of darkness, the Canadian Military, under orders from the federal government, begin preparations for an assault on the school in an attempt to subdue or destroy the terrorists. The government realizes the success of this operation will exonerate them and with a bit of advertising, paid for by the Canadian public, could make heroes of the party in power.

Using night vision goggles and camouflage the soldiers creep to the front and back doors of the blacked out building. They wait, hiding below the stairs and around the corners of the school, concealed from the terrorists inside the structure.

Terrorists, using their night vision glasses observe the soldiers creeping towards the school. Inside the two doorways, they prepare themselves by donning gas masks and the shooter earmuffs or earplugs. One terrorist sentinel watches each doorway and the remaining terrorists cover their eyes, waiting for the impending attack.

Flash-bangs, fired into the schools, mark the beginning of the twin assaults on the terrorists as two waves of soldiers storm the door openings. Suddenly napalm envelops both groups of Special Forces soldiers. Intense light from the flaming napalm blinds snipers stationed around the school sighting through night vision scopes. Terrorists located on the roof of the school lob grenades at the soldiers outside the flames.

An ambulance, siren blaring, moves towards soldiers lying dead and wounded at the front of the school. A rocket arcs from the building, hits the vehicle, and explodes. A second ambulance stops.

A shot rings out. A terrorist on the school roof crumbles, dead from the precise shot of a sniper.

Lights illuminate the ground in front of the school. Five teachers and students exit the school with hands held high, beginning their walk to freedom. Shots ring out and the five hostages crumble to the ground. Terrorists extinguish the lights.

Long into the night onlookers can hear the screams of the mortally wounded soldiers. The cries for help become fewer and more pitiful. The cries cease. The silence of the night becomes deafening in its intensity. The terrorists and the police wait.

With impunity, terrorists stroll around on the roof of the school, openly taunting the police and military personnel who have them surrounded. The price of killing them is too high.

The full impact of the names and addresses of terrorist families Shannon Johansen has been placing on the Canadian Press web site begins to make its presence felt in the psyche of the citizens of Canada. These terrorists in turn find themselves and their families the victims of acts of terrorism. Over the next three days 287 commercial aircraft and U.S., military cargo planes leave Pierson airport in Toronto, and Dorval and Mirabel airports in Montreal, bound for Lebanon, Syria and Libya.

Thursday, November 29.

The Ottawa Citizen carries a full, front-page photograph of Prime Minister Patrick Champlain standing on the Rainbow Bridge at Niagara Falls congratulating the al Qaeda terrorist, Ayman al-Zawahri, on his safe return to Canada.

The Liberal Government can no longer stand up to the press they are receiving concerning their actions, bringing these terrorists into Canada. The terrible deaths and injuries needlessly sustained by members of the Canadian Military and the school hostages, weighs heavily on the minds of the citizens. Protest marches force the government to accede to the demands of the terrorists. On Friday, the government removes the terrorist prisoners from their places of incarceration, placing them on planes destined for their ports of refuge on the Mediterranean. Shortly thereafter two school busses arrive to transport the terrorists and forty hostages to Dorval airport for their flight to Syria.

To curtail further adverse publicity the Federal Liberal Caucus pays the airline bill from the special "Sponsorship Fund" set up to save Canada from separation.

December 5th, the Prime Minister is returning to 24 Sussex Drive in his chauffeured limousine, escorted by two R.C.M.P. vehicles. As his vehicle slows to make the left turn from Sussex drive into his official residence, two armour piercing rockets lance toward the vehicle from the rear of a blue van parked 40 meters away on John Street. The limousine explodes into flames. The van races down the street with an R.C.M.P. vehicle in close pursuit. The back door of the van swings open and the muzzle of a rocket launcher appears. The R.C.M.P., realizing innocent people could be killed during a high-speed chase, call off the pursuit.

Two hours later a blue van is back in the R.C.M.P. impound yard. An armed forces van, used to transport two rocket launchers and a partial case of armour piercing rockets is safely parked and unloaded at Tunney's Pasture, the army base in Ottawa.

One night of violence wipes out five terrorist families. R.C.M.P. forensic specialists from Ottawa, Montreal and Toronto are the first on the crime scenes to conduct the investigations.

Trickles of terrorists continue their exodus from Canada. With their anonymity compromised and the deleterious actions of their comrades in the school in Montreal, their lives and the lives of their families are in constant danger from the citizens of Canada.

Epilogue

In the early afternoon hours of January 29th, 2002 a stranger speaks to the security guard at Choctaw Apartment in Orlando, Florida asking, "Do Joe and Eileen Ferguson live here? Their names aren't on the apartment index."

"I'm not at liberty to say."

The stranger pulls out a letter and examines it, then again addresses the security guard. "This is 1164 Warner Avenue."

"Yes it is."

"Then Joe lives in unit 1823. Is he at home?"

"I'm not at liberty to say."

The stranger presses the intercom button and is soon on the elevator to the 18th floor. The security guard watches as Eileen Ferguson nervously greets the man in the hallway and invites him into the suite.

"My name is Marc Leblanc. I'm with the Canadian Department of Justice and I've been sent to clear up some misconceptions you voiced in your letter concerning your husband."

"Won't you please come in? I was not expecting a member of the Justice Department. I was hoping to get a letter but this is better still."

"There are outstanding warrants on your family but they are only to look at the evidence and help us clear our books." Marc continues, "If a witness fails to appear in court a warrant is obtained to force the person to appear and give his evidence. I have all the documents with me and the authority, from the courts, to clear up this misconception your family has about their personal involvement in the case."

Marc Leblanc removes a piece of paper from his attaché case, hands it to Eileen, and asks, "Would you look at this paper and authorize its authenticity?"

"That's the statement I gave to the Ottawa City Police the night the members of the R.C.M.P. came to arrest us."

Marc gives Eileen a quick glance. It takes him a second to adjust after Eileen's version on the events in question. "Do you remember anything else that could be pertinent to the case?"

Eileen reflects on the night in question, "No I don't."

"Would you initial the statement then this document will be completed?"

Eileen initials the statement, and then Marc Leblanc returns the statement to his attaché case.

Eileen is elated. Everything is so simple and once Joe looks at his documents, they can move back to Ottawa. Back to their friends and families. The boys will see their friends again. Joe will see his paranoia was unfounded and life will be normal again. Joe can go back to his job in the Department of Immigration. He will be happy to see all his misconceptions cleared up and proud of her actions.

In the washroom, Marc Leblanc removes the 45 calibre Glock from his shoulder holster and screws the silencer onto the gun muzzle, then places the gun in the attaché case. It won't be long until he will be putting an end to the family that ruined his opportunity to be Senior Director of C.S.I.S. He will exact his revenge within the hour. Leblanc feels nervous with anticipation.

The security guard watches the car carrying Joe Ferguson, Tom Jackson and Cecil Mann entering the parking garage. Leaving his post, he hurries to the garage where he speaks to Cecil.

"You asked me to notify you immediately if any stranger asked about any of you or rang the apartment buzzer to any of your apartments. This afternoon a stranger asked if Joe and Eileen Ferguson live in the apartment. When I wouldn't tell him he spoke to Mrs. Ferguson on the intercom system and she let him in. He's still waiting with Mrs. Ferguson in suite 1823. "

"Could you arrange for us to see the video of the man?"

"I have it set up."

Looking at the video surveillance tape Cecil comments, "I see Leblanc is out of jail."

Joe immediately contacts his sons, sending them to the Imperial Hotel for the night. He phones the hotel and arranges for his sons to spend the night without having their names registered on the guest list until they leave.

Cecil contacts Marcel Roy in the F.B.I. offices in Washington then phones Marlene.

"Hello."

"Grab my gun and leave the suite immediately. Use the stairs and come down to level one of the parking garages. Bring the phone so I can warn you if I need to."

"What's the matter Cecil?"

"Leblanc from C.S.I.S. is with Eileen in their unit. If he leaves, I'll phone and warn you. Now get out of our suite."

While Cecil continues to monitor the cameras on the 18th floor Joe and Tom leave the security room for the parking garage, waiting for Marlene in the stairwell. The two men hear the light tippity-tap of Marlene running down the stairs. Suddenly they appear in front of

Marlene. Startled she raises her weapon. Both men jump for the safety of the garage, but fail to open the door. Marlene, recognizing them as they sprawl on the floor, starts to giggle – the tension she has been feeling gone.

I'm sorry…. You startled me…. Where's Cecil?"

"In the security room."

Marlene tippity-taps up the stairs.

Tom and Joe give each other a sheepish grin and stand up.

A short time later, a car drives into the underground parking. Joe and Tom acquire two pump shotguns, no questions asked. An elevator technician arrives and Cecil dispatches him to the control room. He is well paid for not being there. Marlene and Cecil wait in the security room watching the monitor for the 18th floor. The security cameras in the parking garage have quit working again and the security guard, with $4,000 in his pocket, will have a very selective memory of what has transpired this day.

At 6:00 p.m., both Eileen Ferguson and Marc Leblanc begin to worry. By 9:00 p.m., they are reaching panic mode.

Marc looks at his watch. "Could I have one more cup of coffee? And then I must leave. I'll come back tomorrow morning and talk to Joe."

Eileen pours them both a cup of coffee. As she returns the pot to the coffee maker, Leblanc drops a liquid into her cup. Five minutes later Eileen has passed out. Leblanc leaves a note for Joe saying, "If you want to exchange your wife for yourself, stay home tomorrow to be arrested and returned to Canada." He knows the letter could be a futile effort because Ferguson must have learned of his presence and is now long gone. Picking up Eileen, he is out the door and stalking towards the elevator.

Cecil is running for the stairs to the parking area as he phones ahead to Joe and Tom. The security guard is on his own phone to the elevator operator.

Marc, carrying Eileen, presses the elevator down button and the door slides open. Stepping inside he presses the main floor button and stands in front of the door waiting for the elevator to stop and the door to open.

The elevator stops. The door slides open. Marc Leblanc is staring into the bores of two shotguns. 'Cecil Mann – what's he doing here? A week ago he bought a pair of socks in Ottawa.' He sees parked cars and realizes he is in the parking compound. Cecil steps into the elevator, slips behind Leblanc, and begins a professional search of his person. Finding no weapon in the shoulder holster, he removes the attaché case from the hand of Leblanc and finds it contains the gun with the silencer. Cecil discovers a second weapon in an ankle holster during a more thorough search.

Standing behind Leblanc, Cecil holds a gun to his head as Joe takes his unconscious wife from the C.S.I.S. agent and places her in Cecil's car. Cecil cuffs Leblanc, then places him in the back seat of Joe's car.

Joe and Marlene take the elevator, which is now working properly, to the 18th floor. Picking up the note left on the table, Joe reads it then leaves.

Inside their hanger at the private airport, the three men remove the shoulder holster, ankle holster and everything else of identification from the pockets of Marc Leblanc, and then throw him roughly onto the floor just inside the door of the Cessna. They use a couple of wraps of masking tape to fasten two fingers together, and then remove the handcuffs. After fastening his feet together with a couple of loops of masking tape, they remove his shoes and socks. Joe, sitting in the seat beside the door, pins Leblanc to the floor of the plane with his feet. Tom sits across from Joe with the 32-calibre ankle gun pointed at Leblanc's head. The Cessna taxis down the runway and is soon rising into the airways. At cruising speed and height, the flight levels out flying in a northeasterly direction.

"Where are you taking me?" Marc Leblanc queries his captors.

Tom Jackson has a pat answer already prepared.

"I have a relative in the F.B.I. in Washington. He'll make certain you go back to Canada and stay there. When we drop you off, you won't be coming back to bother us again."

Ninety minutes out Cecil hollers back to Tom and Joe. "Hang on, I've been ordered to change course. I'm getting too close to the Savannah Airport."

Cecil drops airspeed and begins a roll. The plane continues to roll until the wings are on a vertical plane. Leblanc slips until his feet are braced against the door. Joe lifts his feet and releases the door catch, kicking the door open. Leblanc rips his hands loose – too late. He is already out the door, screaming and clawing at the sky as he plummets down, down, down – down into the Bermuda Triangle.

"**Yahoo!**" Cecil continues the roll, completing the circle. Gunning the motor, he executes two more victory rolls before leveling out. Cecil wags the wings, executes two more victory rolls and begins the return trip. Two hours later, the plane is dropping down to land at Miami International.

Joe and Cecil find Marlene Moore walking Eileen, clearing the drugs from her system. Marlene has already purchased Eileen's ticket for the Air Canada flight to Toronto, and her baggage is loading.

"I'm not leaving!"

Joe is furious. "I have your letter to the Solicitor General telling them where we are. I have the letter Leblanc left, telling me if I want to see you again to stay home tomorrow. We were waiting in front of the elevator when the door opened. We saw the C.S.I.S. agent carrying you. When he threw you into our arms he dropped his briefcase and ran out the security door onto the street, and then ran into the Spanish section of the city. We found his gun with the silencer attached inside the briefcase. He was ready to kill me when I entered the suite. The boys stayed at a friend's house to do a science project or they would be dead now. Whether you go, or whether you stay, this is the last time you'll be seeing the boys or me." Joe, spinning around, leaves Eileen standing.

An hour later Eileen Ferguson is crying to herself on the Air Canada flight to Toronto. Her mother, and members of the Federal Justice System, will be awaiting her arrival.

Six Months Later

Robert Green summons Marcel to his office.

"Marcel I want you to meet Tod Harrington. I believe you'll find him a kindred spirit."

"He tells me that he's started a new job in Ottawa. While working at his job, he discovered a Horse from Troy galloping through the company computer. He followed the hoof prints back to the pasture and lo – they brought him here. He carefully searched throughout the barn and discovered a bin of wild oats where the horse had been feeding. Bagged wild oats from the bin were then delivered to other barns far away. Last week a sprinkling of new wild oats made an appearance."

Marcel glances around nervously.

Robert Green, still looking at Marcel, leans back in his chair.

Tod smiles at him….

"Would you like to stable the horse again?…"

APPENDIX

"Canadian voters only have a six-week memory" is the standing joke among Canadian Politicians in Ottawa. The truth behind this joke is clearly seen in the results of the 2004 Federal Election.

Nearly all men can stand adversity, but if you want to test a man's character give him power. *Abraham Lincoln (1809 – 1865)*

While Abraham Lincoln was president of the United States, he was instrumental in removing First Nation Tribes under the Indian Removal Act, from prosperous reserves in the southeastern United States, to reserves in the deserts in Arizona and Nevada. The tribes were the Creek, Choctaw, and Chickasaw nations. Over 50% of the natives died on these forced migrations from their ancestral homeland and were forced to eke out a meager existence in the strange land they were forced to emigrate to. The First Nations people left behind prosperous farms, homes, barns and livestock. Abraham Lincoln made a fortune as one of the land speculators selling the land from those reserves.

Documentary - 500 Nations.

Canada is the only 'democracy' in the world that elects a dictator. In our system the Prime Minister personally appoints one-quarter of the parliament, the entire judiciary from the level of Queens Bench up, including the Supreme Court, all federal boards including Crown Corporations, agencies and commissions, all deputies and all cabinet ministers. He appoints the Canadian Senators as vacancies occur.

Link Byfield – Red Deer Advocate – March 25, 2005 – Canadian Press

In the last federal election, the Prime Minister appointed some of the candidates for the Liberal Party, and the voters faithfully voted most of those individuals into the House of Commons.

Parliamentarians accused Prime Minister Jean Chretien of using his position to press the Federal Business Development Bank, to grant a loan of $615,000 to Yvon Duhaime, the owner of the Auberge Resort. After the venture failed, the Prime Minister fired Francois Beaudoin, the president of the Business Development Bank. Until pressure was put upon Francois Beaudoin, the bank refused to grant the loan.

A Royal Canadian Mounted Police investigation found the Prime Minister had done nothing wrong.

The same people who control the Federal Business Development Bank, the office of the Prime Minister, control the R.C.M.P. The papers have since been shredded.

Canadian Press – 2004

The Prime Minister appoints and thus controls the Minister of Justice, the Deputy Minister of Justice and the Senior Official of the R.C.M.P. These individuals, answerable directly to the Prime Minister, found he had done nothing wrong.

The Asian Pacific Economic Council Summit meeting in Vancouver, B.C. demonstrated to all Canadians the absolute power the Prime Minister holds over the R.C.M.P.

Canadian Press, September, 2005

C.S.I.S. destroyed the contents of hundreds of hours of tapes of wiretaps and interviews involving suspected bombing mastermind Talwinder Parmer and other suspects in the 1985 Air India flight 182 bombing. The Federal Public Safety Minister, Anne McLellan said there is no point in holding a public inquiry to investigate the Air India Investigation.

Calgary Sun, March 17, 2005. Canadian Press

The Federal Departments of Foreign Affairs, Immigration, Solicitor General and Privy Council officials boycotted a security assessment operation charged with gathering, assessing, and distributing intelligence.

Canadian Press, 2004

Adscam

Prime Minister Jean Chretien directly oversaw the $50 million a year National Unity Fund, A secret source of money to fund the controversial sponsorship program.

Reporters put ex-Minister of Public Works in the Chretien administration, Alfonso Gagliano, on the hot seat. When the problem would not go away, Prime Minister Jean Chretien gave Alfonso Gagliano a diplomatic posting to Denmark.

Gagliano said he had no direct hand in granting contracts to Quebec advertising firms, which were later found to have pocketed $100 million from the $250 million sponsorship program.

Allan Cutler, a public servant in the Public Works Department, has testified that the patronage payments originated in 1994, the second year the Liberal party under Jean Chretien was in power and prior to the Quebec referendum on separation. Cutler testified that Chuck Guite, a senior Publics Works director of advertising and public opinion, effectively removed departmental checks and balances, claiming he had ministerial backing. He was ordered to backdate contracts, give payment for work apparently not performed, approve improper advance payments, and authorize deals that did not comply with the rules.

Among the contracts revealed by Cutler was a march 1995 agreement with Lafleur Communication Advertising worth $3.4 million to buy Canadian flags.

Cutler noted Lafleur received a 17.65% commission under the deal that provided immediate payment upon presentation of an invoice, with no proof of work done.

BC flag retailer Don William's told CBC TV he received $5,000 compensation for fake flag invoices.

Doreen Braverman admitted to CBC TV she was paid for a phony invoice saying it was a kickback. Braverman said she complained for years about the scheme to then-Prime Minister Jean Chretien, Public Works Minister Alfonso Gagliano and Finance Minister Paul Martin.

Sponsorship whistle blower, Myriam Bedard was fired for exposing government patronage. Paul Martin was minister of finance at that time.

Another minister was caught receiving favors from a business given contracts by the government without having to bid for them. Other contracts were paid without the delivery of the product.

Jean Pelletier, fired Via Rail chairman, has been named as the man directly involved in the scandal. He was the Chief of Staff in the Jean Chretien administration, answerable directly to the Prime Minister.

Huguette Tremblay testified, "Charles Guite, the former head of the sponsorship program, met weekly with Alfonso Gagliano, Minister of Public works. He returned from those meetings with instructions that the staff had to follow blindly."

Money under the Public Works sponsorship program was given to the Ottawa Senators, the Ottawa Renegades, the Montreal Canadiens, Montreal Expos, Montreal Alouettes and the Molson Grand Prix in Toronto under the guise of national unity. Montreal Canadiens received $1.2 million in 1996 and millions more in subsequent years.

Jean Chretien approved $975,000 for the schooner "Bluenose 2". It received $658,000. $317,000 went missing.

Chretien cut VIA Rail a cheque for $493,000 in 1996, $1.3 million in 1997 and VIA Magazine $500,000 in 1997.

Jean Chretien personally signed a $900,000 cheque for Canada Post.

Nine Liberal friendly ad agencies received $989,000.00 to design a logo that the people of Quebec would accept. Their billboard design was the word **CANADA**. The Liberal government is blocking the release of the documents on the fund.

The "China TV" series received $1.5 million from the sponsorship program to save the country from separation.

Jean Chretien personally authorized $80 million of the $250 million that was misspent.

Alain Richard, ad executive, received a death threat if he said too much at the Gomery inquiry.

Myriam Bedard testified that Groupaction had to do certain work even though they were charging very high rates for little or no effort. She also testified that Formula 1 racecar driver, Jacques Villeneuve, received $12 million to wear the word Canada on his racing suit.

Yves Bourbonnais, a federal Liberal appointee to the Immigration and Refugee Board is one of eleven people charged with soliciting bribes from newcomers to Canada for favorable Board hearings. The probe was started in the fall of the year 2000, he was suspended in 2001 and charged in the spring of 2004.Why did it take 3.5 years to lay the charges?

The R.C.M.P. in Montreal have been tied to Adscam.

In a poll taken June 28th, 2004, a majority of Canadians endorsed Ad Scam with their vote for the Liberal Party of Canada.

THE MONEY TRAIL:

Groupaction Marketing founder Jean Brault said he was forced to pay the salary and expenses of people working for the Liberal Party – some of whom he never met.

His allegations include:

$ **Daniel Yves Durand** got $500 per week for three months to work for the Liberal Party during the 1993 election. This was the first time Brault made a hefty donation through the back door. It was at the request of Liberal executive member Michel Fournier.

$ **Alain Renaud** received $1.1 million from 1996-2000 to lobby for federal contracts. Brault said once doors began to open in 1997. Renaud worked full-time for the Liberal Party's Quebec wing while continuing to be paid by Groupaction.

$ **Jacques Corriveau's** firm, Pluridesign, got $495,000 which Brault said went to the Liberals. Corriveau is a longtime friend and golfing buddy of former PM **Jean Chretien**, and one of his chief fundraisers.

$ **Joseph Morselli** got an envelope stuffed with $25,000 in cash for his efforts in delaying the re-tendering of a lucrative Justice Department contract held by Groupaction. Brault reneged on a second $25,000 payment. Morselli was a fundraiser for former public works minister **Alfonso Gagliano.**

$ **Serge Gosselin** was paid $84,000 by Brault to do work for the Liberal Party in 1996. In June 1997, Gosselin published a book on Gagliano. He since worked as executive assistant to Liberal cabinet minister **Jacques Saada**

$ **John Welsh** got $97,000 in 1999 at the request of the Liberal Party's former Quebec president, **Benoit Corbeil**. Welsh also got a small office at Groupaction so he could do political work. He is now Heritage Minister **Lisa Frulla's** executive assistant.

$	Commando Communication Marketing, a dormant company, owned by Quebec City Liberal organizer **Bernard Thibotout**, got $79,000. Of that, $22,000 went to the party and the rest went to pay party staff.

$	**Jacques Corriveau,** Liberal bagman, demanded Brault hire **Maria-Lyne Chretien**, niece of the PM. Groupaction paid her for eight months while she worked for the liberal party.

$	**Gaby Chretien** received $4,000 for Liberal efforts on Montreal's south shore.

$	**Alain Renaud** – When Brault tried to fire **Renaud** in 2000 he was threatened with the loss of his Via Rail contracts by **Tony Mignacca, Alfonso Gagliano's** top organizer.

$	**Cameo Productions** - $20,000 plus Liberal invoice for the production of a Liberal video for the 1998 election.

$	**Vercheres Golf Club** – Three 1999 invoices addressed to the Liberal Party for $14,100.

$	**Montreal's Tarentella restaurant** – $8,281 bill sent in 1999 to the Liberals.

$	In 2001, Brault provided tickets for a fireworks show in July for Liberals, including former public works minister **Alfonso Gagliano's** chief organizer, **Tony Mignacca.**

$	Water and juice for 450 golfers at **Gagliano's** annual golf tournament.

One has to question whether the National Security Act is to protect our national security from other nations or our crooked politicians and officials from prosecution.

The Khadr family – a Canadian legacy

<u>Ahmed Said Khadr</u> – Canadian citizen – Patriarch of the clan. Pakistan forces killed him near the Afghanistan border. He was allegedly a close confidant of Osama bin Laden.

<u>Prime Minister Jean Chretien</u> personally went to Pakistan to obtain the release of <u>Ahmed Said Khadr</u> from prison. Chretien spoke to President Bhutto in Pakistan. When released Khadr returned to Afghanistan to fight with al-Qaeda forces against the United Nations coalition forces.

<u>Maha Elsamnah</u> – Canadian citizen. Matriarch of the clan. On national television, she claimed to be a close associate of Osama bin Laden and claimed to embrace the views of al-Qaeda – views which focus on the extermination of the Jews, the killing of peace loving Muslims, and attacking democracies. Since returning to Canada, she claims to have no connection to al-Qaeda.

<u>Abdurahman Khadr</u> – Canadian citizen. He returned to Canada in the fall of 2003 after his release from a U.S. prison camp for terrorist suspects in Guantanamo Bay, Cuba. He said family members fought for al-Qaeda and even stayed with Osama bin Laden. He said our family is an al-Qaeda family.

<u>Omar Khadr</u> –- Canadian citizen. Fighting in Afghanistan against coalition forces, captured by the Americans, interred in Guantanamo Bay, Cuba, as a known Al Qaeda terrorist, interviewed by C.S.I.S., R.C.M.P., and Canada's diplomatic corp. is suing the Canadian government for civil rights violations.

<u>Karim Khadr</u> – Canadian citizen. 14 years of age. Paralyzed when his spine was shattered in the same gunfight that killed his father. Returned to Canada by the Federal Government to receive hospitalization. He is now suing the federal government one week after returning to Canada.

Abdullah Khadr – Canadian citizen. 24 years of age. Wanted by the U.S. government. Supplied arms for al-Qaeda in Afghanistan. Involved in an assassination attempt on the Pakistani Prime Minister. Expressed admiration for the 9/11 attack.

Two daughters of Ahmed Said Khadr are currently living in Afghanistan. They have publicly proclaimed allegiance to al-Qaeda. They are trying to return to Canada.

A top-ranking general in the Iraqi military moved to West Vancouver shortly after Desert Storm.

Mohammad Momin Khawaja, a Canadian citizen, is arrested and charged with terrorism in connection with an attempted train bombing in England.

The auditor general's findings show a government more intent on protecting their own departmental territory than finding terrorists.

After the federal government spent $7.7 billion to combat terrorism, the R.C.M.P. must still manually scan 3.3 million fingerprints.

The Canadian "Financial Transactions and Reports Analysis Centre" uncovered $35 million in suspected terrorist funding in nine months in Canada.

Canadians need never fear a terrorist attack. We raise too much money funding terrorism.

"COLD TERROR" How Canada Nurtures and Exports Terrorism Around the World
By author Stewart Bell

Prime Minister Jean Chretien slammed the door on backing the US, Great Britain, and Australian coalition waging war on Iraq, but one has to wonder if he would have done the same if his son-in-law did not currently have millions of dollars invested in Iraqi oil.

The source of this material has been the Canadian Press.

Worthy of note – Our present Prime Minister, Paul Martin, was the keynote speaker at Taliban fundraiser dinners while Minister of Finance. Other Liberals have also been speakers at other Taliban functions.

Worthy of note – Paul Martin, the current Canadian Prime Minister, purchased Canadian Steamship Lines, a multi-million dollar company, with no money down.
Canadian Press

Worthy of note – During the 2004 Federal Election, Canada Customs discovered a false bottom in a Canadian Steamship Line freighter containing tons of marihuana. The ship was not confiscated, but was allowed to sail. If marihuana was discovered by the police in your home, your home would be confiscated.
Canadian Press 2004

Worthy of note – Canadian Steamship Lines has been charged numerous times for dumping oil bilge in Canadian waters.

In the last Federal Election Prime Minister Paul Martin said,

"I WOULD HATE TO SEE A CANADA RUN BY THE CONSERVATIVE PARTY"

Printed in the United States
57257LVS00003B/67-180